For It's One, Two, Three, Four Strikes
You're Out at the Owners' Ball Game

ALSO BY G. RICHARD MCKELVEY

The Bounce: Baseball Teams' Great Falls and Comebacks
(McFarland, 2001)

The MacPhails: Baseball's First Family of the Front Office
(McFarland, 2000)

*Fisk's Homer, Willie's Catch and the Shot Heard Round the World:
Classic Moments from Postseason Baseball, 1940–1996*
(McFarland, 1998)

For It's One, Two, Three, Four Strikes You're Out at the Owners' Ball Game

Players Versus Management in Baseball

by G. RICHARD MCKELVEY

May. 2002 —
To Bill Eiseman

This is required reading for all baseball fans to get us ready for the next strike; ... maybe in August 2002 ?
Let's hope not.

Richard McKelvey

McFarland & Company, Inc., Publishers
Jefferson, North Carolina, and London

Library of Congress Cataloguing-in-Publication Data

McKelvey, G. Richard, 1935–
    For it's one, two, three, four strikes you're out at the owners'
ball game : players versus management in baseball / by G. Richard
McKelvey.
        p.   cm.
    Includes bibliographical references and index.
    ISBN 0-7864-1192-9 (softcover : 50# alkaline paper) ∞
    1. Collective bargaining—Baseball—United States.
2. Industrial relations—United States.   3. Strikes and
lockouts—Baseball—United States.   4. Baseball players—
Labor unions—United States.   I. Title
GV880.15.M35   2001
331'.041796357'0973—dc21   2001041020

British Library cataloguing data are available

Manufactured in the United States of America

Cover image ©2001 PhotoDisc

McFarland & Company, Inc., Publishers
    Box 611, Jefferson, North Carolina 28640
        www.mcfarlandpub.com

Table of Contents

Preface

People tend to assume that baseball's labor-management difficulties began in the late 1960s when the Major League Baseball Players Association (MLBPA) showed the first signs of becoming a union that the owners would have to reckon with. Marvin Miller, who served as the Players Association's effective and powerful executive director, was the force that drew the magnates' attention and worry. As a result of the direction the MLBPA was taking, the owners formed the Player Relations Committee (PRC) to serve as its labor arm and negotiate for them.

The two groups, through collective bargaining, negotiated baseball's first Basic Agreement, which was signed in February 1968. Since then there have been periods of labor-management peace which were followed by times of labor-management strife. This pattern, however, is not new to the game.

Baseball's two powers— the owners and front office personnel on one hand and the players on the other — have in fact had numerous conflicts since baseball began. There have been curmudgeon owners like Charles A. Comiskey of the Chicago White Sox (1901–1931) who tried to squeeze every bit of competitive drive out of his players while paying them a pittance — or less. This same Comiskey had jumped to the Players League during his own playing days in an attempt to gain a fair level of pay and a measure of freedom and dignity for himself.

Since 1922, when United States Supreme Court Justice Oliver Wendell Holmes issued the seminal ruling that said that baseball was not subject to federal antitrust laws, Congress and the courts have examined and sometimes sought to change that status— so far without success.

Early in baseball's history, a "revolver" was a player who chose to gain a measure of freedom by leaving the team that held his contract — a contract that bound him to that club for as long as the club desired his services. Today, there are free agents. After decades of paltry pay for players came upward-spiraling salaries which owners now claim are out of control and threatening baseball's future.

During the final three decades of the twentieth century, work stoppages became a fact of baseball life. There were strikes—four of them—in 1972, 1981, 1985 and 1994. The players walked out and the games stopped for varying lengths of time during the regular season. The owners were responsible for another form of work stoppage—the lockout—when they closed the spring training camps and kept the players out of the facilities.

A number of books, including *Baseball: An Illustrated History* (New York: Alfred A. Knopf, 1994) by Geoffrey C. Ward and Ken Burns, *Total Baseball* (New York: Warner Books, 1989) edited by John Thorn et al., *A Whole Different Ball Game* (New York: Birch Lane Press, 1991) by Marvin Miller, and *Hardball: The Education of a Baseball Commissioner* (New York: Times Books, 1987) by Bowie Kuhn, provided an overview of some of the historic elements of labor-management relations and the strikes.

Articles from the *New York Times*, the *Boston Globe*, and other newspapers provided day-to-day information about what was happening on the labor front, especially during collective bargaining negotiations.

The book includes photographs of some of the individuals connected with player-management relations down through the years, as well as pictures to illustrate fan reactions to the strikes.

Another resource is the thoughts and remembrances of some of those who were connected to baseball as executives, players, managers, and umpires during the strikes. Some were actively involved in the game at the time and others were retired. In 1981, 1985, and 1994 I wrote to a number of them and asked if they would share some of their opinions about strike. I received many responses, usually handwritten. Many contained interesting, thoughtful, and sometimes amusing comments.

I am indebted to the staff of the Deerfield Academy Library for their guidance in identifying resources and for their assistance in helping me use the available research technology.

CHAPTER ONE

The Early Years

Professional baseball is on the wane. Salaries must come down or the interest of the public must be increased in some way. If one or the other does not happen, bankruptcy stares every team in the face.[1]

Those words, which sound as if they might have come from this morning's sports pages, were Albert Goodwill Spalding's visionary warning in 1881. Spalding had been the ace pitcher for the Boston Red Stockings of the National Association of Professional Baseball Players from 1871 to 1875, leading them to four consecutive championships. In 1876 he jumped to the Chicago White Stockings for the National League's inaugural season. Spalding registered 47 of Chicago's 52 wins that year (47-12), while also serving as the club's manager. He concluded his on-the-field career in 1878 after suffering an arm injury which had forced him to move from the mound to first base. Spalding also needed time to attend to the affairs of his fledgling sporting goods company. He would later take on an executive role in baseball, serving as the White Stockings' president from 1882 to 1891.

When Spalding spoke his words of warning in 1891, he was addressing baseball's challenging economic conditions. He was hoping to capture the attention of those who were responsible for the conduct of the sport for the benefit of all who loved it—be they owners, players, or fans. Spalding's alert serves as a reminder that baseball has long known the struggles between those in ownership and executive positions and those who play the game. The hotly contested struggles have not just recently burst upon the scene.

"The history of baseball is the history of the tension between individual rights on one hand and the priorities and practices of businessmen on the other. Like the game itself, the story is uniquely American."[2] At times, owners and players have worked together and have provided joyful and exciting experiences for those who watched the action from the bleach-ers, grandstand, or luxury boxes. At other times, however, the magnates and their employees have locked horns, and the game has suffered. The reality is that owners and players cooperate and compete in a common enterprise.

The seeds of discontent, which have produced strained relationships between the players on the field and the owners who put them there, were sown during the second half of the nineteenth century, long before four regular-season strikes in the last three decades of the twentieth century rocked baseball. Ironically, the rules of the game as operative in 1866 allowed a batsman four strikes—not three—before he was called out and sent back to the bench in shame. At the time, balls were pitched under-hand!

In 1863 leaders of the National Association of Amateur Base Ball Players, the game's first organization which had been founded in 1857 to codify rules and establish guidelines, began to face a new situation. The foundation of amateurism on which baseball had been built during its early years was being challenged by the advent of paid admissions and the prac-tice of dividing the take among the players.

A year later the National Association, which allowed players who made money in the game to maintain their membership in the organiza-tion, stated that a professional was

> "one who plays baseball for money, place, or emolument." The definition embraced many players, some of whom drew straight salaries, or shared gate receipts, or occupied jobs that were awarded as a subterfuge to conceal their ball-playing activities. What's more, some of the professionals were jumping their contracts for better offers from other clubs. Dubbed "revolvers," they posed a major threat to the shaky authority of the National Association.[3]

The owners sought to stop contract-jumping "revolvers" by adopt-ing a rule that required players to give 60 days' notice before joining another team.

In 1869 professional baseball received a significant impetus when the Cincinnati Red Stockings announced that they were going to put together a salaried team to compete against the best clubs in the country. Other teams had fielded salaried players before the Red Stockings, but they had not been eager to talk about it. Cincinnati's plan was the idea of Arthur B. Champion, a Red Stockings booster and an area businessman. Harry Wright, the team's playing manager, led the club across the country on an amazingly successful tour during which the play-for-pay team racked up 65 wins without a defeat.

The Red Stockings' success on the field—even though they were not successful at the box office—caused a stir in the National Association. The organization's traditionalists wanted to maintain baseball as an amateur . sport. Dissident members left the Association during its annual meeting in 1870, and many of them were involved in the March 17, 1871, meeting at which the National Association of Professional Baseball Players was formed.

The new National Association was baseball's first professional major league. A $10 entry fee assured a club that it had a place in the league. With membership came the requirement that each team play a best-of-five series with each of the other eight clubs. The scheduling was left to the clubs, and the team which won the most series against the other clubs would be crowned the loop's champion.

The league was run by the players and there were mixed results:

> Although the National Association dominated organized ball in 1871–1875, its structural defects portended its coming demise. The player-run organization wielded little control over the players or teams. The easy admission policy made for a chronic dropout problem as disenchanted teams found it easy to turn their backs on ten dollars.... Indeed, most teams lost money, and such losses fueled the tension between the players and investors. Critics accused the player-controlled league of failing to discipline players, especially the contract jumpers, drunkards, and alleged game fixers. Unresolved problems such as these sowed the seeds of the league's eventual collapse, but while it lasted, the National Association also provided spectators with a sprightly brand of baseball.[4]

From eight to 13 teams went to the gate to open the league's five seasons. Wright had moved to the Boston club that was setting the highest standard for players' salaries. They were also the dominant team, finishing in first place four of the five years of the league's existence. Baltimore, Chicago, Cleveland, New York, and Washington were some of the other cities represented, although not all of them fielded a team every season.

William A. Hurlburt, the president of the Chicago White Stockings, raided the Boston team after the 1875 season, signing Spalding and three other Red Stockings' stars. The move was significant in the demise of the National Association which had played its final games. "Problems of competitive imbalance, financial losses and excessive player freedom" were some of the reasons suggested for the league's collapse.[5]

Hurlburt stepped into the void and was the driving force behind the movement to organize a new league. In 1876 he was instrumental in founding the National League that was to be run by businessmen who saw it as an investment opportunity. Eight teams formed the new venture that put the interests of individual players below those of the clubs. The teams issued "tightly written contracts aimed at preventing players from 'revolving.' For the players, this was tough medicine, but with the strongest teams enrolled in the new league, there was little to do but submit."[6]

Membership in the league vacillated during the early years. Teams were expelled for not abiding by the requirement that they play each club ten times. The New York Mutuals and the Philadelphia Athletics suffered that fate in the first season. Many teams suffered financially during the league's early campaigns and, in 1879, there were austerity measures imposed when the circuit returned to eight teams with the addition of Troy, New York, and Cleveland:

> Among them [the austerity measures], salaries were slashed and players compelled to buy their own uniforms and share the cost of meals. Moreover, player mobility was limited by the adherence to a reserve clause in player contracts. Limited to five players per team in 1879, by 1883 the reserve clause system was applied to most player contracts. Thereafter the reserve clause became a major bone of contention between owners and players.[7]

The reserve clause had been the idea of Abraham G. Mills, who would serve as National League president in 1883 and 1884. The National League owners, in a nineteenth century act of collusion, secretly agreed that each team was allowed to "reserve" five players at the end of the season, and other owners were not allowed to seek the services of those five players. The owners also agreed not to sign any of the "reserved" players who refused to play for the club that owned them. Those players would be blacklisted.

The reserve clause effectively gave the club all rights to a player for an indefinite period of time. The player's contract for a given season also contained a clause which gave the team the right to sign him for the following season as well. With that clause in place, a player could not choose to move to another team since he was the property of the owner until he was sold or released.

In a historical perspective, it is ironic that the change from "reserving" five players to having a reserve clause in each player's contract came mainly as a result of the players' wishes. Many who were not "reserved" felt discredited and were often viewed as a lesser part of the club by the fans. In a strange way, it was not positive to be singled out as a nonre-serve player. As long as some were "reserved" it was better for all to be "reserved" and soon, at their behest, all the players on major league teams had the clause in their contracts.

The American Association of Base Ball Clubs (AA), which had come into existence in 1882 to challenge the monopoly of the National League, was recognized as a major league by the 1883 National Agreement. The new six-team league brought Cincinnati, Philadelphia, Pittsburgh, and St. Louis, which were not National League cities at the time, into the game. Since the AA did not operate with or recognize the reserve clause, they were able to draw dissatisfied National Leaguers to their loop for its first season in 1882. That ended with the 1883 Agreement when the AA also required a reserve clause to be included in the contracts of its players.

In 1883 major league baseball drew over one million fans for the first time in its history. The American Association's clubs played before 1,005,000 people and the National League added 616,154 to the season's total. Philadelphia of the American Association led both leagues with 305,000 fans in attendance at their home games.

The following year, the two circuits joined forces to block the insurgent Union League, which had been organized in Pittsburgh the previous fall and was seeking major league status. The new league offered players another opportunity to play for pay without a reserve clause. The Union League folded after one season of operation, having attracted only 411,000 to its games.

Piracy and contract jumping became a thing of the past. Team personnel remained more constant; fans were able to develop longer-term relationships with the players; and interest in the game grew.

By the late 1880s, financial conditions had improved for many clubs, and some were realizing profits of more than $100,000 per year. Most of the money went to the owners, who, at the time, were attempting to increase their profits by imposing salary caps for the players. After the demise of the Union League, the owners established a lowly $2,000 maximum annual salary for their employees on the field. As a result of the profitable seasons, some players had received increases in their pay. However, there was a growing number of concerns, including money, for many who were playing the game.

On October 22, 1885, after citing a string of complaints about their working conditions, nine members of the New York Giants rallied behind one of their own, John Montgomery Ward, and formed the Brotherhood of Professional Base Ball Players.

Negotiations between the Brotherhood and the owners failed to produce the desired results, at least on the part of the players. The talks broke down when the owners refused to budge on key issues including "the unwritten reserve clause, unreasonable fines, and the sale of players from one club to another."[8] It was an omen of things to come!

The owners believed a reserve clause was needed to provide stability for their teams and protection for their investments. The players felt that the owners had created a form of slavery with the reserve clause which eliminated any opportunity for them to choose to play for another team or for other clubs to bid for their services on the open market. When concern grew on the part of some owners that the reserve clause was illegal, "the ten-day notice" was added in an attempt to give themselves a stronger foundation on which to stand. The new wording required that a club owner give a player ten days notice before releasing him. The notice of release ended the contract.

In 1889 William H. "Yank" Robinson, a pitcher, catcher, and outfielder with the St. Louis Brown Stockings of the American Association, experienced the wrath of management when he was berated by Chris Von der Ahe, a club founder and its president, for showing up at Sportsman's Park with dirty pants. Von der Ahe, a hard-drinking, German-born sportsman, viewed baseball fans as potential customers for his St. Louis saloon and beer garden. He wanted his players to look sharp and be responsive to his demands.

After being dressed down by Von der Ahe, Robinson sent a boy across the street for clean pants, but when the boy returned carrying them he was not allowed back into the park. When Robinson's attire didn't improve, Von der Ahe fined his defiant player $25.

Robinson's teammates threatened not to go to Kansas City for the next series unless Von der Ahe dropped the fine. When he heard about the players' demands, the president threatened to fire Yank and blacklist him.

The Brown Stockings decided to make the trip to Kansas City where they lost three games. The suggestion that they had thrown the games as a way of retaliating against Von der Ahe was denied by Charles Comiskey, the Browns' manager. Robinson was reinstated at Comiskey's request.

A writer for the *St. Louis Globe-Democrat* described the series of events as "the most serious revolt ever known in a ball club.... The time has come when ballplayers will, if pressed too far, assert their independence."[9]

On November 5, 1889, the Brotherhood seceded from the National League and formed the Players League. A manifesto reviewing relations with the National League was addressed "To the Public":

There was a time when the league stood for integrity and fair dealing; today it stands for dollars and cents. Once it looked for the ele-
vation of the game and the honest exhibition of the sport; today its
eyes are on the turnstiles. Men have come into the business for no
other motive than to exploit it for every dollar in sight....

Players have been bought, sold or exchanged as though they were
sheep, instead of American citizens. "Reservation" became another
name for property right in the player. By a combination among themselves stronger than the strongest trust they (the owners) were able
to enforce the most arbitrary measures, and the player had either to
submit or get out of the profession. Even the disbandment and retire-
ment of a club did not free the players from the octopus clutch, for
they were then peddled to the highest bidder.[10]

The next day, after the Brotherhood's meetings in the Fifth Avenue
Hotel in New York City, it was reported that the players would make a
proposal regarding the financial operation of the new league and the procedure for dispersing the profits:

After all expenses are paid the first $20,000 to go for the prizes, the
next $80,000 to be divided among the stockholders, and the next
$80,000 to be divided among the players. After that all profits are to
be divided equally between the stockholders and the players.[11]

The Players League also had a new method for distributing the game
receipts between the clubs. The visiting team would receive 50 percent
of the gate and the grandstand receipts. In the other two major leagues,
the visitors received only a portion of the receipts at the gate but none of
the money from the grandstand. The new league was attempting to create financial equity among the clubs. The teams in the smaller cities—
Buffalo, Cleveland, and Pittsburgh—would gain money while those in
Boston, New York, and Chicago would be contributing to the operation
of their "poorer" cousins.

At the meeting it was announced that Comiskey would leave St.
Louis and join the Chicago Players League team. Originally, the Brotherhood's plan was not to include players from the American Association
on the league's rosters, but the addition of the Brown Stockings' popular
manager and first baseman was too much of a coup for them to reject.

Players who left their clubs and jumped to the new league set the
scene for a number of reserve clause test cases. A case involving Ward
served to illustrate some of the issues and the differing points of view.

In 1878 Ward began his major league career as an 18-year-old right-
handed pitcher with Providence of the National League. He led the league

in his rookie year with a 1.51 ERA, and he finished with 47-17 and 39-24 records the next two seasons. An arm injury ended his pitching career and he moved shortstop with New York in 1885 and went on to become one of the best in the game at that position.

Ward wanted to play in 1890 for the Brooklyn team in the Players League. The Metropolitan Exhibition Company (the New York Baseball Club) sought an injunction to restrain Ward, who was attending Columbia University Law School in the off-season, from joining the Brooklyn Brotherhood Club.

The hearing began on January 16, 1890, in the New York Supreme Court chambers. That same day, Samuel Gompers, president of the American Federation of Labor, and three other labor leaders pledged support for the league.

During his presentation at the hearing, Henry F. Howland, a lawyer for Ward, argued that

> the contract signed by Ward with the New York Club in the Spring of 1899 did not bind him for the season of 1890, notwithstanding the reservation clause. That clause, he contended, only bound Ward not to play with any other club belonging to the National League of the National Association, but could not affect his liberty to join a club not in existence at the time the contract was signed.[12]

Joseph H. Choate, who appeared for the New York Club, said the question under consideration was

> whether baseball players, like the rest of mankind, were subject to the laws and bound by good faith and common honesty. The word "contract" is used in baseball parlance to indicate an agreement for the current season, and the word "reserve" an agreement for the successive season. If the reserve clause contained no obligation on Ward, why did it entail an obligation on the club to pay him a salary.[13]

On January 28, Justice O'Brien of the Supreme Court refused to grant the injunction and Ward was free to play for Brooklyn. The players had gained a major legal victory.

Decisions in other cases arising out of the moves to the Players League also supported the players, and the major rationale offered by judges had to do with the apparent inequity between the club's ability to release a player with ten days notice and the player's inability to leave the team that held his contract to pursue a better opportunity for himself.

In an unprecedented mass exodus, about 80 National Leaguers and

30 players from the American Association left their clubs to join teams in the Players League. Included in that number were some of the stars of the game, including Dan Brouthers, Comiskey, Roger Connor, Hugh Duffy, Buck Ewing, Tim Keefe, Michael "King" Kelly, Connie Mack, Jim O'Rourke and Charles "Old Hoss" Radbourne.

Kelly was leaving the Boston team, with whom he had played since 1887, to join the Players League club in the same city. After leading the National League in hitting in 1886 with a .388 average, he had been the first major star to be sold to another team when Chicago shipped him to Beantown for $10,000.

The eight-team major league played its initial campaign in 1890, which turned out to be its only campaign. Kelly's Boston club finished six and a half games in front of Ward's Brooklyn team. Financially, the season was a disaster, and many of the league's financial backers withdrew their support, causing the experiment in "player power" to come to a disappointing end. The new operation had drawn 980,887 fans with Boston leading the way with 197,346. Buffalo and Cleveland brought up the rear, each with an attendance in the vicinity of 60,000 for the season.

With the Players League disbanded, the National League went to war with the American Association over players and cities which had become available after the demise of the third league. After the 1891 season, the AA folded and four of its clubs joined the National League which expanded to 12 teams. In its final season, AA attendance fell to 1,173,000 spectators which was down from its high of 1,313,397 in 1887.

The National League outdrew them by nearly 180,000 in 1891. The National League had regained its monopoly at the major league level. That was a situation which the owners relished:

> Enthralled by their newly created baseball "trust," the league's owners styled themselves as magnates presiding over a million-dollar entertainment industry. The magnates fully expected their monopoly league to produce unprecedented cash and glory.[14]

A national recession and the imbalance in the league prevented the owners from realizing their dreams. Three clubs—Baltimore, Boston, and Brooklyn—won all of the pennant races from 1892–1900. Fans of a number of the "also-rans" lost interest in their clubs and stopped going to the ballparks. Louisville, which never climbed out of the second division during this span of years, played in front of only 53,683 patrons in 1893 and drew fewer than 100,000 during two other seasons. In 1889 Cleveland, with a 20-134 record, could entice only 6,088 fans to come to their park during the entire dismal campaign. That same year Washington, who finished in eleventh place in the 12-team league, saw its attendance fall to 86,392.

In the midst of the hard times, owners imposed a $2,400 ceiling on a player's annual salary. Andrew Freedman, owner of the New York Giants, made a suggestion to improve the conditions in the league. He proposed "the pooling and redistribution of players and profits, provided that the 'strongest and most lucrative franchises' got the best players."[15]

Amos Rusie, who went 23-23 in 1895 for the Giants and led the league with 201 strikeouts, after posting a 36-13 record the year before, staged a rebellion against Freedman, who had withheld $200 in fines from his $3,500 salary for not having tried hard enough.

Rusie, a native of Indiana who was known as "The Hoosier Thunderbolt," was a hard-throwing right-hander whose catcher, Dick Buckley, would sometimes line his glove with lead to deaden the impact of Amos' fastball. Rusie and a few other hard throwers of his era had been responsible for a 5-feet-6-inch increase in the pitching distance in 1893.

When Amos refused to sign his contract for 1886, the Giants tendered him a contract for $3,400 and informed him that he was "reserved." Rusie sat out the 1886 season.

On November 12, after Rusie was informed that he had been "reserved" again for the following season, he filed for an injunction in Federal Court in Chicago. At the time, there was concern on the part of the magnates that there might be a far-reaching impact from the legal action:

> Incidentally, Rusie's application to the Court means more than his personal release, if granted. It means that the right of reservation, exercised by the baseball clubs, has no legal standing, and makes an open field at the close of the season for the contracting of players for the following season.[16]

New York fans supported Rusie against Freedman, and a group of Wall Street brokers called for a boycott of Giants' games until the pitcher received his money. When Freedman refused to give in, other owners paid the fine levied by the Giants' owner and pitched in $3,000 to help pay Rusie's salary. After staging baseball's first successful player holdout, Amos returned to pitch for New York during the 1897 season. The case was settled out of court and, for the magnates, to have it settled in that manner was far more appealing than to have the legal system look too closely at some of baseball's practices.

The owners were always looking for new ways to strengthen the game—from their perspectives. In 1898 they approved two interlocking directorates. The first gave Frank Robison, owner of the Cleveland and St. Louis teams, the ability to strengthen one of his clubs by transferring the best players from the other one. Another example of this approach occurred when the 1899 Brooklyn team was stocked with the top players from that club and the Baltimore franchise. "Wee Willie" Keeler, Joe Kelley, and Dan McGann were three of the players who went from Baltimore to Brooklyn. Manager Ned Hanlon also moved from Maryland to Flatbush.

The Brooklyn Superbas won the championship, but the contrived nature of their victory did not strengthen the league or sit well with some of the owners. Following the 1899 season, the National League decided to drop the Baltimore, Cleveland, St. Louis, and Washington clubs and returned to an eight-team circuit.

Cap Anson, a long-time National League player and manager—most of it spent with Chicago—who had retired from baseball in 1898, criticized the way he saw the game going and the National League's move served as an example:

> Baseball as at present conducted is a gigantic monopoly, intolerant of opposition and run on a grab-all-there-is-in-sight policy that is alienating its friends and disgusting the very public that has so long and cheerfully given it the support it has withheld from other forms of entertainment.[17]

Ban Johnson leapt into the breach created when the National League returned to eight teams, and he proclaimed that the Western League, a strong minor league, was now a major league—the American League. Johnson, the Western League's president, continued in the same capacity with his new operation.

Although Johnson's circuit played its initial season in 1900 as the American League, it would be a year before it was officially recognized as a major league. Before its first campaign, Ban's clubs signed many of the players who had been put out of work when the National League dropped the four clubs.

Comiskey, who had become a magnate following his playing and managing careers, moved his minor league team from St. Paul, Minnesota, to Chicago, and named them the White Stockings, which had been the name of the former National Association and National League clubs in the Windy City. The National League team's name had been changed a number of times before becoming the Cubs. The White Stockings were a formidable city rival for the Cubs in 1900, winning the first American League pennant and having a successful financial season as well.

In early 1901, the National League backed an attempt to revive the American Association, which had folded after the 1891 campaign:

> As the result of a meeting held at the Louisville Hotel this afternoon [January 8], signatures were secured to an agreement which provides for a revival of the American Association under the backing and influence of the National League, and also for the purpose of fighting Ban Johnson and the American League, and preventing him from getting possession of the surplus players of the National League, as under the rule recently adopted [that] each National League team is to be limited to sixteen players.[18]

A further meeting was called for January 18, 1901, at which time a committee from the National League would officially recognize and offer support to the American Association. When Col. John I. Rogers of the Philadelphia club failed to appear at the meeting, his absence sent shock waves through the Senior Circuit's committee. It would later become clear that Rogers would not back the idea of the American Association placing a team in his city. After that happened, the new league lost additional support, and it never received the necessary backing from the National League.

The National Agreement had expired, and Johnson used the opportunity to proclaim that the American League was, in fact, a major league. Weak National League leadership helped set the stage for Johnson's league to gain recognition and strength. Already with a club competing with the National League team in Chicago, Ban and his supporters placed franchises in Boston and Philadelphia for the 1901 campaign.

The new league announced some of its operating procedures, including a new approach to player contracts:

> The American League will submit contracts to its players on the plan advocated by the Players' Protective Association. This plan involves a graded system of contracts of three, four, and five years—no player to be bound for a period longer than five years. At the end of that time he will be free to accept offers from any other club. The plan does away with the "farming" system, a clause in the contracts providing that "no player shall be traded, farmed, or sold to any other club except with his consent."[19]

The American League's action nudged the National League to be more willing to listen to the players' demands. At February meetings in

New York, representatives of the National League and the Protective Association of Professional Baseball Players met together to consider the concerns raised by the players.

The National League's representatives made some concessions:

> The first matter in which concessions were made to the players was regarding the option clause, the abolishment of which the committee will recommend, the old reserve rule to be substituted for it, thus giving the clubs the privilege of holding a player from year to year instead of indefinitely as was formerly the practice.
>
> The League committee also agreed to recommend that the club owners shall cease to farm, sell, and lend players from one club to another, unless the players so to be transferred shall be consulted and shall agree to the changes.[20]

The players had received something through the negotiations; the owners also made gains as they prepared to go to battle with the American League. Charles Zimmer, president of the Players' Association, issued a statement which addressed the American League, which ironically had been the first league to recognize the Association:

> As President of the Protective Association of Baseball Players, and as its authorized representative, I hereby agree in return for the concessions granted by the National League and the American Association of Baseball Clubs, this 26th day of February, 1901, that all National League and Eastern League players who may sign American League contracts will be suspended pending action of the Players' Protective Association as a body.[21]

With a significant amount of money behind the fledgling league, more than 100 National Leaguers crossed the line and suited up for the American League clubs. Among the group were Jimmy Collins, who switched teams in Boston and became the Pilgrims' player-manager; Kid Gleason, who left New York and went to Detroit; Clark Griffith, who suited up for the White Stockings instead of the Cubs; Napoleon Lajoie, who exchanged Philadelphia uniforms; Joe McGinnity, who left Boston for Baltimore; John McGraw, who moved from playing third base in St. Louis to playing third and managing in Baltimore; and Cy Young, who went from St. Louis to Boston.

In the cities where there was a club in each league, the National League often scheduled games to compete with their American League rivals. A report in the *New York Times* on April 25, 1901, noted the opening of the American League campaign the previous day and gave an example of the planned confrontations:

> The American Baseball League essayed to open its season yesterday, and succeeded in playing but one game—that between Chicago and Cleveland. Chicago winning. The Philadelphia-Washington game at Philadelphia was prevented by the rain, and the clash of dates between the American and National League clubs in that city was thus postponed for at least one day. The Detroit-Milwaukee game at Detroit and the Boston-Baltimore game at Baltimore also were postponed, owing to the rain.[22]

The White Stockings held a four-game lead over the Boston Pilgrims at season's end and captured the first official American League pennant. Finishing a strong second, "the Pilgrims quickly supplanted their mediocre NL counterparts in the hearts and wallets of Boston fans."[23] The Pilgrims drew 289,448 fans which nearly doubled the number who went through the turnstiles to see the city's National League team.

Lajoie's signing with the Athletics for the 1901 campaign, like a number of other cases, had fomented a crisis between the player and his previous club. He had signed a contract with the Phillies in 1900 but decided to sign with the Athletics for the following season. The National League team sought an injunction from the Pennsylvania Supreme Court to prevent Lajoie from suiting up for "Mr. Mack's club." Lajoie spent a successful 1901 season with the Athletics. The case took time to resolve and, on April 21, 1902, the Pennsylvania Supreme Court issued its ruling which reversed an earlier decision:

> The Supreme Court to-day reversed the decision of the Court of Common Pleas, No. 5, in the case of Napoleon Lajoie vs. the Philadelphia National League Baseball Club. The decision upholds the validity of the reserve clause in National League contracts.[24]

The Court ruled that the Phillies were entitled to an injunction. There were two factors which led to the decision:

> First, the Phillies' contract reserved Lajoie for only three years and stated what salary would be paid in each of those three years, so it was not simply "a contract to make a contract." Second, Lajoie was a star of the very highest order. Courts are reluctant to order someone to perform a contract for personal services, although they are not at all reluctant to order the defendant to pay monetary damages equal to the harm caused by his nonperformance. Only when the harm cannot be measured in dollars or the contract involves something unique or irreplaceable are injunctions or other nonmonetary remedies granted by a court. The Phillies may have been able to find equally talented replacements for many of their players, but Lajoie—

who led the AL in hits, doubles, home runs, runs, RBIs, batting average, and slugging percentage in 1901—was a unique talent.[25]

The ruling in favor of the Phillies created an optimistic outlook for the Senior Circuit's owners. James Hart, of the Chicago club, was one of them and said, "This decision brings back to the National League over two dozen players who jumped to the American League. I cannot see it in any other light than a fatal blow to the rival league."[26]

Although the Phillies were the victors in the court, Lajoie never played for them again, and other American Leaguers also remained with their new teams. After playing one game for the 1902 Athletics, Johnson arranged a deal between the A's and Cleveland, which sent Lajoie to a new club. The star infielder was not with Cleveland when they played the A's in Philadelphia because the injunction prohibited him from suiting up for any club other than the Phillies in the City of Brotherly Love, and he could end up in jail if he did. The Phillies tried to obtain an injunction that would have prevented Lajoie from playing in Ohio, but they failed to obtain it.

In 1902 Mack's Philadelphia Athletics wore the American League crown after topping the St. Louis Browns by five games.

After the American League's second successful season as a serious big-league rival to the Senior Circuit, leaders from both major leagues sat down in mid–December to find a way for the two leagues to co-exist.

The National League initially proposed a consolidated 12-team circuit which the American League quickly rejected. A report from one of the early sessions described the situation:

> The officials on both sides are astute businessmen, and each organization represents a great deal of invested capital. From any point of view, it was obvious that if the war continued both sides would lose heavily, as they could not stand the financial strain. The salary list of nearly every club in both leagues has been vastly increased, and in some instances almost doubled, by the large financial inducements offered to players by opposition clubs. This could not go on with any certainty of success. In fact, the outlay would be ruinous in a short time, and while neither league was willing to give in, the individual owners saw that something or somebody had to give way, and the suggestion of a compromise was welcomed by those most interested.[27]

Early in 1903, Johnson and Comiskey met with Henry Pulliam, the National League's new president who had been chosen the previous December, and Cincinnati owner August Herrmann. Eventually the two sides negotiated the 1903 National Agreement that addressed a number of issues, including

> the NL and AL would operate as separate and equal major leagues, bound by common playing rules, harmonized playing schedules, and mutually recognized territories and player contracts. The player contract restored the reserve clause and ended the AL's raids. The agreement also allowed an AL franchise to be located in New York, which Johnson secured by moving the financially shaky Baltimore Orioles to Manhattan, where in time the team prospered as the New York Yankees.[28]

There had been discussions about the American League bringing a club to New York to join the Giants, which didn't please the Polo Grounders. Staunch National League adherents argued that there was not room in the city for another team, but Johnson finally won the battle.

Two bartenders, Frank Farrell and Big Bill Devery, purchased the Baltimore franchise for $18,000 and brought the club to Manhattan. A wooden park with seating for 15,000 people was built on Broadway between 165th and 168th Streets to welcome the American League for the 1903 season. The new facility was built on high ground and named Hilltop Park, and the team, which would become the Yankees in future years, was called the Highlanders.

The leagues' leaders also settled a dispute involving Sam Crawford, a Cincinnati Reds outfielder who had hit .333 and banged 22 triples in 1902. He had been signed by both Cincinnati and Detroit for the 1903 campaign. Crawford was awarded to the Tigers because they had signed him first. The American League appeared to be flexing its muscle, and the muscle belonged to Johnson, who soon was known as the "Czar of Baseball."

Sportswriter Bob Considine described Johnson in an article about Mack's managerial career:

> The man who was to be hailed forty-seven years later as perhaps the best manager in the American League was saved from complete oblivion by Ban Johnson, president of the Western League. Johnson, a ruthless dreamer who lived and died believing that baseball was perfected in order to serve him as a gigantic chess board on which to move his living pieces, lifted Mister Mack out of reluctant retirement and set him up as manager and one-fourth owner of the Milwaukee club. Johnson changed the name of his league to the American in 1900 and laid plans to invade the big time monopolized by the

National. He ordered his friend Charles Comiskey, owner of the St. Paul franchise, to move his club to Chicago. He set up other clubs in Cleveland and Buffalo, and took over Detroit and Kansas City. He dispatched Mister Mack to Philadelphia one cold December day in 1900 to raise money for a ball park and to find a club which could successfully compete with the well-established Phillies.[29]

Ban Johnson. The American League's powerful president from 1901 to 1927. (National Baseball Hall of Fame Library, Cooperstown, N.Y.)

The National Agreement created a three-man National Commission to enforce the rules and to keep the peace between the leagues. Johnson, Pulliam, and Herrmann comprised the Commission with the Cincinnati owner serving as permanent chairman. The witty and vocal Johnson, who wielded the most power on the Commission until it was replaced by baseball's first commissioner in 1920, usually received the support of Herrmann. That meant that Ban's positions and ideas usually had the weight of the majority behind them. By comparison, during the years of the Commission's existence, the National League was represented by four rather weak presidents—Pulliam, John Heydler, Thomas Lynch, and John Tener.

Under the new National Agreement, the major leagues entered a period of prosperity. Part of the prosperity was due to the revival of the World Series in 1903. The postseason extravaganza became a financial boon for the game and especially for some of the owners.

The Fall Classic had first been played in 1884, with the National League's Providence Grays defeating the American Association's New York Mets. The season-ending competition between the two leagues continued annually through 1890. With the leagues warring with each other in 1891, the series was discontinued. A year later the postseason competition was revived with the winners of the National League's first and second halves of the campaign battling for the World Championship. The divided season was eliminated the following year and so was the World Series. Pittsburgh sportsman William C. Temple sponsored a postseason series between the top two National League clubs from 1894 through 1897. The winner of the Temple Cup was considered Organized Baseball's champs. Two seasons without a postseason followed but, in 1900, the top two finishers were back at it competing for the Pittsburgh "Chronicle-Telegraph Cup." Two seasons without a culminating match-up followed until the return of the World Series in 1903.

However, in 1904, McGraw, the manager of the National League champion Giants, refused to allow his club to meet the Junior Circuit's Boston Pilgrims who had beaten the Pittsburgh Pirates the previous October. After that the World Series had clear sailing.

New and larger ballparks were built to meet the needs of the growing cadre of baseball fans. Player salaries also grew as a result of increased profits. At the end of the first decade of the twentieth century, some players were making as much as $12,000. By 1915, superstars such as Ty Cobb, Tris Speaker, and Walter Johnson had salaries in the "stratospheric" $20,000 range.

With the agreements made between the leagues and the resultant prosperity experienced by many teams, major league baseball entered a period of relative stability between the club owners and the players. The working relationship between the two parties had been clearly defined. For the next seven decades, with but a few exceptions, a player would have the option of playing for the team which held his contract or finding employment in another field.

CHAPTER TWO

Peace and War

Following the 1903 National Agreement between the Senior Circuit and its Junior counterpart, major league baseball moved into an era of relative peace. A large measure of the peace came because players had lost significant power and could not mount a united stand against the owners, who had the reserve clause and the practice of blacklisting on their side.

The National Commission, with Ban Johnson as the power on the throne, handled disputes between the leagues, clubs, and players:

> As men of their time, the Commissioners shared proprietors' beliefs in the sanctity of property and the subservience of labor, and rigorously upheld the reserve clause and ten-day clauses, while assiduously avoiding any legal test of their validity. Yet despite this tilt toward their employers, they showed their best side in the justice of many difficult decisions affecting the commerce in players.[1]

However, besides the National Agreement and the National Commission there was another powerful force at work:

> The Agreement was inspired less by a regard for players than by assurance of an open market for owners, so that by offering opportunity to baseball's best prospects the clubs would enjoy a competitive balance and hold fan interest. Yet for the owners a gentleman's agreement was always more compelling than the national one. They connived with each other to diddle the draft, waiver, and option processes, and, incidentally, to limit salaries and rosters, hold up the pay of injured players, and burden the released players with the travel costs of getting wherever they were being sent. Such sharp practices and cheese-paring economics were considered shrewd business, and the Commission, when it did not agree with them, was hard put to remedy any but the most egregious injustices.[2]

Along with peace there was also a sense on the part of some that the game was undergoing a discouraging change as mentioned in an editorial in the *New York Evening Journal* on October 7, 1908:

> In the earlier days of baseball there was a sentiment attached to the national game that made games take on the appearance of real battles between cities and sections, but sentiment no longer figures in the sport. It is now only a battle of dollars.[3]

It wasn't long before the owners' control was tested as the players' concerns began to percolate. On August 7, 1912, an article in the *New York Times* reported that a union of baseball players had been formed at a secret meeting in the office of David Fultz, a former outfielder for Philadelphia and Baltimore of the National League and Philadelphia and the New York Highlanders of the American League. The ballplayer-turned-lawyer had retired from baseball in 1905.

Fultz was not ready to say much about the new organization—the Baseball Players' Fraternity—which would be a precursor to the modern day Major League Baseball Players Association. After news of the organization leaked out, he said:

> This will be an association ... but will have no trade union features. The aims and objectives of the body will be to have a better understanding among all the members of the baseball clubs and the club owners, and, in short, to systemize the playing of baseball.[4]

The organization claimed to have 286 members—almost all the players in the two major leagues. A number of managers expressed an interest in joining, but Fultz said that would not happen because it might put them in an untenable position between the players and the owners.

The Baseball Players' Fraternity was incorporated in the State of New York on September 6, 1912. In the announcement of the incorporation, Fultz, who had been named the fraternity's president, mentioned a number of cases which indicated that players needed representation through such an organization.

He spoke about a player who had been released from a major league team to a minor league club without passing through waivers. Fultz said that two other major league teams were interested in signing him to a contract for the same amount he was currently earning, but he was "railroaded" to the minors for a salary below his major league contract.

Fultz noted another player who had signed a three-year contract for 1911, 1912, and 1913 for $4,000 per season. In July the player had been sold to a minor league club and was being paid $2,000 per season. The organization's president mentioned others who had been sold to the minor leagues and were suffering financially as a result of their demotions.

Fultz outlined the purposes of the new organization:

> The general purposes of the fraternity are as follows: To have every reasonable obligation of the player's contract lived up to by both contracting parties. To secure adequate protection from abusive spectators. To discountenance and abolish, as far as possible, rowdyism on the field. To be of financial assistance to deserving ball players. To advise the player concerning any real or fancied grievance, and, in the event the former exists, to prepare his case for him. To instill into the player a pride in his profession and to use the strongest possible influence to induce him to keep himself in condition, and to give his employer the best service of which he is capable.[5]

When Charles A. Comiskey, the owner of the Chicago White Sox, and Johnson learned of the fraternity's purposes, they offered no objection to the organization. In fact, Johnson expressed optimism:

> It looks to me ... as if a lot of good might be done both the players and the owners with such a body at the head of the men engaged in the game. I don't think any unreasonable demands will be made, and I don't believe the players intend to wreck the game, which just now is at the height of its prosperity. With sensible men at the head of fraternity, who will confer with league officials on important questions, it looks to me as if all sides should profit.[6]

The Detroit Tigers' Ty Cobb, one of baseball's superstars, became a pivotal player in the struggles between those on the field and those in the front office. Cobb, who had balked at signing his contract in prior years, refused to sign for the 1913 season, and the Tigers suspended him.

In 1911 the three-time batting champion had demanded a $10,000 salary, but Frank J. Navin, owner of the Tigers, refused to oblige. Cobb responded by sitting out the first 14 games of the season. Detroit struggled, the fans bellowed, and Navin gave in. Cobb went on to capture another batting crown with a career-best .420 average.

Cobb sat out again in 1912, but for a very different reason. On May 15, Cobb belted a fan who, for three days, had been with a group sitting behind the Tigers' bench verbally abusing him during the games with New York in Hilltop Park. A newspaper reporter described the fourth-inning set-to:

Everything was very pleasant at the Detroit-Yankee game on the Hilltop yesterday until Ty Cobb johnnykilbaned a spectator right on the place where he talks, started the claret, and stopped the flow of profane and vulgar words. Cobb led with a left jab and countered with a right kick to Mr. Spectator's left Weisbach, which made the peeper look as if some one had drawn a curtain over it. Silk O'Loughlin [umpire], without a license from the boxing commission, refereed the go. He gave the decision to Cobb and then tossed him out of the ring. The spectator went to a lawyer's office to make out his will.[7]

Johnson, the league president, suspended Cobb indefinitely. Both Ty and his teammates were angry, believing that Ban had dealt unfairly with the Detroit player. The Tigers went on strike, saying they refused to play any games until Cobb was reinstated. On May 17, in Philadelphia, Detroit manager Hugh Jennings gathered up a bunch of local players, many from St. Joseph's College, to be Tigers for a day. The collegians lost to the A's, 24–2, on the day of baseball's first players' strike.

The Tiger players realized that the public was against them, that Johnson would not yield, and that Cobb was urging them back into action—and so they ended their walkout. They were back on the field against the Washington Senators on May 21. Johnson fined each of Cobb's sympathizers $100 for striking, but he said he had not yet determined the length of Ty's suspension or the amount of his fine.

On May 25, Johnson announced his verdict and Cobb's sentence:

After a careful investigation into the causes and circumstances of the encounter between Player Cobb and Claude Lucker, a spectator at the New York grounds on May 15, I find that direct responsibility for the unfortunate occurrence rests upon the player....

As a lesson to the accused and a warning to all other players, I fix the term of the player's suspension at ten days and impose a fine of $50. He will be eligible to play on May 26.[8]

When Cobb, the 1912 batting champ with a .410 mark, asked to have his salary raised to $12,000 for the 1913 campaign, Navin said, "Cobb is becoming a real threat. He may not belong on the team. Does he want to wind up owning it?"[9]

After Cobb and Navin had gone round and round for some time, Hugh McKinnon, who was prominently recognized in baseball circles, came to Ty's defense:

My belief is ... that Cobb is the victim of a plot to run him out of base-ball because he is becoming too expensive. Ban Johnson, president of

the American League, has threatened to suspend him if he contin-
ues these every-season hold-outs. Now, Cobb is well aware of this
plan to make him knuckle under, and rob him of his prestige.

But the salary future of every player in baseball is at stake here.
Cobb is out to create new pay standards, for not only himself, but
every other underpaid man in the profession. Baseball has become a
major big business. In Detroit, Navin is doing such a box-office that
he upped Bennett Field from 11,000 to 14,000 capacity and currently
is ripping out the old wooden stands and building a concrete single-
decker seating 23,000. Since 1910, we have seen a great stadium-
building spree. Comiskey Park has risen in Chicago, Griffith Stadium
has been opened in Washington and a new Polo Grounds has been
erected in New York. Fenway Park has just opened in Boston, Ebbets
Field in Brooklyn will be inaugurated soon and Wrigley Field in
Chicago is in the design stages.

Hard times for the magnates? Phaugh![10]

On April 19, 1913, Cobb, "the Georgia Peach," received a wire from
Hoke Smith, a United States Senator from his home state. Smith asked
for a copy of Ty's contract, including the reserve clause, so that he could
investigate whether or not the contract violated any federal statutes. Three
days later, Representative Gallagher of Illinois introduced a House Resolution in Washington which called for a special committee to investigate the interests controlling baseball. Gallagher wanted to discover
whether

unjust discriminations have been practiced in favor of or against players; whether players are now or have been prejudiced, coerced, or
restrained from the exercise of their just rights to enter into contracts
of a fair equitable nature, and whether such a combination has been
effected among baseball magnates throughout the country as would
preclude competition and operate in restraint of trade.[11]

Former Philadelphia Phillies' owner Horace Fogel (1909–1912), writing to Gallagher, raised his own concerns:

I think you have struck the popular chord in the movement against
the baseball trust, as the public at large are sour on the methods of
this monopoly, and you will have the people with you in demanding
the investigation.[12]

While things were heating up in the nation's capital, Fultz, in
response to criticism about the Baseball Fraternity's silence regarding
Cobb's situation, announced that the organization would not take any

action in the case unless requested to do so by either Cobb or the Tigers. He said that "he regarded the matter as a purely business transaction between Cobb and President Navin, and that it was not only unfair but silly to attack the fraternity for not settling it."[13]

The federal government's sudden interest in the Cobb case, along with language being used on the floor of Congress which linked the Sherman Antitrust Act and baseball for the first time, sent Navin and other magnates scurrying to get the Tigers' star inked to a 1913 contract for $12,000.

The National Commission fired the final shot in the skirmish. In May they fined Cobb $50 for holding out, which they judged was an action "detrimental to the game."[14]

On September 25, the Detroit club confirmed that it had received a report in which the Players' Fraternity had listed a number of demands for the Commissioners and the clubs to consider seriously. One focused on players who were in the midst of lengthy careers—ten years in the majors or 12 years in the majors and minors combined. The Fraternity demanded that a club holding the contract of one of those players give him his unconditional release rather than trade him to another team. Another issue concerned the use or lack of use of the waiver system. The Fraternity wanted a guarantee that any player on a major league team's payroll until July would be put on waivers so that any American or National League team could claim him before he was released to the minors.

The National Commission's opinion about the Fraternity and Fultz had changed since September of the previous year when Comiskey and Johnson had extolled its virtues. August Herrmann said that the Commission would not discuss the players' demands as long as Fultz was representing them. He added:

> If a committee of the players meets the commission … and we discuss both sides of the question at issue, I am sure that both sides will concede something, and the agreement will be agreeable. Of course, I am only talking for myself, and not for the commission.[15]

The change in the Commission's attitude had come primarily because Fultz had involved himself in a July case involving Phillies' pitcher Addie Brennan, who had assaulted New York Giants' manager John McGraw. When Fultz attempted to have a $100 fine against Brennan annulled, Thomas Lynch, president of the National League, expressed his strong opinion that the Fraternity's president was making demands in a situation where he didn't belong.

The Commission stirred up another hornet's nest after Chief Bender, star pitcher for the 1913 World Champion Athletics with a 21-10 record and a pair of wins in the World Series, had pitched for a semi-pro team in Brooklyn. Also, on a ball field in the Bronx, the A's $100,000 infield of Stuffy McInnis, Eddie Collins, Jack Barry, and Frank "Home Run" Baker had played a game with a local club.

Although it was thought that manager Connie Mack had given permission for the five A's to play—as was the policy at the time—the Commission sought to put an end to the practice. They believed that baseball was being cheapened by stars who participated in games where the price of admission was only 15 or 25 cents: The spokesman for the Commission said that the practice

> detracts from the dignity of the game to have such great players mingling on the same lots with any pick-up team which is willing to give them a little money.[16]

It was not long before the Commission and the owners had to face a threat that was much greater than players' demands and stars performing during the off-season on local ball fields.

On December 29, Herrmann, chairman of the National Commission, expressed concern about plans that were being made for the operation of a third major league—the Federal League:

> Heretofore not a great deal of attention has been paid to the new league officially by the commission. It is the general impression now, however, that more attention will be given to the new organization by the National Commission.[17]

The Federal League had some wealthy individuals who were prepared to go to war against the American and National Leagues (Organized Baseball). Jim Gilmore was a coal and paper magnate, Charles Weeghman owned a string of lunch rooms and billiard halls in the Chicago area, Phil D. Ball was in the ice business in St. Louis, Bob Ward owned bakeries, and Harry Sinclair was an oil magnate. On the same day that Herrmann expressed his concern about a possible new league, it was announced that infielder Joe Tinker and pitcher Mordecai Brown had signed contracts with teams in that league—Tinker with Chicago and Brown with St. Louis.

Brown had played for the St. Louis team in the National League during his rookie year in 1903, had spent nine seasons with the Chicago Cubs and was then traded to the Cincinnati Reds for the 1913 campaign. He won 20 or more games six times with Chicago.

Tinker had been the Cubs' legendary shortstop since 1902, and, in 1913, he had also been their manager. Following that season, he was traded to the Brooklyn Superbas.

Tinker reportedly signed a three-year $36,000 contract with the Chicago Whales. Weeghman was providing the major money for the new club. Tinker's salary had been guaranteed by a bonding company which meant that Joe would receive his money regardless of the league's fate.

John Heydler, the National League's secretary, appeared confused as to why Tinker would have accepted Weeghman's offer:

> The fact that Tinker would positively receive a $10,000 [bonus] for signing with Brooklyn makes the report of his jump appear all the more improbable to me, because no ball player would turn down such a large bonus for an uncertain proposition. It is, of course, possible that the Federal League banked all that money to Tinker's credit, but I cannot believe it.[18]

The impending competition with the Federal League, which had created a plague of player pirating and contract jumping, drove the owners and the Players' Fraternity to the bargaining table. At the January 6, 1914, meeting in Cincinnati between the National Commission and the Fraternity, the players' requests, which had first surfaced the previous September, were discussed and acted on. There were 17 requests in all and, when all was said and done, the players had made major gains. Two of them were:

> When waivers are hereafter asked on a player in the National League and no club in that league claims him it will be the privilege of an American League club to take him up if it wants him, and vice versa. Heretofore, a player had a chance of being claimed by only seven other clubs in a league before going to the minors.
>
> The new rules about a player receiving his unconditional release after ten years of service, if no major league team claims him, will also work for much good among the old players, for it will give them a chance to get minor league managerial positions instead of being tied up by contract with some minor league club.[19]

As a result of the changes, many players in Organized Baseball had to sign new contracts in place of the one they had already agreed to for the 1914 season.

Harry N. Hempstead, president of the New York Giants, was pleased with the results of the talks and said:

The granting of practically all the requests of the players will put an end to a great misunderstanding that has existed about the feelings and relations of club owners toward the players.... The same results could have been achieved just as peacefully at any previous time, but the impression had been that the club owner was inclined to disregard the desires and rights of the players. The requests which did not go through will be just as beneficial to the players as those which were agreed to, as the player was really getting the better treatment under the old conditions.

When the players asked that the old contract be binding in cases of transfers, they seemed to overlook the fact that the major leagues place 90 per cent of the players, who have outlived their usefulness in the majors, in good paying conditions—much better, in fact, than these players might be able to obtain if they had the record of being unconditionally released.[20]

At the end of January, the Superbas made a last-ditch effort to retain Tinker. Earlier, they had offered a $10,000 bonus and a $5,000 salary, which was the same annual pay he had received while he was with the Cubs. Brooklyn owner Charles Ebbets sweetened the pot, offering Tinker a $7,500 salary, which was what Joe had originally asked for. However, Tinker didn't budge from his commitment to the upstart Chicago Whales.

Lured by the promise of increased salaries and welcoming the opportunity to get out from under the control of the reserve clause, Brown and Tinker were among 81 American and National Leaguers and 140 minor leaguers who jumped to the Federal League which opened operation in 1914 in eight cities. Four of the cities—Brooklyn, Chicago, Pittsburgh, and St. Louis—also had teams in the majors. The other clubs in the eight-team league were located in Baltimore, Buffalo, Indianapolis, and Kansas City.

The players' movements to teams in the Federal League resulted in a new round of court cases. One of the most celebrated involved Philadelphia Phillies' catcher Bill Killifer. Killifer had played for the St. Louis Browns in 1909 and 1910. He then went to the Phillies and was with them through the 1913 campaign when he was in 120 games and batted .244. Killifer signed with the Chicago Whales on January 8 for three years at a total salary of $17,500, which was a substantial pay increase for him.

Twelve days after signing with the Whales, the Phillies offered him more money to return to Philadelphia and he accepted their offer. On March 20, the Federal League club brought suit in the United States District Court in Grand Rapids, Michigan, which was the jurisdiction in which Killifer resided. They were seeking an injunction to restrain the catcher from returning to the Philadelphia team.

On April 10, Federal Judge Clarence W. Sessions denied the application for an injunction, although he ruled that the reserve clause was invalid and unenforceable. He said:

> The leading authorities, with possibly one exception, are agreed that executory contracts of this nature can neither be enforced in equity nor form the basis of an action at law to recover damages for their breach. The reasons for the decisions are that such contracts are lacking in the necessary qualities of definiteness, certainty, and mutuality.
>
> The 1913 contract between these defendants, relative to the reservation of the defendant Killifer, for the season of 1914 is lacking in all of these essential elements.[21]

Sessions' ruling was based primarily on his belief that the Federal League club had not come to court with "clean hands." He noted that the plaintiff was well aware that Killifer was under a moral obligation, if not a legal one, to play with Philadelphia when he was induced to repudiate his obligation and sign with Chicago. Sessions said, "In so doing, a willful wrong was done to the Philadelphia club, which was none the less grievous and harmful because the injured party could not obtain legal redress."[22]

The Federal League club appealed the ruling in the United States Circuit Court of Appeals in Cincinnati, but that court supported Sessions' decision. Killifer returned to Philadelphia and played for the Phillies.

The victory in the case involving Killifer had gone to the National League. Another decision would go the other way. Hal Chase began the 1914 campaign with the Chicago Americans. He had played with New York of the Junior Circuit from 1905 to 1913 and had managed them for a year and a half. He was traded to Chicago early in the 1913 season and played 58 games with the team the following year. Since Chicago could release him by giving him a ten-day notice, Chase decided to give them a ten-day notice that he was leaving. At that point, he signed with the Buffalo club in the Federal League. On June 25, while he was with Buffalo, Chase was served with injunction papers which prohibited him from playing for his new club. The Federal League sought to invoke the Sherman Antitrust law because they believed that Organized Baseball was operating in restraint of trade.

On July 21, New York State Supreme Court Judge Herbert P. Bissell, after hearing the arguments, granted the motion to vacate the injunction which restrained Chase from playing for Buffalo. Although the judge ruled that Organized Baseball did not involve interstate commerce and was not in violation of the Sherman Antitrust law, he said:

The plaintiff can terminate the contract at any time on ten days' notice. The defendant is bound to many obligations under the remarkable provisions of the national agreement. The player's contract, executed in accordance with its terms, binds him not only for the playing season of six months from April 14 to Oct. 14, but also for another season, if the plaintiff chooses to exercise its option, and if it insists upon the requirement of an option clause in each succeeding contract, the defendant can be held for a term of years. His only alternative is to abandon his vocation. Can it fairly be claimed that there is mutuality in such a contract?[23]

Other players used the Federal League threat to gain a salary increase for themselves. Walter Johnson, the ace of Washington's staff, having gone 36-7 in 1913, agreed to terms with a Federal League team but returned to the Senators for the 1914 campaign after they offered him a raise.

The Federal League would have pulled off a monstrous coup if they could have gotten Cobb in the uniform of one of its clubs. Sinclair offered the American League batting champion a three-year contract worth $100,000. He also gave Cobb a guarantee that he would receive the money even if the league folded. Ty, who had battled Navin almost annually for what he thought was a decent working wage, did not accept Sinclair's offer. He had signed a $12,000 contract with the Tigers and, of all people, believed that he should honor it.

Navin, however, was not convinced that Cobb was committed to play for Detroit, and he had a terrible fear that his star outfielder might depart for a more lucrative salary. Cobb, aware of Navin's concern about losing him, played the waiting game and then took on the team's owner. Ty eventually squeezed a new three-year, $45,000 guaranteed contract out of Navin.

Cobb was asked to sign a new type of contract which the American and National Leagues had just initiated. It included a new approach to players' rights:

> Now an option contract was issued by the AL and NL by which the player reserved his own services to his team for the following season, and paid for the reservation out of his salary. By signing, the player tacitly agreed to put himself on option (the club's option, not his), and so rendered the courts unable to act. As smooth as goose grease was this agreement, and few players understood the number of rights they signed away.[24]

The Federal League's Indianapolis club took the first season's pennant with an 88-65 record and one and a half game advantage over

Chicago. The team owners, by and large, suffered significant financial losses over the course of the campaign, but the season had been played and the war had been waged.

Early in the off-season, there were some signs that the outlaw league and Organized Baseball were trying to reach an agreement before the start of the next campaign. The talks broke down when it appeared to the Federal League's leaders that the other two circuits would not officially recognize them as a third major league.

Relations were further strained when, on January 5, 1915, the Federal League's owners filed an antitrust suit in Chicago against Organized Baseball. They knew that Federal Judge Kenesaw Mountain Landis had the reputation of ruling against antitrust practices, and they asked him to rule that the reserve clause and blacklisting practices as provided for by the National Agreement be declared illegal.

Less than two weeks later, the suit was expanded to include individual players in the Federal League as well as the league itself. The court was specifically asked to adjudicate the relation which a player has to Organized Baseball:

> The contracts signed by players in organized baseball were cited, and the court was asked to determine whether the agreements and their interpretation amount to a violation of the laws against enforced servitude, peonage, and the right of every citizen to enter into a free contract.[25]

Organized Baseball responded by submitting a number of affidavits to represent its position. Leaders of the leagues spoke up in support of what they had been doing, with Comiskey serving as one of the leading advocates:

> Charles A. Comiskey, giving his history as a ball player since he entered the professional game at Milwaukee in 1876, at a salary of $70 a month, declares he never broke a contract, and never objected to the ten-day clause in any of the contracts he had signed. He complains of the loss of Hal Chase and Ted Easterly, who left his club for the Federals, and also of the effect that Federal bidding had on the minds of other players.[26]

Heydler was seriously concerned about the Federal League's suit:

> The impression that seems to prevail in some quarters, that the Federal League attack on the National Agreement is a laughing matter, is not shared in by the gentlemen who took part in the Chicago

preliminary conference. On the contrary, the action brought is considered the most serious attack made on the fundamental principles of professional baseball....

Nothing can possibly be accomplished by this proceeding in Chicago next Wednesday except to tear down what has been built up by years of vigilance, backed by the absolute control of the game vested in a central power. Professional baseball has been made by the iron hand of discipline and control. No professional sport has ever lived, or can live, without such controls.[27]

The trial was completed in January, 1915, but Landis did not make his ruling, and the Federal League's second season began without any change in the relationship between the three circuits. The only change in the makeup of the Federal League was that a team in Newark, New Jersey, had replaced the pennant-winning Indianapolis club.

In May another round of peace talks began. It was understood that Landis would withhold judgment until June 1 to allow the parties to reach a peaceful out-of-court settlement. On June 1, there was no peace and, through the summer months, there was no ruling.

In July the Federal League began to talk about further player raids on teams in the other two leagues. Johnson, who was convinced that the Federal League could not financially succeed much longer and that players in Organized Baseball wouldn't be foolish enough to accept their offers, was, nevertheless, furious about the outlaw league's plans:

> Why, it is almost unbelievable.... The Federal League is doing exactly what it asked Judge Landis to prevent. They went into court praying that organized baseball be enjoined from interfering with the players and business of the Federal League. Now, without waiting for the decision of Judge Landis, they announce that they are going out to get players from our leagues, regardless of contracts. No greater anarchy in baseball could be imagined than that. I understand they have already obtained a player from the International League and one from the American Association. That's certainly fine business.[28]

At the conclusion of the 1915 season, a new round of discussions began, and, on October 2, Landis announced another delay in his decision until at least December. Additional filings had been added to the considerations regarding the case, the most recent of which was a suit brought by the Philadelphia National League club against the Chicago Whales and Weeghman, the team's president.

The discussions went into December, with charges and counter-charges flying between the warring factions. Organized Baseball wanted the Federal League to withdraw its suit as a condition for peace. The outlaw league wanted to see signs that it was being taken seriously by the other side.

On December 22, peace was achieved. The Federal League disbanded and Weeghman and Ball, owners of the Chicago and St. Louis franchises, became owners of the National League clubs in their cities. With Weeghman came the Whales' ballyard, Weeghman Park, which would later be renamed Wrigley Field. The historic home of the Chicago Cubs stands today as the last vestige of the Federal League.

The agreement also gave immunity to all minor and major leaguers who had jumped to the outlaw league, and all players, with the exception of those on the Chicago and St. Louis Federal League clubs, would be available to the highest bidder. Robert B. Ward, the league's vice president and the owner of the Brookfeds, also benefited from the agreement. It was reported that "The Ward interests will be reimbursed (an estimated $400,000, payable at the rate of $20,000 per year), by both major leagues assuming this responsibility."[29] The Federal League's suit against Organized Baseball was dropped and another legal test of baseball's monopoly status was avoided.

However, all was not well everywhere. After the peace agreement, Boston Red Sox owner Joseph Lannin wanted to roll back star outfielder Tris Speaker's $18,000 salary to his pre–Federal League rate of $8,000. Speaker threatened to sit out the season rather than accept such a pay cut. Johnson stepped in and worked out a trade between the Red Sox and Cleveland, and a disgruntled Speaker was shipped out of Beantown.

The owners of the Baltimore Federal League franchise were not happy either. They wanted to buy an existing American or National League club and move it to Baltimore. When that didn't happen, the owners raised the money necessary to file a suit based on the Sherman Antitrust Act against Organized Baseball and the Federal League, who they thought had sold them out.

The core of the Sherman Antitrust Act was contained in the following three sections of the suit:

> Section 1 ... Every contract, combination in the form of trust or otherwise, or conspiracy, in restraint of trade or commerce among the several States, or with foreign nations, is hereby declared to be illegal....
>
> Section 2 ... Every person who shall monopolize, or attempt to monopolize, or combine or conspire with any other person or persons, to monopolize any part of the trade or commerce among the several States, or with foreign nations, shall be deemed guilty of a misdemeanor....

Section 3 ... Every contract, combination in form of trust or otherwise, or conspiracy, in restraint of trade or commerce in any Territory of the United States or of the District of Columbia, or in restraint of trade or commerce between any such Territory and another, or between any such Territory or Territories and any State or States or the District of Columbia, or with foreign nations, or between the District of Columbia and any State or States or foreign nations, is declared illegal.[30]

Testimony in the case began in March 1919, and the Baltimore franchise won an award of $264,000 in damages. Organized Baseball appealed the decision. The centerpiece of their appeal was the position that baseball was not involved in interstate commerce, and was not, therefore, subject to the Sherman Antitrust Act. On December 6, 1920, the District Court of Appeals in Washington, D.C., overturned the earlier decision, ruling:

The transportation in interstate commerce of the players and the paraphernalia used by them was but an incident to the main purpose of the appellants, namely the production of the game. It was for it they were in business—not for the purpose of transferring players, balls, and uniforms....

So, here baseball is not commerce, though some of its incidents may be.[31]

The Baltimore club appealed the ruling to the United States Supreme Court, and Judge Oliver Wendell Holmes, writing in 1922 for a unanimous court, reinforced the earlier opinion that baseball was not involved in interstate commerce. Holmes ruled that baseball was basically a sport, conducted in local ballparks before local fans, and was not subject to prosecution under antitrust laws. The historic decision appeared to give baseball an antitrust exemption.

Concurrent with the most important legal decision in baseball history, the game also made its most important structural change—the naming of a commissioner.

On November 12, 1920, Landis became baseball's first commissioner, and he was to become both the judge and the jury over the game.

His first major decision was to ban the eight White Sox players who he believed had been involved in throwing the 1918 World Series. After they had been tried and found innocent in a civil court on August 2, 1921, Landis barred the group from the game for life.

During the trial, it had become apparent to many that Comiskey, the Chicago owner, had been very tight with his money and was paying

Charles Comiskey and Chicago Cubs president William L. Veeck, Sr., in a Chicago courtroom in 1920. (National Baseball Hall of Fame Library, Cooperstown, N.Y.)

his players as little as he could get away with. In 1918 he had promised his club a pennant-winning bonus—it turned out to be a case of cheap champagne! Some of the players, both those who were on trial and some who were not, used the miserly Old Roman's unwillingness to adequately pay his players as a rationale for their actions. Dickie Kerr, one of the honest White Sox, who had won two World Series games in 1918, and had 21-9 and 19-17 records the next two seasons, quit the team when Comiskey refused to raise his $4,500 salary for 1921. Kerr left to play semi-pro baseball where he made more money. Ironically, this was the same Comiskey who had jumped to the Players League in 1890 in an attempt to increase the salary he was receiving from the St. Louis club of the American Association.

With the warfare over and Landis, who was often referred to as the game's "High Commissioner," in office, baseball entered a golden age. It was the "roaring twenties," with the charismatic Babe Ruth and Lou Gehrig helping to build the New York Yankee dynasty, with Frankie Frisch and the Giants in the Polo Grounds, the Waner brothers in Pittsburgh, and general manager Branch Rickey along with second baseman Rogers Hornsby leading the St. Louis Cardinals to prominence. Americans had money to spend on entertainment, and baseball claimed an important place in the entertainment field.

CHAPTER THREE

Baseball Faces Challenges
on a Number of Fronts

The Great Depression brought austerity to the nation and delivered a financial blow to baseball's owners and players. Teams, both in the major and minor leagues, had known prosperity in the 1920s. Major league attendance had soared to an average of 9.6 million a season over the years 1924–29 and reached 10.1 million in 1930. Sunday baseball games, which had been legalized in all states with major league clubs except Pennsylvania, helped to increase attendance figures. However, the Depression depleted citizens' wallets and pocketbooks, and major league clubs began to realize that there were increasing numbers of empty seats in their ballparks. Major league attendance fell to 8.4 million in 1931 and plummeted to 6 million two years later. The minors also experienced a drastic decline. A promising recovery began in 1935 and major league attendance from then through the 1940 campaign averaged 8,650,000.

Player salaries, which had risen to an average of $7,500 in 1929, fell to $6,000 by 1933 as teams struggled with their financial limitations. The average salary was up to $7,300 by 1939, but it was still below what it had been a decade earlier.

Average attendance and salary figures were just that—an average. Some clubs made out better than others. During the down years from 1931 through 1934, the New York Yankees had the highest annual average attendance with 864,000 at the Stadium while the St. Louis Browns pulled up the rear with an average of 123,500 fans in the seats at Sportsman's Park each season. In the National League the Chicago Cubs led the way, averaging 840,000 fans at Wrigley Field. The Philadelphia Phillies' 219,000 patrons were the fewest in the Senior Circuit on a yearly basis.

Tom Yawkey, the wealthy owner of the Boston Red Sox, who took control of the club in 1933, represented a small group of magnates who had the resources available to purchase players. During the lean years, Yawkey bought Lefty Grove and Bing Miller from the Philadelphia Athletics, Heinie Manush from the Washington Senators, Rick Ferrell from the Browns, his brother Wes from the Cleveland Indians, as well as other players. Three of them—Lefty, Heinie, and Rick went on to become Hall of Famers.

Commissioner Kenesaw Mountain Landis had been a strong leader and, at times, an arbitrary one. During his tenure in office, he had solidified the integrity of the game. In the latter part of the 1930s, a couple of clubs took a hit from him when they went beyond the rules of the game as he understood them.

The commissioner believed that local ownership and operation of minor league clubs were in the best interest of baseball, and he did everything within his power to curb the practice of major league clubs owning farmhands. He thought that the depth of some minor league systems worked against those clubs' players having a fair opportunity to make it to the majors.

Landis said:

> From the beginning ... the commissioner has regarded the farm system as evil; evil not because ownership of several non-competing clubs is bad in itself—although it questionably is preferable every club is independently owned and operated—but evil because such ownerships are operated to control great numbers of players, imperiling their essential rights, if the rules do not prevent such operation, and also because it reduces minor league clubs to subserviency.[1]

Landis' war against farm systems worked to the benefit of some minor leaguers. In 1938, under the rule that no major league club could control two teams in the same minor league, the commissioner took action against the St. Louis Cardinals and their expansive minor league system which had been developed by Branch Rickey. On March 23, Landis declared that an estimated 100 players who belonged to six Midwest teams were free agents. Although the final number of players affected was fewer than that, the action had a major impact on the Cards and sent a clear message to other clubs. Landis reported:

> [the] investigation establishes beyond doubt or question that the Cedar Rapids club and its affiliates in 1936 and 1937 were merely adjuncts to the St. Louis system and that St. Louis controlled the players of two clubs in each of three Class D leagues in 1936 and in each of four Class D leagues in 1937.

Commissioner Kenesaw Mountain Landis looks over the game. (National Baseball Hall of Fame Library, Cooperstown, N.Y.)

Throughout this period ... St. Louis and Cedar Rapids represented that there was no agreement or understanding between them, and so certified officially in purported compliance with the rules.[2]

Two years later, Landis took similar action against the Detroit Tigers. In 1940 he freed players who were in higher classifications than the Cards' farmhands had been. Four major leaguers and 87 others in Double-A and below were declared free agents. Detroit management said that the value of the players they lost was in excess of $500,000. The commissioner felt that the Tigers were in violation of the rules by using its farm clubs to hide dozens of players.

John Kieran wrote in the *New York Times*:

> Maybe he should have been named Abraham Lincoln Landis. If he keeps going in his recent stride, the Commissioner of Baseball may wind up freeing more slaves than the Great Emancipator....
>
> As this distant observer understands these emancipation proclamations of "Abraham Lincoln" Landis, the slaves are freed because the Commissioner of Baseball interprets the rules one way and the shocked club owners interpret them another way. Every so often they get together and talk over the rules and apparently no agreement comes of it. The magnates and "Honest Abe" Landis do not speak the same language.[3]

Landis used the Detroit situation as an opportunity to issue five new rules regarding players' contracts:

1. Players must not be signed to blank contracts and a true copy of the contract must be delivered to and left with the player.
2. Players must not be signed for other clubs, directly or indirectly, whether owned, affiliated or independent.
3. Players must not be placed with other clubs, except under proper transfer agreements, duly filed for promulgation, which agreements must be optional assignments if the assignor desires to retain a right of acquisition exercisable before the player has passed through a selection period at which he is subject to selection.
4. "Working agreements" must be truthfully set forth in the officially filed document "the actual consideration, terms and conditions" of that agreement and there must be no "agreement not embodied in the document as filed."
5. "Working agreements" must be executed by the club actually making same, and must not be executed in the names of affiliated or subsidiary clubs to whom the major or other higher-classification club supplies the necessary funds therefore by loans, advances, capital stock subscriptions, player purchases, or other methods whatsoever.[4]

The "High Commissioner" also put in a variety of responses in place for those who violated the new rules. A club would be fined from $500 to $1,000 for each offense and the officials or employees who committed the wrongdoing would also be punished for their actions.

It was ironic that Landis, as commissioner, "worked for" the owners but often made decisions that benefited the players. Perhaps, his intention was to create a more level playing field for all.

Shortly after baseball witnessed Landis's battle with the major league clubs that had acted contrary to the rules regarding their involvement with the minors, the game became part of a much bigger war—World War II. The shortage of players with legitimate major league ability had the greatest impact on the game. During the 1942–1945 seasons, 5400 of the 5800 professional players at the time of Pearl Harbor spent some time in the military. Transportation was curtailed by the war effort. The quality of baseballs and bats was also affected by shortages of rubber and wood. A number of franchises suffered great economic hardship. Philadelphia's National League club went bankrupt and was purchased by Robert R. M. Carpenter, Jr., of Delaware's duPont family. The 1945 season took place although it looked for a time as if it would be canceled, but the All-Star Game was not played that year. And lights in baseball parks on the East Coast, which were thought to create a security risk, were turned off.

After peace was achieved, the 1946 campaign promised a return to the quality of prewar baseball. Many stars were returning to their teams. Some had made it back during the 1945 season. Hank Greenberg rejoined Detroit in July and sparked them to the 1945 World Championship. The Tigers also welcomed Virgil "Fire" Trucks home. He worked five innings in a late-season game and then pitched the second game of the Fall Classic, beating the Cubs, 4–1. Cleveland's Bob Feller returned and went to the mound for the Indians in August.

Not all the players, however, headed for baseball in the United States. The Mexican League had launched raids on major league talent, offering them fabulous opportunities to play ball south of the border. In mid–February, 1946, there were rumors that five Mexican Pasquel brothers—Alfonso, Bernardo, Girardo, Jorge, and Mario—were planning to sign players in Organized Baseball in the United States to add to the talent in Mexico for a major league in that country. The Pasquels were engaged in an import-export business and there were reports that they had $40 million (American) behind them to entice "poorly paid peons" (players) in the American and National Leagues to leave their clubs for a new life of baseball and riches in Mexico. Organized Baseball went to war against the new outlaw league.

Danny Gardella, a second-year outfielder with the New York Giants in 1945 and a player of modest ability, was the first to sign a contract to play in the Mexican League. Jorge Pasquel, who was primarily a liquor dealer, had met Gardella at a New York City gym and told the 25 year old that riches awaited him and other players in Mexico City, Vera Cruz, Monterrey, Tampico, Neuvo Laredo, Puebla, San Luis Potosi, and Torreon. Pasquel offered Gardella $15,000, which was about three times the salary he was making with the Giants, and Danny accepted it. The new Mexican Leaguer also became a recruiter for the inviting new enterprise.

As yet, major league owners were not taking the prospect of losing some of their players very seriously. Gardella, with a .267 batting average in 1945 against pitching staffs that had been severely depleted by the war, was not a great loss for the Polo Grounders. With better players returning from the battlefields to reclaim their places on the playing fields, it was anticipated that Gardella would probably be spending the 1946 season in the minors.

During the next couple of months, the Pasquels set their sights on and aimed their money at some of the best major leaguers. Feller, Greenberg, Stan Musial, and Ted Williams were among those mentioned as possible defectors, but none of them took the offer. An offer was also made to a young Brooklyn farmhand—Jackie Robinson. He, too, turned the Pasquels down.

Some owners began to take the situation more seriously. The Brooklyn Dodgers lost Luis Olmo, a native of Puerto Rico and a .313 hitter with 110 RBI in 1945, pitcher Adrian Zabala, and catcher Mickey Owen. Vern Stephens, the Browns' 25-year-old starting shortstop, was one of the first players to sign to play in Mexico. On March 31, the Giants watched as second baseman George Hausmann, pitcher Sal Maglie, and rookie first baseman-outfielder Roy Zimmerman packed their bags and departed. Maglie had signed a Mexican League contract which paid him five times more than he would have made with the Giants. During the season, the Cardinals lost the services of left-hander Max Lanier, who was off to a 6-0 start but was hiding a sore arm from his manager for fear that he would be sent down to the minors or sold if owner Sam Breadon heard about the injury. Rookie right-hander Fred Martin and infielder Lou Klein also left the Cards with Lanier and headed for Mexico.

Although the leadership of the three New York teams—the Dodgers, Giants, and Yankees—spoke publicly that all was well with their clubs, each would seek a restraining order in the courts to forbid further raids by the Mexican bandits. In May, Larry MacPhail, the Yankees' president, went to court in his club's battle against the insurgents.

Bernardo Pasquel, brother of the league president Jorge, reacted to MacPhail's legal action and promised that his organization would go to the United States Supreme Court to establish our right to offer better salaries than are now open to baseball players on the North American continent.... We have offered players better salaries, improved working conditions and reduced working hours to play in Mexico and we have no apologies for these actions.[5]

Even though MacPhail was successful in the courts, not all the owners were happy with his attempt to handle the Pasquels and the Mexican League in that manner. They were willing to give the Mexican League time to disappear and were fearful of having the question about the legality of a player's contract find its way into the courts.

A ruling on May 5, 1946, had alerted Organized Baseball to the role that the courts could play in disputes between a player and his team. In an unprecedented decision, Assistant United States Attorney Tom A. Durham ruled that the Seattle Rainiers of the Pacific Coast League must reinstate infielder Al Niemec, who had played for them before entering military service. The Rainiers had released Niemec, and he appealed to the Selective Service Board for reinstatement to his former job. Referring to the GI Bill of Rights, Durham ruled:

> Baseball is no different than a store or a machine shop.... The law is simple. A veteran rates his job back and we intend to see that the law is carried out. We are not interested in whether or not Niemec plays with the Rainiers, but they will have to carry him on the club and pay him his salary.[6]

With an increased sensitivity to the role the courts might play in player disputes, some of the owners were jittery:

> in doing so [going to the courts], the clubs had invited legal attention to the potentially explosive issue of the Uniform Player's Contract with its reserve clause and ten-day severance provision. In the hearing for the injunction sought by the Yankees the Pasquels' attorney argued that Organized Baseball constituted an illegal monopoly, but he also raised the issue of the player's contract and characterized it as a form of peonage. New York State Supreme Court Justice Julius Miller eventually granted the injunction the Yankees sought, and he chastised the Pasquels for seducing employees to break contracts they'd voluntarily entered into. But before he made his decision, Miller asked what were to prove troubling questions about the contract and whether in its present form it was absolutely essential to the continued health of the game.[7]

The Pasquels had plans for luring more than players to Mexico. Commissioner A. B. "Happy" Chandler was offered a $50,000 salary to become high commissioner of the Mexican League. The five-year contract plus living expenses did not interest Chandler. What interested Happy was making sure that the players who left for Mexico would not have an easy return to Organized Baseball. He threatened all the "contract breakers" with at least a five-year suspension if they didn't return by the start of the major league's 1946 regular season.

The Mexican League opened its season on March 21, with American imports in the clubs' lineups. Nineteen players would spend time during the campaign south of the border. Not all who signed to play in Mexico were satisfied with their new lives. Stephens and Owen discovered that conditions were not what they were told they would be. Accommodations and the ballparks were far below what they were in the United States. Stephens returned to the Browns on April 6, even though Jorge Pasquel offered him an increased salary to stay and play in Vera Cruz. He negotiated a contract with St. Louis which was better than his pre–Mexico offer had been, and he played 115 games for them in 1946.

Owen's experience was far different from Stephens'. Rickey, the Dodgers' president and general manager, had been willing to renegotiate Olmo's contract in February after he had signed with the Mexican League. However, "the Mahatma" believed that to take Owen back in April, under any circumstances, would be to go against the sanctity of the contract which was the foundation of the game. He said:

> I hope Owen goes to Mexico.... If he returned to the Brooklyn club he would get not a cent more than his previous contract called for ... if he does come back he will be immediately for sale or trade. I do not want him on this club.[8]

Without a welcome in Brooklyn and not wanting to retire from baseball, Owen returned to Mexico and resumed his position as player-manager of the Vera Cruz club.

The Mexican raiders were not overlooked in Boston on opening day. In pregame ceremonies at Braves Field, a trio of musicians sporting sombreros stood in front of the visiting Dodgers' dugout and played "South of the Border." After finishing their musical rendition, they tossed fake pesos into the stands.

In addition to the Mexican onslaught from the south, another force was positioning itself in the north to take on Organized Baseball. Boston labor lawyer and baseball fan Robert Francis Murphy was organizing the American Baseball Guild (A.B.G.) to help major leaguers obtain better working conditions. A.B.G. chapters were formed by a number of teams, player representatives were elected, and the subject of higher salaries, increased pension and benefit plan was discussed. A strike was mentioned as a potential weapon in the players' arsenal in any upcoming war against the owners.

On June 4, 1946, Murphy said that a majority of players on six teams had enrolled in the A.B.G., and that those on the Tigers, Red Sox, and Yankees were proving to be the toughest to attract. He had begun his work with the Pirates since "Pittsburgh is a highly unionized city covered by both National and State Labor Relation acts."[9] After Pittsburgh owner John W. Galbreath refused to meet with him and a committee of players to discuss working conditions with the club, Murphy called for the Pirates to strike before a June night game in Forbes Field. Chandler got wind of the proposed strike from Pirate pitcher Rip Sewell, and the commissioner helped line up a team of old timers to play in place of the regular Bucs. Hall of Famer Honus Wagner, Pittsburgh's 72-year-old former superstar, was one of those on deck. Sewell was successful in convincing his teammates not to strike, and the game went on as scheduled. Chandler presented a gold watch to Sewell as a token of his appreciation.

The A.B.G. had also drawn interest from players in the Pacific Coast League. Murphy said he had not talked with anyone in that league because his time was being taken up working with the major leaguers. He said that if a majority of players on any team in the Pacific Coast League wanted to join the A.B.G. that he would help them organize.

The loss of players to the Mexican League and the threat of unionization by those who remained made the magnates more willing to negotiate with their employees. It was a reminder of the forces that had been at work during the time of the Federal League and Baseball Players' Fraternity in 1914, when management and the players sat down to rewrite some of the operating conditions of the game.

On July 8, the leaders of Organized Baseball set up the Major League Steering Committee, with MacPhail as its chairman. National League president Ford Frick and owners Phil Wrigley of the Cubs and Breadon of the Cardinals were their league's representatives. President William Harridge, MacPhail and Yawkey were the members of the committee from the Junior Circuit. Leslie M. O'Connor of the Chicago White Sox (and a former associate of Landis) joined the committee in an advisory capacity.

On July 18, in a precedent-setting move, the Steering Committee initiated the formation of a management-sponsored players' committee which was invited to bring their concerns to the owners. Three players from each league were selected to serve as spokesmen during the meetings with the Major League Steering Committee. Cleveland's Mel Harder,

Chicago's Joe Kuhel, and New York's Johnny Murphy represented the American League. The National Leaguers were St. Louis' Marty Marion, Boston's Billy Herman, and Brooklyn's Dixie Walker.

Chandler would become known as the players' commissioner. Happy, who had been elected partially because the owners thought that they could . control him easier than they had been able to handle Landis, encouraged the players as the first meeting drew near. He told the owners

> they're going to make more money this year than at any time in the history of baseball, and now's the time to give the men who play for them something which should have been granted long ago.
>
> Only by dealing generously with their players are the magnates going to combat such an item as the invasion of Pasquel. You can't blame kids for grabbing the big money he's putting out, but he can't keep that up, and won't.
>
> However, it is our duty to help our players rise above such a temptation by providing for them where they really want to play. Then we can talk to Pasquel and anyone like him on our terms.[10]

The two sides sat down together on August 5 in the Yankees' office to engage in a new exercise—collective bargaining. MacPhail presented the owners' need to retain the reserve clause. The players spoke about salaries, fringe benefits, and a pension plan.

By the end of August, the players had been promised a number of improvements in their working conditions in a new Uniform Player's Contract. There would be a $5,000 minimum salary (although not the $6,500 the players had sought), a pension plan (MacPhail had already inaugurated baseball's first such plan with the Yankees), and a modification of the ten-day release clause. As a result of the negotiations, the players were promised that there would be a 25 percent limit on pay cuts, expansion of postseason barnstorming from 10 to 30 days and $25 a week for incidental expenses during spring training. The players called the latter "Murphy money" because they viewed it as a payoff for rejecting the A.B.G. and Murphy. Also, a new Executive Council, which included an elected player from each league, was put in place. The players, however, were not granted another of their requests which would have been a significant coup had they gotten it—that the player receive one-half of the sale price when he was sold. The owners still retained the reserve clause. MacPhail reported that "not more than 1% [of the players] wanted any change."[11]

The major source of revenue for the players' benefits would come from national radio and television income. The players had suggested a series of inter-league games as a way of raising the funds to financially support the agreement. They proposed that late in the season the first-place teams in each league play each other as a prelude to the Fall Classic. The other teams, based on the standings on July 1, would play the corresponding club from the other circuit. The proposal was rejected by those who sat on the other side of the table.

The new agreement was approved in December 1946, at the Major League meetings in Los Angeles. There was also an agreement made between the two major leagues and the National Association, which was the governing body for the minor leagues. It established a new bonus rule which put a $6,000 limit (reduced from $7,500) on the amount a major league club could pay a player as an extra reward for signing a contract. If a team signed a player and paid him a bonus in excess of the limit it would be fined.

The players were feeling more empowered and much happier as a result of the victories they had achieved through negotiations. The A.B.G. quietly disappeared. A disappointed Murphy said, "The players have been offered an apple ... but they could have had an orchard."[12]

The disappearance of the threat from the A.B.G. was followed a short time later by the players' disillusionment with the Mexican League. Those who had left Organized Baseball for promises of riches south of the border had pocketed more money but also had suffered through endless rain, long and uncomfortable bus rides, strange food, and inferior lighting in substandard ballparks—one of which had a railroad track running through the outfield!

The Mexican League came upon hard times as the 1947 season approached. Many native players threatened to strike if they did not receive the same level of salaries that had been eagerly handed out to the visiting Americans. Two teams did not survive financially and dropped out of the league before the new season got off to a late and rocky start.

The 18 contract jumpers returned home with the intention of rejoining their major league teams for the 1947 campaign. That was not to be. Chandler's threatened five-year suspension was in effect and the players would not be allowed to participate in Organized Baseball until their penalty was paid and they were removed from the blacklist. Some owners saw more than a baseball infraction in the players' actions. Rickey viewed their disloyal act, along with their questioning of the reserve clause, as a sign of "avowed Communistic tendencies."[13]

After the players were informed by Chandler that they were suspended for five years, as he had said he would do in March 1946, three of them headed to the courts to ask for a ruling that would require Organized Baseball to reinstate them immediately. Gardella was suing for

$300,000 in treble damages; Lanier and Martin were suing for a combined $2,500,000.

Gardella's lawyer was Frederic Johnson, an attorney who knew both the law and baseball. Since Gardella had not signed a contract with the Giants for the 1946 season before leaving for Mexico, Johnson believed that his client had a legitimate case. In the affidavit, Johnson challenged the legality of the reserve clause. He also introduced a novel dimension, arguing that the presence of radio and television had extended the game into interstate commerce.

Organized Baseball filed a motion to dismiss the suit in New York District Court. On July 14, 1948, Judge Henry W. Goddard did so, citing United States Supreme Court Justice Oliver Wendell Holmes' seminal ruling in 1922 in the case involving the Federal Baseball Club of Baltimore v. the National League of Professional Baseball Clubs.

The three players appealed the decision, and the case involving Gardella was heard first by the United States Court of Appeals for the Second Circuit. The three-man appellate court heard Johnson's argument and, on February 9, 1949, issued a 2–1 ruling in Gardella's favor. It was the opinion of the majority of the judges that the case was strong enough to merit a trial. Judge Jerome N. Frank made it clear that he thought the reserve clause of the standard baseball contract was illegal. Judge Learned Hand, in a separate opinion, indicated that he felt the reserve clause would have to go if baseball was declared a monopoly. The Court of Appeals directed the Federal District Court to determine whether television and radio broadcasting had brought Organized Baseball within the scope of antitrust laws and whether it had violated those laws.

Gardella, who was working as an orderly in New York City's Mount Vernon Hospital, had scored a victory.

In the event that the trial's verdict went against Organized Baseball, certain members of Congress were attempting to pass legislation which would legalize the reserve clause and grant baseball an exception from antitrust laws. Arkansas congressman Wilbur Mills introduced such a bill in the House of Representatives. Nothing came of Mills' bill, but it wouldn't be the final time that Congress, antitrust laws, the reserve clause, and baseball would become intertwined. Whereas Mills was supportive of the reserve clause in this instance, that would not always be the position taken by other members of Congress.

Owen, along with a number of the other jumpers who had appealed to Organized Baseball for reinstatement, was not pleased with Gardella's legal fight. On the day following the Court of Appeals' decision, Mickey reacted strongly:

I hope Danny Gardella loses his suit against baseball....

Baseball didn't force us to go to Mexico; we went because of our own weakness. Baseball needs the reserve clause, and while I am in the same boat as Gardella, I would not file suit to try to break it.[14]

That same day, U.S. Representative A. S. Syd Herlong, a Democrat from Florida and the former president of the Florida State League, addressed the House of Representatives and urged Gardella to withdraw his suit:

Organized baseball received a stunning blow yesterday when the Court of Appeals ruled in effect that the contract of a player is not binding.... Players and club and league officials have traditionally had a complete understanding that the particular type of contract under which they operated was necessary to perpetuate our national game....

I sincerely hope that any player who would destroy baseball for personal gain, will, for the sake of American youth, reconsider his actions before it is too late....

[This action] could well sound the death knell for the sport that has kindled the fires of ambition in the breasts of so many thousands of young Americans.[15]

Arthur Daley, writing in the *New York Times*, painted a picture of the game without the reserve clause:

Let us suppose that the Supreme Court eventually rules that the reserve clause is a monopolistic practice and illegal. At the end of each season every player then is on the open market. So Dan Topping of the Yankees, Tom Yawkey of the Red Sox, Walter Briggs of the Tigers and Phil Wrigley of the Cubs—assuming that they are the wealthiest owners in the major leagues—begin bidding for players. It would amount to the boyish pastime of choosing up sides, except that money is involved....

This, mind you, is no attempt to pass on the legalistic merits or demerits of the reserve clause. It is merely an effort to report how impossible it would be for baseball or any professional team sport to survive its abolition. Up till now no one in the diamond game—including those oppressed peons, the players—has made any effort to subject a player contract to court scrutiny. They were willing to let well enough alone and keep the Government out of the business of athletics.[16]

On June 2, Gardella, Lanier, and Martin lost their appeal for a quick reinstatement. The Circuit Court in New York affirmed the District Court's earlier ruling that to compel reinstatement of the players through the court "would restore them to positions they resigned voluntarily.[17]

Three days later, Chandler announced that he was granting amnesty to all 18 players who had been placed on the ineligible list for having gone to Mexico, and said that he was welcoming them back to Organized Baseball. Speaking about the court cases, which he felt had tied his hands with regard to the question of reinstatement, the commissioner said:

> While this situation was still before the courts and could be interpreted as a threat, however, I could not even consider taking such action voluntarily. Baseball will not ever surrender to threats of force, and it cannot afford to take any action which could be interpreted as such a surrender....
>
> The attempt to force immediate reinstatement through the courts has now failed.[18]

Olmo returned to the Dodgers for the 1949 season, and Owen, who had been rejected by Rickey upon his brief return in 1946, ended up playing for the Cubs.

Gardella, Lanier, and Martin, who were among those granted amnesty, continued to fight through legal channels. When the 1949 campaign began, they were playing semi-pro baseball in the Quebec Provincial League. Martin and Lanier dropped their suits on August 27, and the pitchers rejoined St. Louis in their pennant fight with Brooklyn. Martin went 6-0 and Lanier was 5-4 down the stretch as the Cards finished one game behind the Dodgers.

Believing that Gardella was facing a long and extended ordeal, Johnson urged him to settle out of court. On October 8, 1949, Gardella accepted a settlement from Organized Baseball which amounted to $60,000. The owners were happy to settle before the trial, thereby avoiding another legal test of the reserve clause.

By the 1950 season, Gardella had received his unconditional release from the Giants and had signed with the Cardinals. He played one game for St. Louis before retiring.

Even though the issues that had been created by the Mexican League jumpers were behind Organized Baseball, the battles about the reserve clause were not.

In July 1951, Brooklyn Congressman Emanuel Celler, chairman of the House Monopoly subcommittee, launched an investigation to determine whether organized baseball was violating antitrust laws. Celler reported that President Harry S Truman was wholeheartedly in favor of the investigation. The congressman said, "The President, I am very glad to say, completely endorsed our plan to hear testimony from club owners and players."[19]

Hall of Famer Ty Cobb, the 64-year-old former star who had almost annually challenged the Tigers' owner about his salary, was the first to testify. The legendary "Georgia Peach is"

> defended as essential to the orderly and successful operation of baseball the reserve clause in players' contracts and the franchise system under which club owners control territorial rights. He rejected insinuations that the clause made the players "peons."[20]

Many other players who appeared before the subcommittee also staunchly defended the reserve clause. Even those who were against it testified that some form of the clause was necessary for the conduct of the game.

When the House bill came up for a vote more than a year later, it was defeated by an overwhelming majority. A bill in the Senate at the same time never made it out of committee and a vote on it was never taken.

There were a number of cases in the courts at the time and, perhaps, they would serve as the avenue for resolution of the issue.

In 1953 the United States Supreme Court, with Chief Justice Earl Warren presiding, reaffirmed the ruling in the 1922 "Federal Case" in a suit brought by Yankee farmhand George Toolson. Toolson had been placed on the ineligible list after he refused to accept a demotion from Triple-A Newark of the International League to Binghamton of the Eastern League, which was a lower classification team. Major league clubs would keep top talent in the minors as protection against being caught short-handed if one of their major leaguers was injured. Toolson, who could probably have played for a number of other major league teams, found himself in that situation. He believed that he was being denied the opportunity to play in the majors because of the depth of the Yankees' farm system.

Toolson's case, along with others of a similar nature, went all the way to the Supreme Court, where, on November 9, the Holmes' decision was left standing by a 7–2 vote in a brief per curiam decision. A per curiam decision is by the court instead of a majority opinion written by an individual justice.

The decision reaffirmed baseball as a sport and not as a business:

> In Federal Baseball ... this court held that ... professional baseball ... was not within the scope of the federal antitrust laws. Congress has had the ruling under consideration but has not seen fit to bring such a business under these laws by legislation having prospective effect.... The present cases ask us to overrule the prior decision,

and, with retrospective effect, hold the (antitrust laws) applicable. We think that if there are evils in this field which now warrant application to it of the antitrust laws it should be by legislation. Without re-examination of the underlying issues, the judgments below are affirmed on the authority of Federal baseball.[21]

Baseball had become the ball in a ping-pong match between Congress and the courts. As reported in the *New York Times*, the Supreme Court looked to the legislative branch of government, which it said had had ample opportunity to change the law but had not availed itself of the opportunity:

> The Supreme Court threw a hard, high fast one to Congress, however, by noting pointedly that, if the character of baseball's operations had changed since 1922, it was the business of Congress to do something about it.[22]

Former National League president Ford C. Frick, who had replaced Chandler in 1951 when the commissioner did not receive the necessary 75 percent of the clubs' votes for him to gain another term in office, expressed baseball's relief:

> Naturally I am pleased with the decision.... I have always felt that baseball was primarily a sport and not the kind of business which Congress intended to bring under the Federal antitrust laws. The decision clarifies that point.
> Until this decision baseball was in a fog of uncertainty. From now on the responsibility is ours of modernizing baseball; of stepping from the past into the changing present and making sure always that our decisions and our policies are based on honesty, on fairness, on true sportsmanship, and with the best interests of the fans and the players and those who make baseball our great national game.[23]

The decision had been rendered and there was optimism for the future. But the fog would return.

CHAPTER FOUR

The Brewing Storm

After World War II, baseball entered a new era—a golden era. Interest in the game grew rapidly. Major league attendance, which had been 10.8 million in 1945, exploded to 18.5 million a season later. In both 1948 and 1949 over 20 million fans came to big league ballparks.

Minor league baseball was a hit as well, and teams sprang up all over the country. A person could watch the game in the majesty of a major league stadium or in a minor league park in classifications from lowly D to AAA.

The New York Yankees were at the top of the game, winning the World Series in 1947 and every season between 1949 and 1953. Joe DiMaggio and Mickey Mantle patrolled the Yankees' outfield in 1951 when the "Yankee Clipper" was finishing his Hall of Fame career, and "The Mick" was just beginning his.

Off the field, the players found themselves in another power struggle with owners. In 1953 the players hired New York attorney J. Norman Lewis to represent them as part-time legal advisor to the newly created Major League Baseball Players Association [MLBPA]. The organization was led by player representatives Ralph Kiner of the Pittsburgh Pirates and Allie Reynolds of the Yankees. One of their first actions was to seek improvement in the existing pension plan. A number of owners were outraged by the players' demands—"requests" might be a more suitable term at that point. These organized efforts by the men on the field would eventually result in the MLBPA arguably becoming the most successful union in history—and not just in sports history.

Agreements and court cases were beginning to claim more space on the sports pages. In 1957 there was positive player-owner activity in a number of areas. On February 1, the 16 club owners adopted a new five-year pension plan, which had been approved by the players. It would be financed from the $16 million which baseball expected to receive in the following five years from the sale of radio and television rights to the World Series and All-Star Games. The plan also included improved hospital and disability benefits. Commissioner Ford Frick said that the agreement "was as generous as anything ever written for any group of men in America."[1]

The owners were not as generous the next day when they rejected the players' request for an increase in the minimum salary from $6,000 to $7,500. The owners did agree to schedule an annual meeting at which all 16 player representatives, one from each team, could discuss their desires, problems, and grievances with their employers.

The same month the Supreme Court, by a 6–3 vote, declared that the National Football League (NFL) was no longer exempt from antitrust laws. The case had been filed on behalf of William Radovich, a former all-pro guard with the Detroit Lions. Radovich believed that he had been denied a position as the player-coach with a team in the Pacific Coast League because he had played in the All-American Conference, which was a rival to the NFL.

NFL commissioner Bert Bell was confused by the justices' decision because it left baseball as the only professional sport specifically held by the courts to be outside the antitrust laws. Bell was confused and, also, angry:

> I always thought that under the Constitution of the United States all people were regarded as being equal.... Evidently under the Supreme Court decision, baseball, a team sport, is different from football, a team sport.[2]

It would not be long before the government turned its gaze back to the "business of baseball." The House of Representatives was considering a pair of bills aimed at placing the national pastime under antitrust laws. One of the bills was sponsored by Emanuel Celler of Brooklyn who had failed in the same effort in 1951. California congressman Patrick J. Hillings was the sponsor of a second bill. Hillings cited the $1 million offer by the Boston Red Sox to the Cleveland Indians for left-handed pitcher Herb Score as "clinching evidence that baseball is a business—big business."[3]

Major League Baseball began lining up its team to face Congress. A four-man committee, including Frick, National League president Warren Giles, American League president William Harridge and National Association (minor league organization) president George Trautman, was appointed to handle all legislative matters on behalf of baseball at the hearings in Washington.

According to the *New York Times*, Frick, Giles, and Harridge were subpoenaed on June 4 to appear before the House Monopoly subcommittee. The following day, Celler said that the baseball executives had been invited, not subpoenaed, since the latter would have been necessary only if they had refused to appear. Lewis, the players' attorney, was also invited along with a number of players including the Yankees' Jerry Coleman, the St. Louis Cardinals' Stan Musial, the Philadelphia Phillies' Robin Roberts, and the Washington Senators' Eddie Yost. Roberts was the National League's player representative and Yost held the same position for the Junior Circuit. Bob Feller, who had retired following the 1956 season, was also summoned to the hearings.

During the hearings, the daily reports regularly appeared on page one of the *New York Times* rather than on the sports pages.

Frick, in his testimony on June 19, reasoned:

> If the result of the proposed statute should be the elimination of the reserve clause ... a chaotic scramble for player talent will ensue. The natural result will be a concentration of the best player talent on the clubs which are able to spend the money to outbid other clubs.... I see baseball set back fifty years.[4]

The commissioner used the hearings as an opportunity to announce a proposed change with regard to drafting minor leaguers. He hoped the owners would consider and approve the measure at their December meetings. Frick's plan provided that any player who had been in the minors for four years would be eligible for an unrestricted draft by any of the 16 clubs in the majors. As a result, a minor leaguer might no longer be owned by a club for an entire career and that, according to Frick, would "eliminate the opportunity for unfairness in that direction."[5]

Frick described what he thought was necessary for the game:

> As between the American League and National League, and between teams in the minor leagues, the reserve rule is the foundation of professional baseball. If one league is permitted to raid another league for players without the limitation of the reserve clause, the lower-class minor leagues could not exist. For as they developed players and promoted public interest in them, clubs in larger cities would snatch them away without any compensation, thus depriving the club of its players, its team organization, its public interest and support, and its involvement in the development of these players. The unique structure of baseball, with the reserve system as its keystone, provides a nationwide system of apprenticeships for developing players' skills and experience and, at the same time, protects the player and assures

advancement commensurate with his ability, through the draft and waiver rules....

To preserve competition on the field, the competition for players must be regulated. This is an axiom to which all baseball operators agree and which experience had proved.[6]

In their testimony on June 24, Coleman, Roberts, and Yost backed the need for the reserve clause. However, the following day Feller told the House panel that he thought baseball was a business and there could be places for antitrust controls. He spoke about a number of possibilities, including

Limiting the reserve clause to three years, with conditions. If a player got at least a 15 percent rise in pay the club could extend the clause for two more years.

Subjecting minor-league players to a "free draft" after they showed what they could do for three years.

Lifting of restrictions on playing winter ball, or other sports, and barnstorming under which players could earn money in the off-season.

Loosening of restrictions on moves of franchises from one area to another.

Giving players an equal voting share in the selection of the Commissioner of Baseball.

Strengthening of existing bargaining proceedings for pay of star players.[7]

When a planned appearance by Feller two weeks later at a baseball school for young boys at Wrigley Field in Los Angeles was suddenly cancelled, there was suspicion that baseball officials were trying to intimidate "Rapid Robert" because of his remarks to the committee. Hillings said that Congressional investigators were looking into that possibility.

On the day of Feller's testimony, baseball officials released, for the first time, a report of the teams' payrolls. The statistics showed that the Brooklyn Dodgers had the highest average salary at $18,880 with the Red Sox second with a $17,590 average. The Phillies and the Pirates were at the bottom of the list. Each had a payroll which averaged $9,940 per player on the 25-man roster. Musial's $75,000 yearly income was the major leagues' highest. It was thought that Yankee catcher Yogi Berra topped the American League with a $58,000 salary.

Arthur Daley, writing in the *New York Times*, described the contents of a letter which Hall of Famer Rogers Hornsby, who had retired as an active player in 1937, had sent to Celler. In the letter Hornsby supported the reserve clause, but then made a number of suggestions which did not sit well with the owners. According to Daley, Hornsby, in his unsolicited letter to the subcommittee, had

> blasted the draft system, the farm system and unrestricted broadcasts. The Rajah's belt at the draft could not help but hit the owners in one of their most vulnerable spots. This is a phase of the game that's screaming for reform.
>
> The player draft is an annual ritual that should be both impressive and important but is neither. The sixteen major league teams solemnly assemble and pick minor league stars for promotion to the big time. It sounds noble but it's a ridiculously empty gesture. The cupboard is always bare because the juiciest plums have been hidden elsewhere.[8]

The major league clubs had developed an effective system for holding on to their best minor leaguers. The big league teams were permitted to expand their rosters from 25 to 40 players before the draft. To go along with that, a team's brightest prospects were often moved to one of their minor league club's roster. The Dodgers might shift their hopefuls on the St. Paul roster to the Montreal team. The drafters could select only one player from Montreal and all the rest were effectively protected. Hornsby believed that the practice prevented many of the top players in a strong farm system from having a fair shot at making the big leagues with another club. Daley said:

> The Have-Nots will support Hornsby on the question of an unrestricted draft while the Haves will charge that it's socialistic and that it penalizes them for having greater enterprise. Yet the Congressional hearings have had a sobering effect on all baseball men and the impression grows that a draft limiting one to a customer is on the way out.[9]

While the owners waited to hear what would result from the hearings, the players were seeking a change in the minimum salary. That was one of the three requests made by the 16 player representatives during their discussions with club owners on December 4, 1957, in Colorado Springs, the site of the annual winter meetings.

The players sought a raise in the minimum salary from $6,000 to $7,000. They also requested that there be extra money paid to players moving to the West Coast. That need was created because the Dodgers and Giants would be playing in Los Angeles and San Francisco in 1958 rather than in Ebbets Field and the Polo Grounds. The request for a group insurance plan which would make families of the players beneficiaries as well as the ball clubs was also on the players' agenda.

The owners approved the minimum salary increase and agreed to a maximum of $1,200 for increased transportation and moving costs for those affected by the Dodgers' and Giants' move from New York to California.

They also scrapped the bonus rule that required all free agents—usually untested high school and college players—who signed for more than a $4,000 bonus to remain with the major league team for two years before they could be optioned to the minors. The rule had slowed the development of most of the young "bonus babies" and was suspected of having led to under-the-table payments as a way of avoiding the impact of the rule.

The concept of paying large bonuses to unproven players confused Jack Barry who had finished his American league career in 1919:

> It makes me laugh when I read where a club has given an untried youngster $50,000 or more to sign a contract. They called us the "$100,000 infield" when I played with [Stuffy] McInnis, [Eddie] Collins and [Frank] Baker, but I'll bet it didn't cost Connie Mack more than $50 to land us all. I know that all it cost him to get Collins and myself was carfare.[10]

The owners were thinking along the lines of Hornsby when they modified the draft system involving minor leaguers. The existing seven-year wait in the minors before draft eligibility was lowered to four years. Perhaps as important as lowering the number of years for draft eligibility was the change which allowed any number of players to be drafted from any one minor league club. The new rule promised to provide increased opportunity for the best minor leaguers, but as suggested:

> The slickies, of course, will still find a way to protect their interests. But it won't be so easy as in the past. Also, the wealthier clubs gained some measure of victory with the provision that the price tag on all minor leaguers regardless of classification should be $25,000 for a major league club.[11]

The owners saw an impending battle with the minor leagues on baseball's horizon. The center of the controversy was television broadcasts of major league games. CBS, one of the three national networks, had begun making contracts with some big league clubs to televise their Sunday contests on the "Game of the Week." CBS was already airing Saturday games, and had lined up the Baltimore Orioles, Chicago White Sox, Indians,

Yankees, Cincinnati Reds, and Phillies for Sunday telecasts. Minor league executives insisted that the move to televise Sunday games would threaten the existences of their clubs. They were planning to use every means available to them to fight the plan.

Meanwhile, on January 11, 1958, Celler and Hillings announced that they were dropping their attempts to have the bills passed which would have brought baseball under antitrust laws. Celler said that he was heading back to the drawing board and would be working on a compromise approach that would exempt all except the purely business aspects of all professional sports from antitrust regulation.

All was not well between Lewis and some of the players. He had suggested that the players support Celler's compromise bill to regulate the game, and that upset many of them. In March an effort to oust Lewis from his position as the players' attorney failed when the players, coaches, managers, and trainers on a majority of the clubs voted to retain him.

While the House was preparing their compromise bill, the Senate began their own investigation. The Senate Antitrust and Monopoly subcommittee held hearings on legislation that would have legally insured that baseball had immunity from antitrust action against the game. The bill would have extended the same status to other professional sports as well. Tennessee Senator Estes Kefauver was the chair of the subcommittee that heard testimony from a star-studded group of players and others connected with baseball. Active players Mantle, Musial, Roberts, Ted Williams, and Yost were among those who appeared before the subcommittee.

The hearings, which began on July 9, 1958, the day following the All-Star Game in Baltimore's Memorial Stadium, did not provide a clear answer to the question regarding antitrust immunity, but they did produce a host of interesting witnesses. Yankee manager Casey Stengel, who was the first to speak, provided the most memorable and entertaining testimony as his Stengelese allowed him to talk for forty-five minutes without actually saying much on the subject. At one point when he was asked why he thought that Major League Baseball wanted the bill passed, he said:

> I would say I would not know, but I would say the reason they want it passed is to keep baseball going as the highest paid ball sport that has gone into baseball, and from the baseball angle—I am not going to speak of any other sport.[12]

Mantle followed Stengel to the witness chair and, when asked by Kefauver if he had any observations about the applicability of the antitrust laws to baseball, he said, "My views are just about the same as Casey's."[13] Mickey's answer brought an uproar from many in the room.

Throughout the testimony, none of the players expressed major dissatisfaction with the reserve clause which bound them to their teams. They said that if they were starting over they would do things the same way. Williams did add that he would have wanted to have a clause in his first contract with San Diego of the Pacific Coast League which would have provided him with some of the $25,000 which the Boston Red Sox paid to obtain him. The Senate bill died before it reached the floor.

Major League Baseball's next opponent appeared in New York City when, on November 13, 1958, William A. Shea, chairman of Mayor Robert F. Wagner's baseball committee, unveiled plans for a third major league. Branch Rickey was named the fledgling Continental League's president. The 78 year old, who had revolutionized farm systems while he was with the Cardinals and had helped revolutionize the game when he brought Jackie Robinson to Brooklyn in 1947, had a new dream:

> With all his customary grandiloquence, he announced the formation of a brand new Continental League with plans for teams in New York (where the bereft Dodger and Giants fans had found shifting their allegiance to the hated Yankees inconceivable), as well as Atlanta, Houston, Dallas, Denver, Minneapolis-St. Paul, and Toronto. "Twenty great cities cannot be ignored," he rumbled. The major leagues weren't keeping up with the population's steady shift westward; all he and his associates wished to do was to spread the game to new markets. "We are not looking for a war," he told the owners. "We pretty much prefer to come in as friendly members of organized baseball.... All we request is that you gentleman grant us major league membership as a third league. All we ask is that you give us a chance."[14]

Rickey believed that it was time for Major League Baseball to expand to other parts of the country. The American and National Leagues had been reticent to think beyond the cities of the existing sixteen teams. The new league, which Rickey hoped would be welcomed as an equal partner in Major League Baseball, would remedy that situation. Most owners didn't see things the way Rickey did and were talking about "the Mahatma's" dream creating a new outlaw league. Lewis was saying he didn't think that many players would be eager to leave their clubs and their pension and other benefits for positions in the new circuit.

Branch lashed out at a press conference:

I do not have to have a job. Mother (Mrs. Rickey) and I can go along all right. At the moment I am lily white in motivation. I am not accustomed to the emotions of defeat. I never have been—in St. Louis, Brooklyn or Pittsburgh. The Continental League is as inevitable as tomorrow morning. The present position of the majors means the funeral for professional baseball. I do not plan to attend the funeral. The Continental League does not intend to be a pall-bearer. If we go down they will write an epitaph that "They did their best. They died trying." But we have just begun to fight.[15]

A number of important player issues were addressed at the 1958 winter meetings. The players were defeated in their bid to obtain a salary budget equivalent to 20 percent of a club's gross income. Earlier in the discussions with the owners, the players had demanded a 25 percent cut of a club's profits.

Not all the owners' decisions were contrary to the players' wishes. Farmhands were given a break when the magnates agreed to a measure which the minor league executives had previously approved. Under the new rule, a player could be drafted after his first season of minor league ball. If he wasn't selected at that point, he would not be eligible again until he had played four seasons in the minors. The owners also voted to allow unrestricted trading in the major leagues from November 21 through December 15. During that period no waivers would be required on a player being traded to a club in his league or in the other circuit.

Despite the players' continued advancements on the labor front, on March 24, 1959, they dismissed Lewis as counsel to the Major League Baseball Players Association. He left the position expressing pride in his accomplishments during his tenure in office. The salaries of 75 percent of the players had risen to the $10,000 to $25,000 range, and DiMaggio, Musial, and Williams had broken the $100,000 barrier.

The movement to replace Lewis was led by Roberts and Sherm Lollar, a catcher for the Chicago White Sox, but they had the support of many players. Their bone of contention continued to be the statements that Lewis had made without their knowledge or approval the previous year during the congressional hearings. Lewis had survived the vote in 1958, but he was gone 12 months later. Marvin Miller, who would become the executive director of the Players Association in 1966, said that Lewis' removal was a joint effort, writing, "by the spring of 1959 the owners had had enough and urged (*read*: told) the player reps to fire him."[16]

When the owners and player representatives gathered for the 1959 winter meetings, Robert C. M. Cannon, a Wisconsin Circuit Court judge, was in attendance. He had been engaged as the players' new legal advisor. Cannon's father had been counsel to the 1918 Black Sox in the Illinois criminal case against them.

The signing of a new, lucrative World Series and All-Star Game radio and television contract to replace the one set to expire in 1961 was the major matter on the docket for the players and owners. The existing contract called for a $16,000,000 package over five years. The players received 60 percent of that amount to help underwrite their pension fund. Because there had been two All-Star Games in 1959—the first in Pittsburgh on July 7, and the second in Los Angeles on August 3—a huge pot of money was now available. The pair of games would continue through the 1962 season.

Author Arnold Hano wrote about the dramatic change in the game brought about by television, which would become a major player in baseball's future:

> This game of baseball has again become a tool of the club owner. Not a gambling tool, as it once was, but a tax-break tool. Stories about baseball might as easily slip onto the financial pages as the sports pages. And they do. The biggest story of the baseball year is the amount of money television people will give to baseball for the privilege of presenting a distorted image of the sport to millions of lethargic, uncaring spectators. You measure your sports today by their respective Neilsen ratings. A man flicks his fingers over a bank of computerized buttons, and neon lights flash on a scoreboard showing the figure of a man playing a bugle. In response, 20,000 people mechanically cry: "Charge!" Fans cheer when they are ordered to.[17]

Roberts was sensing that the commissioner and the owners were more cooperative with the players than they had been in some time. He was satisfied with Frick's approach to the new contract, saying:

> The commissioner already has been keeping us fully informed on negotiations he is conducting with reference to a new TV and radio world series contract.... We understand fully it's up to him to make the final decision and whatever he does will be all right with us.[18]

For the first time, the owners had submitted a draft of the next season's schedules to the players for examination. The owners had listened to the players' request that night games not be scheduled the day before an afternoon game in another city. The players had discovered only one such date in the American League schedule and four in the National League schedule, which was a significant improvement over previous years.

As the Continental League's plans continued to be firmed up, the American and National League magnates began to consider expansion more seriously.

In 1961 the Junior Circuit was the first to expand to 10 teams when it placed a franchise in Los Angeles (the Angels) and a new team in Washington to replace the unhappy Senators who had been given permission to move to Bloomington, Minnesota, and become the Minnesota Twins. The National League added a pair of clubs for the 1962 campaign when the Houston Colt .45s and the New York Mets began operation. The moves were partially an attempt to undercut the threat of the Continental League. Expansion also brought money to the original 16 teams. Each of the four new clubs contributed $2 million for the other teams to divide. The schedule was expanded from 154 to 162 games. Cannon, who would run the Players Association as a friend of the owners, endorsed the expanded schedule even though it did not provide the players with a commensurate salary increase. The players were given a small increase in their daily meal money.

Major league expansion was monumental since "16" had seemed to be an inviolate number. That was but the first of a number of changes in the game during the decade of the '60s—a time when the entire country was undergoing significant and sometimes violent upheaval.

William D. "Spike" Eckert, who had retired as a one-star general from the Air Force in 1961, replaced Frick as commissioner in 1965. He brought a financial background to the job, but he was lacking one important thing—a knowledge of baseball. Lee MacPhail, who left as president and general manager of the Baltimore Orioles, became Eckert's guide through the game. MacPhail would be followed a year later by John McHale.

Eckert's relationship with the media was shaky from the start. He was both an unknown name and an unknown quantity; in fact, there was a story that some owners thought that they were voting for a much more familiar general, Eugene Zuckert. Because of his limited baseball knowledge and his low-key, cautious public style, the media found Spike to be a less than scintillating interview.

One of Eckert's first calls to action involved the proposed move of the Milwaukee Braves to Atlanta for the 1966 campaign. The Braves had migrated from Boston to Milwaukee in 1953 and had enjoyed many outstanding years on the field and at the box office in the Wisconsin city. They won two pennants, captured a World Championship, finished in second place five times and never suffered a losing season. In 1954 they became the first club to play before 2 million fans and they continued to draw more than 2 million to County Stadium the next three seasons.

The Braves' move to Atlanta threatened to leave Milwaukee without a major league team, and that prompted Wisconsin Attorney General Bronston LaFollette to file a petition for an injunction to keep the club in Wisconsin. He argued that although other major league teams had moved to new places, this would be the first time that a city was left without a big league club to play there. Although the Dodgers and Giants had gone to greener pastures in California, the Yankees still provided New York with major league baseball—although not everyone who bled National League blood would have agreed.

Milwaukee Circuit Court Judge Elmer W. Roller launched a second legal attack when he ruled that baseball must stand trial in a state court on charges of violating antitrust and monopoly statutes. The trial lasted over seven weeks in the Milwaukee County Court. Bowie Kuhn, later to become baseball's fifth commissioner, argued the case for the National League:

> It soon became apparent to defense counsel that Judge Roller had no sympathy for anything we had to say. Inescapably, he became known in our private conferences as "Steam Roller," an appellation he reinforced with a decision enjoining the move of the Braves.[19]

The Braves were caught in a legal impasse. Along with the legal procedures in Wisconsin, they were also under order of Georgia's Fulton County Superior Court to comply with the team's lease to play its 1966 home games in Atlanta Stadium. MacPhail spoke about the counsel he gave Eckert:

> One of the first bits of advice I had given to the commissioner was never to say something "was a league affair." Ford Frick had often taken that position. It irritated the press and damaged his image. So I advised the commissioner not to consider that anything was outside his jurisdiction.[20]

Eckert let National League president Warren Giles and the circuit's owners resolve the dilemma. On January 31, 1966, they voted not to put a replacement team in Milwaukee.

The season began with the Braves in Atlanta. The National League had appealed Roller's decision and, on July 27, the Wisconsin Supreme Court rendered its opinion:

> In a 4–3 decision, the justices ruled that baseball was a monopoly and agreed that leaving a city without a major league franchise clearly harmed its economy. But the majority ruled, "The state is powerless to deal with it."[21]

Miller explained why the justices could not have ruled any other way:

> The reason, they said, and it was quite logical, is that the state laws
> against trusts and restraint of trade are overruled when there is a fed-
> eral law. You are dealing with a matter of interstate commerce, and
> the federal law controls that. The court correctly ruled that the state
> antitrust laws are trumped by the federal law.[22]

Eckert and MacPhail were involved in another matter with the
Braves. The first-ever draft of amateur players, which ended a free-enter-
prise approach to acquiring young prospects, had taken place in June 1965.
Each major league club, in turn from the lowest to the highest finish the
preceding year, picked from a nationwide pool of high school and college
players. Under the previous system, the best players could negotiate with
a number of clubs, and they had begun to command increasingly large
amounts of money to sign a contract. The newly designed draft was aimed
at doing away with a financial opportunity for players and a financial
problem for the clubs.

In 1936 Cleveland had signed Feller, an Iowa farm boy, for one dollar. Fourteen years later, the Pirates gave 18-year-old, untested, left-handed
pitcher Paul Pettit $100,000 for signing with them. The "bonus baby" won
only one major league game before being forced to retire with an injured
arm. In 1959 Milwaukee raised the previous ceiling by paying outfielder
Dave Nicholson $120,000 for signing. In 1961 Bob Bailey, a high school
shortstop from Long Beach, California, received $175,000 of the Pirates'
money and, three years later, Gene Autry, the "Singing Cowboy" and
owner of the Los Angeles Angels, parted with $205,000 for the services
of Rick Reichardt, a University of Wisconsin junior.

Tom Seaver, a talented pitcher at the University of Southern California, was chosen by the Dodgers in the June 1965 draft. Seaver opted
to wait for the next draft, which would be held in mid–January 1966,
rather than sign with Los Angeles who, in his opinion, had not offered
him enough money.

The Braves made Seaver their first choice in the January draft, and he
signed with them on February 24. He received a $51,500 package—a $40,000
bonus, $4,000 to replace his scholarship and a $7,500 incentive bonus.

Because Seaver had signed with the Braves after his university's season had begun, which was a violation of baseball law, Eckert voided the
contract on March 2. MacPhail devised a solution which would eliminate the prospect of a bidding war which might result in Seaver receiving more money than the Braves had been willing to give him. MacPhail
explained:

Lee MacPhail leaves his desk in Baltimore as president and general manager of the Orioles to lead commissioner William Eckert through the game. (Baltimore Orioles)

> The ideal for us would be to have him sign with another club for the same terms. So it was my idea to advise the clubs of the Braves' terms and invite any club that would match them to advise us by a certain deadline. That would make them eligible for a drawing.[23]

Miller disagreed with the approach and believed that it was an indication of how much the players were pawns in the hands of the owners. He asked:

> Why was the "ideal" that Seaver sign for the same amount with another club? Here was a player who had never signed a contract with any club, who had great value, and MacPhail asserted that no one should offer him more than the first club. Why was that?[24]

The "Seaver raffle" took place on April 2. The Indians, Mets, and Phillies had entered with a bid of $51,500. MacPhail drew the name of the winner: It was the Mets.

The Dodgers, who had originally drafted Seaver, did not enter the drawing. They were focusing on a novel and intriguing labor situation involving pitchers Don Drysdale and Sandy Koufax, and general manager Buzzy Bavasi had forgotten to notify the commissioner about his club's continued interest in Seaver.

Drysdale and Koufax, the aces of the Dodgers' staff, were seeking a three-year deal in which they would divide $1 million equally. Two months before the start of the 1966 campaign, Drysdale, a 6-foot-6-inch, 215-pound overpowering right-hander, and Koufax, an outstanding lefty, had gone to Walter O'Malley, the club's owner, with their joint demand. Since they could not seek work with another club because of the reserve clause, they told O'Malley that they would try their hands at acting if their demand was not met. They also informed O'Malley that their agent, J. William Hayes, would be handling the negotiations. O'Malley, angered by both the demand and the involvement of an agent, told the pair, "Baseball is an old-fashioned game with old-fashioned traditions.... I have never discussed a player contract with an agent and I like to think I never will."[25]

Los Angeles had captured the World Championship in 1963 and 1965 and the pair of pitchers had been the workhorses of the staff. In the years from 1963 through 1965, Koufax had won 70 games and Drysdale had picked up 60 victories. Koufax had gone 26-8 and had been selected as the Cy Young Award winner (only one award was given at the time), and Drysdale was 23-12 during the season before they made their joint demand. The pair had also won three of the games in the Dodgers' 4-3 victory over Minnesota in the World Series.

While Hayes was negotiating, the pitchers were acting. Bavasi wasn't as adamant about not dealing with agents as was O'Malley. There were a number of reports about conversations between Hayes and himself. On March 29, after Bavasi made the Dodgers' "final offer," the two men spoke over the telephone. Buzzy reported:

> He [Hayes] graciously informed me that the boys had turned down an additional offer of $25,000....
>
> The reason they turned [the offer] down is simply a matter of economics.... It simply is not enough money.
>
> I must assume Mr. Hayes is speaking for the players when he says they will do other things than play baseball.
>
> I'm sorry to hear it. We need them; so does baseball.[26]

The following day, after all hope appeared to be lost, Drysdale and Koufax agreed to a combined package of more than $210,000 for one year. According to reports, the pair had made slightly more than $70,000 apiece in 1965.

Although Drysdale and Koufax had not received what they were asking for, they had accomplished something of value through their novel approach. It would serve as a sign that the old style of owner-player relationships was changing. They returned to the mound and left the stage behind. The proposed title of the film they were doing, *Warning Shot*, contained an ironic message.

Years later, Koufax talked about the purpose of their approach:

> The goal ... was to convince [the owners] that they would have to approach us, not as indentured servants, but as coequal partners to a contract, with as much dignity and bargaining power as themselves.[27]

While the Dodgers' pitchers were fighting their battle, a new force was making his way through the 1966 major league spring training camps. Miller was addressing groups of players, managers, coaches, and trainers about a new direction for the Players Association.

By 1965 the player representatives believed that the scope of baseball's current issues mandated that Cannon's job needed to become a full-time position. They also saw a need to have the Players Association's office—although it contained only a single, battered file cabinet at the time—located in New York City. Cannon had maintained the "office" in Milwaukee so that he could also continue his career as a judge.

Baseball's Executive Council, which was comprised of three owners from each league, was receptive to a plan for a full-time advisor and voted a $150,000 allocation from the proceeds of All-Star Games to pay his salary and the association's office expenses.

It was in the owners' best interest to keep Cannon in the job. During his service with the MLBPA, Cannon had:

> publicly endorsed the reserve clause, praised the pension fund as the "finest in existence," and told a congressional committee in 1964 that the "thinking of the average major league ballplayer" was that "we have it so good we don't know what to ask for next.[28]

The Pittsburgh Pirates' Bob Friend, a leader of the Players Association and a friend of Cannon, sought to keep him in the post. Meanwhile, the names of other candidates began to circulate. Feller, who had retired as an active player in 1956, and John Gabel, actuary of the Pension Fund, were two possibilities for the position.

Roberts, who was president of the Players Association at the time, asked George William Taylor, a professor at the University of Pennsylvania's Wharton School of Finance, for his recommendations. Taylor and Roberts had never met, but the professor recognized the name of the Phillies' star hurler. Taylor suggested Marvin J. Miller, an economist and negotiator with the United States Steelworkers of America. The players had another candidate to consider.

In January 1966, the player representatives approved Cannon to be the Players Association's first full-time executive director. However, Cannon wanted to maintain his home and other interests in Milwaukee. He also became involved in a dispute with the player reps when he asked them to match his judicial pension.

Roberts said, "after he pissed off a number of player reps by demanding additional conditions,"[29] they began to look for another person to fill the post. That is when the attention moved to Roberts' favorite for the job—Miller.

Miller was upset with some aspects of the process and especially with being the Association's "second choice." It took some convincing from Roberts and Friend before he consented to be considered for the post.

Roberts suggested that Miller visit Eckert. While in New York on business, Miller made an appointment to meet the commissioner. While waiting for Eckert to finish another meeting, Miller met MacPhail for the first time:

> I was sitting in the waiting room and a man came out of one of the offices and introduced himself as Lee MacPhail. He mentioned in conversation that he had heard that I was planning to leave my job with the Steelworkers and I was considering a number of options. I said that I was, and told MacPhail that I had had conversations with Derek Bok, later the president of Harvard. Bok was interested in having me lecture at graduate seminars in Labor Relations as well as do some writing. Lee illustrated how little those in the commissioner's office understood about the future nature of the executive director's job when he said, "That position sounds interesting. Perhaps you could do the Harvard job and the Players Association job at the same time."[30]

Miller was chosen for the post at the player representatives' meeting on March 6. However, he would not formally become the executive director until the members of the Players Association ratified his selection.

In advance of the ratification vote, Miller headed to spring training camps to introduce himself and his approach to his future constituents.

He started with visits to the West Coast training camps of the Angels, San Francisco Giants, Chicago Cubs, and Indians. He received a rather cold reception at each camp, even though he had chosen to address a topic which he thought would be of special interest to the players—baseball's unreasonably low $7,000 minimum salary. Miller reminded the players that they only received that amount after they had spent more than 60 days in the majors in a given season. Those who failed to meet that standard received the $6,000 minimum salary. Miller spoke about one of the difficulties he was encountering:

> They had no experience with unions. Not in baseball and, obviously, not in other parts of their lives. They [the players] were very young people. And in most every case, they didn't have prior working lives and so they had all of the natural fears of an inexperienced young person confronted with organizing and forming a union for the first time.[31]

Miller found a more welcoming audience in the spring training camps in Florida where he had Friend, Roberts, the Phillies' Jim Bunning, and others running interference for him.

On April 13, the result of the ratification vote was announced, and it was in Miller's favor, 489–136. Most of the negative votes had been cast by managers, coaches, and trainers.

Baseball was headed in a more militant direction. The Players Association would be a far different organization than it had been under Lewis and Cannon. Miller awakened the Dodgers to that fact during his meeting with them:

> I want you to understand that this is going to be an adversarial relationship. A union is not a social club. A union is a restraint on what an employer can do otherwise. If you expect the owners to like me, to praise me, to compliment me, you'll be disappointed. In fact, if I'm elected and you find the owners telling you what a great guy I am, fire me! Don't hesitate, because it can't be that way if your director is doing his job. The owners loved Judge Cannon. Don't make the same mistake with your new executive director.[32]

CHAPTER FIVE

Strike One: 1972—The "Flood" Gates Are Open

It was not long before the magnates realized that life with Marvin Miller would be difficult, and they were certainly not going to pitch in and make things easy for him and the Major League Baseball Players Association (MLBPA). On May 4, 1966, the 20 club owners overruled the Executive Council's earlier decision to provide $150,000 for Miller's salary and the expenses of the Players Association's New York office. Marvin commented about the owners' action:

> Baseball was making a biblical statement: "The Lords of Baseball give and the same Lords take away!"; that is, they give if they can hand-pick an owners' man to head the players' organization, but they take away if the players exercise their legal right to choose an experienced union man as their executive director. The point the owners made was not lost on the players.[1]

Miller was actually disappointed when the Executive Council's earlier vote was overridden. Had the original plan been followed it would have served as another indication of how much baseball's executives had to learn about a players' union:

> That [paying the $150,000] would have given me the opportunity to refuse it because it would have been illegal for them to pay the salary of the executive director of the union and the expenses of running the office. I don't know why Paul Porter [Major League Baseball's chief lawyer] wouldn't have known that.[2]

The players found another source of funding for the Association— themselves. They had been paying $2 per day during the season into baseball's benefit plan, which amounted to about $160,000 a year. At Miller's urging, the owners made the benefit plan noncontributory by the players. Marvin suggested that the players pay the daily $2 as dues to the organization, and that became the primary source of the Association's revenue.

Thanks to the presence of the Association, players were soon receiving increased income from another source. The Topps Chewing Gum Company was the only company that could sell players' pictures alone or with a confectionary product. They had been paying minor leaguers $5 a year and major leaguers $125 with no royalties for the right to print and sell their cards. In 1968 Topps negotiated a new contract with the Players Association after hearing threats from players that they would not renew their contracts with the company. The pact doubled the payment to the players and paid royalties of 8 percent on sales up to $4 million and 10 percent on sales above that amount. It was one of the game's earliest "licensing arrangements," and it set the wheels in motion for payoffs which, over the years, put millions of dollars in the pockets of all connected with Major League Baseball. The Players Association also arranged for players to grant the use of their pictures of a certain size to other companies, thus ending Topps' monopoly on baseball cards.

On the management side, Eckert was forced to resign on December 6, 1968, with four years remaining on his contract, and a search was begun for his replacement. On February 4, 1969, the mantle fell on the broad shoulders of 6-foot-5-inch Bowie Kuhn, a 42-year-old Wall Street lawyer with Wilkie Farr & Gallagher. The firm had the National League as one of its clients, and Kuhn had worked as counsel for the Senior Circuit in the trial involving the Milwaukee Braves' move to Atlanta and other cases.

Kuhn was given a one-year contract to serve as commissioner pro tempore. Baseball had devised a reorganization plan and it would be Kuhn's job to implement it. Elements of the plan were:

1. Doing away with traditional procedures which now require separate League consideration of those matters which concern baseball as a whole;
2. Exploring ways to improve the presentation of the game;
3. Developing a plan for the reorganization of the governing bodies of baseball and the revision of their constitutions; and
4. Developing a plan for the consolidation of the office and staffs of the Commissioner and other officials of baseball.[3]

When Eckert entered office, he discovered the Braves' move to Atlanta and the Tom Seaver draft situation staring him in the face; Kuhn saw an impending players' strike on the horizon. As Kuhn came into the commissioner's office, there were signs that the MLBPA had been skillfully led by Miller, who had infected some of the players with a sense of militancy which had become a credible force for improving the players' working conditions.

Baseball had made its way into what for them were the uncharted waters of collective bargaining. As Miller recalled:

> The first agreement in all of sports arrived at through bona fide collective bargaining was the benefit plan agreement of December 1966. It was a landmark, but it covered only pensions and insurance. The next big goal was to negotiate a basic agreement that would cover all other terms and conditions of a major league player's employment. This effort got under way in early 1967, and as you might guess, the first subject we tackled was the minimum salary.[4]

In 1967 the owners formed the Player Relations Committee (PRC) to serve as their negotiating body. The committee was comprised of the presidents of the two major leagues as ex-officio members and four owners from each league. John J. Gaherin, former president of the New York City Publishers Association, served as the PRC's chief negotiator.

In February 1968, the first Basic Agreement was signed as a result of negotiations between the PRC and the MLBPA. The agreement, which covered the 1968 and 1969 seasons, was a significant achievement for the players in that it took precedence over major league rules whenever the two were in conflict. The agreement incorporated the Uniform Player's Contract. No longer would the owners and their lawyers be able to unilaterally change an individual player's contract. The first formal grievance procedure was also outlined in the agreement.

On February 3, 1969, the day before Kuhn was chosen commissioner, 130 players who were seeking a new pension agreement with the owners attended a four-hour caucus with the tone of a town meeting in the Biltmore Hotel in New York City. They had announced they would refuse to sign their contracts for the upcoming season until they reached agreement on a new pension plan. The old benefit agreement was due to be renegotiated by the end of March 1969.

The owners had gone on the offense early, seeking to keep the payments to the pension fund at the current level. Even though more money would come from the new radio and television contracts, the magnates were not willing to increase the pension fund money.

Negotiations between the PRC and the MLBPA, which the players had wanted to start in July and hadn't begun until November, had broken down. On December 5, after the players accused the owners (there were now 24 of them because of expansion) of foot-dragging, Paul Richards, executive vice president of the Atlanta Braves, remarked:

> Miller speaks mainly for a few rabble-rousers and greedy ballplayers.... As for the players who want to leave, I say to them: good luck, we could replace them with Triple-A minor leaguers and keep all the TV money, and be better off.[5]

The owners appeared to be expecting that the MLBPA's "solidarity" would break down before any of their threats became reality. Such was not the case; the players' resolve increased as the owners continued to resist. Most of baseball's major stars, including Hank Aaron, Roberto Clemente, Mickey Mantle, Roger Maris, Willie Mays, and Carl Yastrzemski, were solidly behind the MLBPA.

In February, with the two sides not talking to each other, Kuhn moved into the silence and called the teams back to the negotiating table. Kuhn remembered:

> I called Miller and asked him to resume bargaining. He responded warmly, pointing out that he had not favored the break-off in the first place. While Gaherin was not anxious to make further concessions to Miller, he was a good soldier and recognized the practical necessities. Negotiations were resumed and an agreement was promptly reached.[6]

On February 25, 1970, nine days before the first scheduled spring training game, the PRC and the MLBPA agreed to a new pension agreement. A $5.45 million a year package, which represented a $1.35 million increase, and a provision lowering the time it took a player to become eligible for a pension to four years were features of the three-year agreement. Benefits for former players were increased along with those who were still playing the game. And a strike was avoided.

Miller, writing about Kuhn's efforts, said:

> Whatever the reasons, and granted that his own self-interest surely was involved, his efforts to persuade the owners to drastically revise the regressive position they had taken in the pension negotiations were in the best interest of the game, and they were successful. The owners' position on the issues changed 180 degrees. John Gaherin's prior marching orders were rescinded.[7]

Miller's influence on the changing status of contracts was witnessed in the New York Yankees' spring training camp. A club would issue a ten-day notice to a player if he had not signed a contract by March 1. If he did not sign within the ten days, the club renewed the contract for one additional season.

Left-hander Al Downing, who had been pitching in the Yanks' regular rotation since 1963, arrived in camp without having signed a contract. After Downing did not sign a contract for 1969 during the ten-day notice period, New York renewed his contract. However, the club would not let Al draw a uniform, receive expense money, or participate in the camp until he signed the renewed contract.

Miller spoke about the advice he gave Downing and the ramifications of the Yankees' position:

> My position was that Al was already under contract since the Yankees had renewed it according to the Uniform Player's Contract. They were in violation by not letting him begin spring training. I went over my position with Downing, told him to write it down and send a note to [Lee] MacPhail. After a short negotiation with Downing, Lee made Al a slightly better offer and he signed for the 1969 season.
>
> I wondered why it was so important that Downing sign the renewed contract. They had to have a reason. And then it came to me. They were not satisfied with their own procedure. Once the renewed contract is signed they can say, "You accept the fact that your contract has been renewed." Then they would be in a stronger position to renew it again if the player did not sign for the following season.[8]

In 1970 the players chalked up another victory when a new agreement, baseball's second, was signed early in the season. The minimum wage was raised to $12,000 (an increase of $2,000) and, for the first time, players were given the right to be represented by an agent.

In 1971, with salaries on the rise, some owners and players were thinking about future limits. Los Angeles Dodgers' president Peter O'Malley said:

> I believe salaries are at their peak, not just in baseball, but in all sports. It's quite possible some owners will trade away, or even drop entirely, players who expect $200,000 salaries. There's a superstar born every year.... But there is no way clubs can continue to increase salaries to the level some players are talking about.[9]

Dodger Wes Parker, who was about to begin his eighth year with the club, held a similar opinion:

I think $200,000 for one year is the limit any star can hope to make.
I also think that the player who seeks and gets that much may be
pricing himself right out of the game.[10]

In Detroit, Tiger outfielder Al Kaline, who was in his nineteenth year
with the club, expressed an eye-opening approach to his contract. Commenting about Detroit general manager Jim Campbell's offer in 1971 to
make him the team's first $100,000-man after years of excellence, Kaline
said:

I don't deserve such a salary.... I didn't have a good enough season
last year. This ball club has been so fair and decent to me that I'd
prefer to have you give it to me when I rate it.[11]

In 1971, after rebounding from the earlier sub-par season and leading
the Tigers with a .294 average, Kaline accepted the six-figure contract.

Baseball and the courts were drawn into another examination of the
reserve clause. In the 1950s, George Toolson had not been able to legally
bring it to an end; perhaps in the 1970s, Curt Flood would succeed. On
October 8, 1969, Flood, a 12-year veteran with the St. Louis Cardinals
(he had also made brief appearances with the Cincinnati Reds in the two
seasons before joining the Cards) was traded to the Philadelphia Phillies
in a seven-player deal.

The 31-year-old outfielder, who was one of the premier defensive
players at his position, was paid $90,000 in 1969 by the Cardinals. He
had helped the Cards win three pennants and two World Championships
in the past five years. He did not want to go to Philadelphia and hoped
to be able to choose where he would finish his career.

Flood was upset about the way he heard about the trade:

I got the news about the trade one afternoon by phone. I have known
Bing Devine, the Cardinal general manager, for much of the thirteen years, and he has been good to me and I think I have made a
few dollars for him. He didn't call. One of the lower-echelon people
in his office called and, with a voice that sounded like a tape record-
ing, he told me I had been traded to Philadelphia along with Tim
McCarver, Joe Hoerner, and Byron Browne for Richie Allen, Cookie
Rojas, and Jerry Johnson.[12]

Flood asked Miller for his help in challenging the reserve clause.
After discussions with Curt, Miller was deeply impressed with his com-
mitment to take a stand on the question of his freedom. He and Dick
Moss, the union's general counsel at the time, arranged for Flood to attend

the executive board meeting in Puerto Rico to talk with the player representatives.

Flood, a quiet, sensitive man who had endured racial prejudice while playing in some Southern cities during his minor league career, remembered the meeting well:

> This winter, on a bright day in San Juan, Puerto Rico, I walked into a meeting at the Americana Hotel. Seated in the room, waiting to listen to me, were the player representatives of the big league clubs— people like Reggie Jackson, Tom Haller, Jim Bunning, Tim McCarver, Joe Torre, Bob Clemente, Dal Maxvil. There were twenty-six ballplayers in all, the executive board of the Major League Baseball Players Association. Now I was going to try to tell them why I planned to challenge baseball's reserve clause in a case that could revolutionize the structure of baseball and stop twenty-four millionaire owners from playing God with thousands of players' lives.[13]

During the meeting, the question was raised about whether Flood would be willing to stay for the long haul or whether he might be willing to settle out of court as Danny Gardella had done. Curt assured them that he was in the battle to the end, and he impressed them with his sincerity of purpose. The Association voted to support Flood and cover his legal fees and travel expenses from St. Louis to New York for the preparation of the case and his court appearances.

Flood retained Arthur Goldberg to work as one of his lawyers along with Allan H. Zerman of St. Louis. Goldberg had been Secretary of Labor, an Associate Justice of the Supreme Court (he left the bench in 1965) and an associate of Miller at the Steelworkers. Goldberg was so interested in the case that he agreed to charge for expenses for himself and his assistants, but no fee.

On December 24, 1969, Flood sent a letter to Kuhn and asked him to bypass the reserve clause so that he could make his own choice about where to play. Flood wrote:

> Dear Mr. Kuhn:
>   After twelve years in the major leagues, I do not feel that I am a piece of property to be bought and sold irrespective of my wishes. I believe that any system that produces that result violates my basic rights as a citizen and is inconsistent with the laws of the United States and several states.
>   It is my desire to play baseball in 1970 and I am capable of playing. I have received a contract from the Philadelphia club, but I believe

I have the right to reconsider offers from other clubs before making any decisions. I, therefore, request that you make known to all major league clubs my feelings in this matter, and advise them of my availability for the 1970 season.[14]

Kuhn's response was dated December 30, and read in part:

You have entered into a current playing contract with the St. Louis club, which has the same assignment provision as those in your annual major league contracts since 1956. Your present contract has been assigned in accordance with its provisions by the St. Louis club to the Philadelphia club. The provisions of the playing contract have been negotiated over the years between the clubs and the players, most recently when the present basic agreement was negotiated two years ago between the clubs and the Players Association.

If you have any specific objection to the propriety of the assignment, I would appreciate your specifying the objection. Under the circumstances, and pending any further information from you, I do not see what action I can take and cannot comply with the request contained in the second paragraph of your letter.[15]

Before the 1970 season began, Kuhn asked to meet with Flood to see if they could find a solution to the impasse. Flood didn't accept the invitation. Monte Irvin, an assistant to Kuhn, informed Curt that the commissioner was willing to allow him to arrange a deal with any National League club and that it would not damage his litigation. Flood felt that if he accepted the offer he would be weakening his suit, and he sat out the season.

The case was filed on January 15, 1970, in Federal Court in New York City. The commissioner, the presidents of the two major leagues, and the 24 club owners were named as defendants in the $3-million damage suit.

Flood's suit struck at the reserve clause and presented arguments as to why baseball belonged under antitrust laws. Those issues had been argued unsuccessfully a number of times before. Flood's case included two new allegations:

1. The St. Louis Cardinals have violated the Sherman Act by arranging to limit all sales of beer in their park to the beer produced by their affiliated company. (The Cardinals are a subsidiary of Anheuser Busch, Inc.) Such a violation tends, the complaint argues, "to increase the revenues of the beer company and diminish the revenues of defendant St. Louis National Baseball Club, Inc., available for player salaries, including that of the plaintiff."

2. The Columbia Broadcasting System, because it owns the New York Yankees, has refrained from bidding for national baseball broadcasts and it is one of the three national networks that could bid. This "injury to competition" is a violation of Federal antitrust laws and reduces the revenues in which "players such as the plaintiff would share."[16]

The trial began on May 19, and the case was argued before Federal District Court judge Irving Ben Cooper. Flood and Miller testified during the first day of the trial, with Cooper asking Flood a number of questions abut his salary during his time in baseball. When he was unable to remember the exact figures, a lawyer representing Major League Baseball quoted from information provided by Curt's former employers. The figures showed that Flood was paid $4,000 a year during each of his first two minor league seasons, had made $23,000 in his seventh major league campaign, and had earned $90,000 in 1969 with the Cardinals. The Phillies had offered him $90,000 plus $8,000 spring training expenses for the 1970 campaign.

The trial was concluded on June 10 and produced about 2000 pages of testimony from the 15 sessions. On the final day, Bill Veeck, Jr., a former owner of the Cleveland Indians, Chicago White Sox, and St. Louis Browns, as well as one of the greatest characters and promoters in the history of baseball, gave his testimony. Veeck, who had retired in 1961, said that the complete elimination of the reserve system would be chaotic, but some sort of orderly modification of the system over a period of years was possible.

Robert Lipsyte, writing in the *New York Times* the day after the trial, said:

> Ultimately, after all this talk of balance of power, honor, reputation and serfdom, this case, too, is about money. The owners are fighting the suit so hard because their tightly-structured control of the acquisitions and movement of talent keeps the costs down. That such a tight control is best for baseball has yet to be proven.[17]

On August 12, Cooper, in a 47-page opinion, ruled against Flood. He suggested that the players and the owners work together to make changes in the reserve system. In the opinion, the judge said in part:

> Since baseball remains exempt from anti-trust laws, unless and until the Supreme Court or Congress holds to the contrary, we have no basis for proceeding to the underlying question of whether baseball's reserve system would or would not be deemed reasonable if it were in fact subject to anti-trust regulation.[18]

Flood's lawyers appealed the District Court's ruling to the United States Second Circuit Court of Appeals which, in 1971, upheld the lower court's ruling. The next stop was the United States Supreme Court. On October 19, 1971, the Supreme Court agreed to hear the case.

Leonard Koppett, writing in the *New York Times*, didn't see any immediate and drastic changes even if the nation's highest court ruled in Flood's favor:

> It is highly unlikely that chaos will result from any decision. A victory for Flood will only begin the process of working out new contractual arrangements between club owners and athletes, and these new arrangements will be arrived at gradually....
>
> An analogy can be drawn to the school desegregation decision of 1954. Technically, segregated schools immediately became illegal. But lower courts were given considerable time to work out provisions for specific cases.[19]

Before the Supreme Court could issue its ruling, the game of baseball was lurching toward its first strike—the first-ever in professional sports.

With the current Basic Agreement due to expire March 31, 1972, the Players Association was seeking a cost of living increase in pension and health insurance. The cost of living had risen 17 percent and the players' health care had increased $500,000 a year since the 1969 pact was ratified.

Early in the negotiations, the PRC made a marginal offer that did not satisfy the players, especially since the owners had signed a new $71.75 million, four-year television contract with the National Broadcasting Company (NBC) for rights to the World Series, the All-Star Games and the Game-of-the-Week.

The PRC's membership was mainly conservative and consisted of National Leaguers Francis Dale (Reds), Donald Grant (New York Mets), Dan Galbreath (Pittsburgh Pirates), and Dick Meyer (Cardinals), and American Leaguers Calvin Griffith (Minnesota Twins), Jerold Hoffberger (Baltimore Orioles), Ewing Kauffman (Kansas City Royals), and Dick O'Connell (Boston Red Sox). The two league presidents, Chub Feeney of the Senior Circuit and Joe Cronin of the Junior Circuit, were ex-officio members.

On July 5, 1971, the Players Association had filed an unfair labor practice charge with the New York regional office of the National Labor Relations Board (NLRB) against the 24 major league clubs. In the filing they cited the clubs' refusal to release the terms of the new television contract. The Players Association said that they needed the figures in order to adequately prepare for the new round of negotiations.

Gaherin had made an offer of a $500,000-a-year contribution to health care. Even though there was surplus income from the pension fund which could be used to increase retirement benefits, the owners were not willing to use the money for that purpose. From Miller's perspective, had they been willing to do that it would not have cost them any additional money to increase their contributions to the players' retirement fund.

Baseball's pension fund was a complicated and sophisticated structure. The fund was started in 1946 on a relatively small basis, but had grown throughout the years, largely as a result of the increased bargaining power of the players. In 1957 the owners agreed to contribute 60 percent of the television revenue from the World Series and 95 percent from the All-Star Game to the players' pension fund.

In the previous agreement the owners had contributed $5.45 million annually to the pension fund. By 1971 the fund had sizable assets—$60 million. The money was invested in two vehicles. Forty-four million was in a fixed account that was expected to earn 4½ percent a year. The remaining funds were in common stocks and other equities, and that income varied with the market.

Because of the healthy nature of the economy, the accounts had produced more than the expected return, creating a surplus. The Players Association also knew of other sources of surplus. First, the owners had over-funded the amount of money needed for permanently disabled players. Also, even though money was set aside for every player on the major league rosters, a number of those players never met the four-year requirement for collecting a pension and, according to Miller, that money was also in the surplus category.

In both 1967 and 1969, the owners had designated some of the surplus to increase the funding of the pension program. Miller was asking the PRC to do that again in 1972. By his estimate there was a current surplus of $817,000, and it rightly should benefit the players. The owners, however, believed that it was their money and they were free to do with it as they wished.

On March 1, while negotiations continued, Miller and the Players Association's counsel Moss began a tour of spring training camps. They updated players on the progress of the talks and said that there appeared to be reason for optimism about getting a new and acceptable contract.

However, while they were at the Chicago White Sox camp in Sarasota, Florida, there was a significant change in the owners' position. Miller and Moss heard that they had decided not to make any additional contributions to the pension fund, as they had attempted to do in 1969, and they were going to reduce their health care offer.

Miller assessed the situation, saying:

> Reducing a bargaining proposal which Gaherin knew was inadequate
> in the first place was an unmistakable signal: management was bait-
> ing us into a strike. Their position was, "Take it or leave it! There's
> nothing you can do or the players can do about it."[20]

Before Miller and Moss left the White Sox camp, the players there
voted 31–0 to support a strike. That was the beginning of a new tenor
among the players—the idea of a strike as a method of obtaining an acceptable agreement came to the fore.

During the remaining 17 visits on Miller's itinerary (he had already
visited seven camps, some of which he and Moss revisited and he spoke
with players by telephone in the others), the subject of a possible strike
was the central item on the agenda. He received strong support for that
action from the players in the camps who were beginning to sense the
power that was in their hands.

The lines were drawn and the magnates were not going to surren-
der to the players. After an owners' meeting in St. Petersburg, Florida, a
red-faced and angry Cardinals' president August A. Busch, Jr., threw
down the gauntlet, bellowing, "We voted unanimously to take a stand....
We're not going to give them another god damn cent! If they want to
strike—let them."[21]

Miller found a few pockets of resistance among the players. By the
time he arrived at the Red Sox' camp, the combined vote for the strike
was 349–0 (with two abstentions). Boston's Rico Petrocelli, Reggie Smith,
and Yastrzemski were vocal spokesmen against a strike and their team's
tally was 19–4. Interestingly, Yastrzemski had been a solid supporter of
the MLBPA in 1969 when the union battled the owners about an increase
in the pension fund. A few Dodgers were also opposed to the union's recommended action. The final vote of the players, managers, coaches, and
trainers was 663–10 (with two abstentions) in favor of a strike. They had
shown their resolve at the ballot box. Would they do the same when they
weren't receiving a pay check? The owners thought not!

Kuhn, who was now firmly entrenched in the commissioner's office
after being given a full seven-year term, had his own ideas about the vote
and the strike:

> Why the strike vote? Either Miller's inexperience as a bargainer was
> showing and he was having difficulty knowing when to close a deal or
> he had decided to precipitate a strike as part of a strategy to intimidate

the owners in the following year's negotiations on the basic agreement, which included the reserve system. By this point, having lost the Flood case on two judicial levels, and certainly with no reason to feel optimistic about the Supreme Court, after the oral argument there on March 20, it could have made sense to lay groundwork for the future. Either answer is plausible, and indeed both might have been correct. Still, I am inclined to think he was trying to deliver a message for the future.[22]

While negotiations over a new pension agreement and discussions about a strike continued throughout spring training, the legal battle had again heated up in Washington, D.C. On March 20, the Supreme Court heard the arguments in Flood v. Kuhn. Each side was given 30 minutes to state its position. Goldberg, representing the union, contended that the pivotal issue was the legality of the reserve clause. Paul Porter and Lou Hoynes, attorneys for Major League Baseball, argued that Flood v. Kuhn was basically a labor dispute between Baseball and the Players Association since the latter was paying the legal costs of the suit.

On March 29, two days before the 1969 Basic Agreement was due to expire, and sensing that the owners were not about to change their stand, Miller proposed that the dispute be decided by an impartial arbitrator. Gaherin, speaking for the owners, rejected the proposal.

Arthur Daley, writing in the *New York Times*, wondered why all the fuss over the pension plan. He described the situation of former player and manager Leo Durocher, who was 66, retired, and collecting a pension of nearly $2,000 per month. Daley wrote:

> The player pension scale is so generous that it may be the best pension plan in the country. The only one that might challenge it is that of the airline pilots, another group of high-flyers. But the pilots must wait for the usual retirement age of 65 after perhaps 30 years of service before collecting in full. The ballplayers can collect—at a lower early retirement rate—at the age of 45 and after only four years of big-league play.
>
> But Marvin Miller, the professional unionist who directs the players' union, has jostled the complacent ballplayers into threatening a strike that could begin tomorrow. Virtually no one close to the situation, however, believes that there will be a strike because such a strike would go counter to every principle of logic.[23]

Miller, in a meeting with the player representatives and their alternates on March 31 in Dallas, Texas, suggested that they remain on the field while negotiations continued during the season. However, after extended discussions, the players voted 47–0 (with one abstention) to strike.

A victim of the strike. A forlorn youngster waits for a game that will not begin.
(UPI-Bettmann/Corbis)

Baseball's first strike began on April 1, prematurely ending spring training. The following day, tragedy and sadness struck the game in another form when 47-year-old Gil Hodges, former Dodger star and current manager of the Mets, dropped dead of a heart attack following a round of golf in West Palm Beach, Florida. The attention of many in the game was turned to a much deeper concern.

With spring training halted, and the April 5 opening of the regular season in serious jeopardy, most in the media faulted the players for precipitating the unthinkable event and took the side of the owners. C.C. Johnson Spink, editor of the *Sporting News*, was one of the most outspoken critics, calling the walkout, "the darkest day in sports history ... the whole idea of pensions for major league players may have been a mistake growing out of a misconception of what constitutes a career."[24]

Dick Young, a writer for the *New York Daily News*, lashed out at Miller, who he called "Svengali," saying:

> Ball players are no match for him [Miller]. He has a steel trap mind wrapped in a butter melting voice. He runs the players through a high-pressure spray the way an auto goes through a car wash, and that's how they come out, brainwashed. With few exceptions, they follow him blindly, like Zombies.[25]

Columnist Red Smith, one of the few writers to support the players, countered:

> From time to time, owners and mouthpieces of the establishment picture Marvin Miller as a master pitchman who hypnotizes players. The 663–10 vote in favor of a strike suggests that if the players aren't in earnest, Marvin Miller has to be the glibbest con man this side of Soapy Smith.[26]

Richards leveled another shot at Miller, exclaiming, "Tojo and Hirohito couldn't stop baseball but Marvin Miller could."[27]

Most former players who had lived through management-controlled careers were nevertheless on the side of the owners. They were, after all, drawing respectable pensions from baseball. Rip Sewell was one of them. The 64-year-old, former blooper-ball pitcher charged:

> First, the players wanted a hamburger and the owners gave them a hamburger. Then they wanted filet mignon and they gave them a filet mignon. Then they wanted the whole darned cow and they got the cow. Now they want a pasture for the cow. You just can't satisfy them.[28]

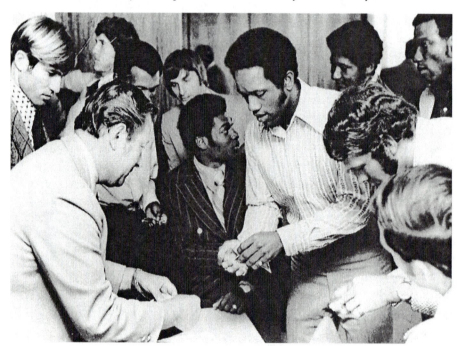

Oriole players draw money as the strike begins. (UPI-Bettmann/Corbis)

Some teams experience internal strife. Hoffberger, owner of the Orioles, blasted his players, and he had the support of manager Earl Weaver and pitcher Jim Palmer. A contingent of Dodger players, led by Maury Wills, voted to open the season on April 7, but others on the team successfully led a movement against Wills' plan.

The White Sox, Phillies, and Pirates bucked the leagues' guidelines and attempted to entice their players to come back by opening their stadiums for them to prepare for the season. Arthur Allyn, outspoken owner of the White Sox, refused to be dictated to by anyone, even his fellow owners, and barked, "Nobody is going to tell me what to do with my team!"[29]

On April 9, President Richard Nixon became involved with the shutdown, suggesting that the two sides meet with J. Curtis Counts, director of the Federal Mediation and Conciliation Service. Miller and Gaherin went to Washington and met with Counts the following morning.

That afternoon, April 10, after returning to New York City, Gaherin announced that the owners were willing to use $400,000 of the surplus to support the pension fund. In addition, $500,000 would be made available for an increase in health care premiums. Miller came back with a demand of $600,000 for the pension fund and, ultimately, the two sides compromised at $500,000, which represented a 14 percent increase in the payment to the pension fund.

Charles O. Finley, the owner of the Oakland Athletics who had made his fortune in insurance, had changed dramatically from his earlier position when he had said that he was against using the surplus for the pension fund. He became one of the leaders in the owners' discussions that led to the final agreement about health benefits and the pension fund.

A settlement appeared imminent, but another issue took center stage. The two sides began to discuss the regular season games that had not been played because of the strike. Most National League owners held out for a way to reschedule the missed games. Those in the Junior Circuit, who for years had favored a shorter schedule, were not adamant about playing them.

National League owners wanted the games made up on off-days and by turning single contests into doubleheaders; the players expected to be paid extra for playing them. Miller suggested that the games be made up, but without admission being charged and without the players receiving any extra salary. He saw it as a way of repaying the fans for any inconveniences caused by the strike. Gaherin and the owners turned down Miller's idea.

Negotiations about the missed games took place over three days. The owners gathered in Chicago on April 12 and the player representatives were at the Association's office in Manhattan.

The 13-day strike came to an end about 4:15 P.M., Central Time, on April 13, 1972, with the two sides having negotiated a new benefit and pension agreement. The health care and pension contributions were as they had been decided on April 10. The last decision was that the 86 games in question would not be played. Both the owners and the players would suffer financially because of the cancellations—no admissions, no receipts, and no pay.

The season began on April 15. Irv Kupcinet, writer for the *Chicago Sun-Times*, noted a missed opportunity:

> Somebody in baseball has no sense of humor. Marvin Miller should have been invited to throw out the first ball on opening day. After all, he helped throw out the first 86 games of the season.[30]

Not all the owners were happy with the scheduled opening. Kauffman announced that he would protest to the American League office about any games his team had to play against the White Sox the first weekend. He said that Allyn had disregarded the owners' wishes by opening Comiskey Park and that had given his club an unfair advantage.

Robert Howsam, general manager of the Reds, fired a parting shot at Marvin:

> Look at Mr. Miller's background.... He has not played one inning as a professional player. He has never worked for a baseball club. Baseball is not the steel industry, and he can't use the tactics of a steel negotiator.[31]

Some teams would have 153 games on their schedules in 1972 and others would play as many as 156 of the 162 regularly scheduled contests. In the American League East, the Tigers played 156 times, and they won the division by one-half game over the Red Sox, who played one fewer contest.

Fans didn't stay away from the ballparks in any great number as a protest against baseball's first regular season stoppage of play. Although official attendance was down by 2,225,148, that number represented an average loss of 25,873 fans for each of the 86 games that were not played because of the strike.

On June 19, 1972, a little more than two months into the season, the nation's highest court upheld the two lower courts' decisions in Flood v. Kuhn. Oliver Wendell Holmes' judgment a half century earlier, which supported baseball's exempt status from antitrust laws, was still the law of the game.

Chief Justice Warren Burger, who voted with the majority, "recognized the error of baseball's ways, but wrote that the lives of too many people would be affected by the reversal of the errors."[32]

Justice Harry Blackmun said:

> Professional baseball is a business and it is engaged in interstate commerce—and thus normally subject to federal business law. But it is in a very distinct sense an exception and an anomaly. The aberration is an established one.[33]

A dissenting opinion was filed by Justice William O. Douglas:

> If Congressional inaction is our guide, we should rely upon the fact that Congress has refused to enact bills broadly exempting professional sports from antitrust regulation.... There can be no doubt that were we considering the question of baseball for the first time upon a clean slate, we would hold it to be subject to Federal antitrust regulation. The unbroken silence of Congress should not prevent us from correcting our own mistakes.[34]

Kuhn believed that the decision sent a number of important messages. He wrote:

> The decision was hailed by many as a great victory for baseball, but it carried another message—that the immunity was an "aberration," and that it would be Congress's job, not the Court's, to correct it. I called the decision "constructive," and said, "It opens the way for renewed collective bargaining on the reserve system after the 1972 season. I am confident that the players and the clubs are in the best position to determine for themselves what the form of the reserve system should be and that they both will take a more responsible view of the respective obligations to the public and to the game."[35]

By the time the Supreme Court issued its ruling, Flood's playing career had ended. He had been traded by the Phillies to the Washington Senators on November 3, 1970, for three players—Greg Goossen, Gene Martin, and Jeff Turpko. Flood signed a contract with Robert Short, owner of the Senators, to play for the American League club in 1971. He appeared in only 13 games for Washington, hitting .200, before retiring. The layoff had cost him too much.

Former commissioner Ford Frick, writing about the Supreme Court's decision, concluded:

> All of which leaves the whole question of legality and future procedures very much up in the air.... Congress must decide two questions.

Marvin Miller, Bowie Kuhn, and Congressmen Frank Horton and Emanuel Celler discuss baseball and antitrust issues in Washington in August 1972. (UPI-Bettmann/Corbis)

> First, does the unique competitive nature ofl professional team sports justify broad exemption from antitrust laws? Second, how can Congress best provide leeway to permit player development and honest competition and still come within the letter of the law as written? Those are the $64,000 questions.[36]

Those questions had been asked many times over many years. They, in fact, still remain unanswered.

CHAPTER SIX

No Strikes, but
Two Close Calls

"Ruling Is Seen Raising Prospect of Baseball Strike Next Spring."[1] The headline on the Sports page of the *New York Times* the day following the Supreme Court's 5-to-3 decision in Flood v. Kuhn put a scare in many who, once upon a time, thought that a baseball strike could never happen. The owners' and players' differences had always been settled by an agreement or by one side—usually the players—backing down in time for the games to be played. That belief had been shattered in 1972 and there was growing sentiment that it could happen again.

The article suggested two avenues for settling the issues that would face the negotiators before the start of the 1973 campaign. Either Congress could settle the question about the reserve clause or the two sides could come to an agreement through negotiations. As reported in the *Times*:

> But unless Congress acts fast, only the second course will remain. And the indications were growing that any direct negotiations might become lengthy and crippling. The reason: Every basic relationship in the sport, from minimum pay to the length of the season, is scheduled to be argued before the teams play in 1973.[2]

Shortly after the difficult negotiations in 1972, the Player Relations Committee (PRC) had a makeover in preparation for the next round of negotiations. In July the committee's size was reduced from ten to six voting members and the voting rule for player matters was changed to a simple majority of the major league clubs rather than a majority in each league.

The collective bargaining which led to the 1973 Basic Agreement, which was baseball's third, was lengthy. When it appeared that an agreement might not be reached before the opening of spring training, the owners, fearful of another costly player walkout, announced on February 8 that all the early camps which were mostly for pitchers and catchers would be cancelled. The announcement was issued by the American and National League offices and advised players who had been invited to report to spring training prior to March 1 not to report until further notice. In the players' view the owners' action constituted a lockout. The owners wanted to call it neither a lockout nor a strike; they simply didn't want to start anything before an agreement was reached.

Marvin Miller contended that the lockout could be interpreted as a breach of contract that made all the players' contracts null and void. He said:

> If a player negotiated a contract for $100,000, or whatever salary, and he's locked out of spring training and doesn't have a good year he could claim he was denied the right to get into shape.[3]

On February 16, Phillip K. Wrigley, long-time owner of the Chicago Cubs, reasoned:

> We aren't anticipating a strike but if they (the players) won't work without a contract why should we? I don't know why we should train somebody for a season that might not happen.[4]

Negotiations continued without much fanfare. Unlike the previous year, the press was not regularly informed about the areas of agreement or disagreement or about progress being made.

A three-year agreement was reached and announced on February 25, 1973, and spring training was set to start on March 1. The minimum salary was increased from the 1972 level of $13,500 to $15,000 for the 1973 and 1974 seasons with an additional adjustment to $16,000 for the following year.

A couple of changes that affected the reserve clause were of more long-term importance. The first was a new ten-and-five rule that said that any ten-year major league veteran who had been with his club for the last five years could not be traded without his permission. That policy would have been helpful to Curt Flood when he was traded to the Philadelphia Phillies in 1969.

Also, the players gained salary arbitration for the first time. The owners had proposed that a player had to have three or more years in the majors to file for arbitration and the player could not file more frequently than every other year. The final agreement was the players' proposal which granted eligibility for arbitration after two or more years with no restriction on frequency.

The offer of salary arbitration served as a compromise between management and labor. Owners wanted to retain the services of players they had purchased, traded for, or developed through their minor league systems; players wanted free agency which would give them a choice of where they wanted to play and would be influential in determining their market value. For the owners, salary arbitration at least allowed a club to retain the player while giving the player power with regard to his market value.

The salary arbitration procedures as outlined were straightforward; the criteria for decision making were not as clear cut.

If a player did not believe that the money the club offered him was what he thought he was worth, he filed for arbitration by a specified date in December. If the two sides were unable to reach agreement by the middle of January, the player and the club each submitted a salary figure. Within twenty-four hours the player, the club, the commissioner, the Major League Baseball Players Association (MLBPA), and the PRC were notified of the two amounts that had been submitted.

Not every case would go as far as reaching an arbitrator's decision. According to the guidelines, the two sides could reach agreement on a new contract as late as right before the arbitrator was to give his ruling. That would happen on only a few occasions. A more common pattern would be for the club and the player to settle the dispute before the hearing began.

A three-hour hearing for each player filing for arbitration would be held separately sometime during "arbitration season" which was between February 1 and 20. Both the player and the club could be represented by counsel and both sides paid for their own representation. The two sides shared the cost of the arbitrator(s). A change was made by the 1996 Basic Agreement which provided that a three-member panel of arbitrators rather than a single arbitrator hear and rule on each case.

The role of the arbitrator(s) was to hear the presentations made by both sides and then, within 24 hours, award the player either the salary amount the club offered or the salary he sought. The amount stated by each side was known as "the last best offer," and the arbitrator(s) could not decide on a compromise between the two amounts. The decision was final and binding.

The criteria to be applied in determining the proper salary was stated in the Basic Agreement:

> a. The quality of the Player's contribution to his Club during the past season (including but not limited to his overall performance, special qualities of leadership, and public appeal);

 b. the length and consistency of his career contribution;

 c. the record of the Player's past compensation;

 d. the existence of any physical or mental defects on the part of the Player;

 e. and the recent performance of the Club, including but not limited to its League standing and attendance as an indication of public acceptance.[5]

At the start of the hearing, the two sides exchanged briefs. Representatives for the player were the first to present their position (for one hour) and management would then have the same amount of time to argue their case. After a period of recess, the player's representatives would make a 30-minute rebuttal which was followed by a 30-minute rebuttal by management.

The arbitrator(s) would make his decision known within 24 hours. In the beginning, the form of the arbitrator's response was not as sophisticated as it would become later. The arbitrator would write the amount of his salary decision in the appropriate space on an American League or National League standard contract which had already been signed by the player and the appropriate representative of the club. The arbitrator did not have to present a written opinion in the case.

A *New York Times* editorial on February 28 pictured baseball as a pioneer at the bargaining table:

> Major league baseball, until now a squalling infant in the ranks of unionized industries, has set an admirable example of creativity at the bargaining table in the new three-year agreement between the club owners and the players.
>
> By accepting arbitration as the device for settling future disputes over individual salaries, the bargainers not only warded off long and mutually painful holdouts by the game's brightest stars but also did much to ease the unfairness of the tyrannical reserve clause. No longer must the players accept as conclusive the owner's decision on how much they will earn, though it is still his right—not theirs—to decide whether they will stay with his club or be traded. The remedy for that form of indentured labor will have to come through overdue action by Congress to void baseball's present exemption from the antitrust laws.[6]

While new relationships between the owners and players were being forged at negotiating tables, new records were being set at the box office. Attendance during the 1973 season reached 30 million for the first time. It would grow to more than 40 million in five years.

The new ten-and-five rule first made headlines during the winter meetings in Houston. On December 5, 1973, Ron Santo, the 14-year veteran third baseman for the Chicago Cubs, informed the club's vice president and general manager John Holland that he wouldn't approve a trade which would send him to the California Angels for pitchers Andy Hassler and Bruce Heinbechner. Three other players who had veto privileges—Willie Davis, Claude Osteen and Juan Marichal—agreed to trades early in December.

Following Santo's refusal to go to California, the Angels' general manager Harry Dalton attempted to change the recalcitrant third baseman's mind, but he failed to do so. The Cubs applied pressure and threatened to cut his salary the maximum 20 percent. Santo informed the Cubs that he wanted to remain in Chicago and would only accept a trade to the White Sox, who subsequently signed him to a two-year contract and raised his annual salary from $110,000 to $117,000. In exchange for Santo, the Cubs received pitchers Steve Stone, Ken Frailing and Jim Kremmel along with catcher Steve Swisher, who had been the White Sox' first choice in the June 1973 draft. Santo played one season on the South Side of Chicago and then retired.

An angry Wrigley, who at one point threatened to give Santo his unconditional release (a move that would have been acceptable to the third baseman), commented about the new rule:

> I don't think anybody realized the rule was there ... and now it's created a big turmoil. I think it's going to be tough on a lot of players. I don't think anybody will keep any players for more than five years from now on. Then you could use them in a trade without their consent.[7]

In January 1974, New York Mets right-handed pitcher Tom Seaver assessed the salary scene from a player's perspective:

> Whenever a player raises the top salary in any sport, it has to help everybody below. The owners might not want to admit it, but it's absurd to think that it won't help. The one thing it definitely does is to give us a better understanding of our worth. Pitchers with comparable records and ability have a valid point in seeking a comparable salary.[8]

Prior to the start of the 1974 campaign, one of the most momentous labor-management events began to take shape. Jim "Catfish" Hunter signed a two-year agreement with the Oakland Athletics for a $100,000 annual salary. The contract for the A's star pitcher, who had won 21 games in each of the previous three seasons and had led his club to consecutive World Championships in 1972 and 1973, included a provision that half ($50,000) of his salary would be remitted by the club to an insurance company, named by Hunter for a deferred annuity. The money was to be paid to the Jefferson Insurance Company of North Carolina on a semi-monthly basis during the two baseball seasons covered by the contract.

Charles Finley, owner of the Athletics, realized that the payment of deferred money created unfavorable tax consequences for him since he could not declare it a deductible expense for tax purposes until Hunter received his deferred annuity payments years later. Finley did not follow the agreed upon details of Hunter's contract and, late in the season, Miller saw an article in a newspaper about the pitcher's situation. After Miller and MLBPA counsel Dick Moss read a copy of Hunter's contract, Marvin said:

> The case was an open and shut case. The Uniform Player's Contract, which existed long before there was a union [it had been in existence for more than 40 years], had been drawn up by the owners' lawyers, and if my memory is correct, one of the very first sections of the contract described what the player's rights were if the contract should be breached by the club. It basically provided that if that should happen, the player could bring this to the attention of the owner in writing and the owner would have ten days in which to rectify the wrong. And if he hadn't done so ten days after being notified in writing, the player had the right to notify the club owner that he was declaring the contract at an end.
>
> I told Hunter that he would have the right to file a notice because he told me that he had already talked to Finley and Finley had refused to give him any satisfaction. All of this had been going on all season long, and now it was very near the end of the championship season. I said to Hunter, "You know you have time on this. Do you want me to hold up on this until the off season? You know it could be a distraction." He said, "No. It doesn't bother me. File the notice, file the ten-day notice."[9]

Miller and the Players Association sent a letter to the Oakland club calling for it to correct the default within ten days in accordance with the Uniform Player's Contract. Finley ignored the ten-day notice, prompting Miller to send notices to Finley, American League president Lee MacPhail, Kuhn, and the PRC's John Gaherin, stating that Hunter was terminating his contract, that a grievance had been filed to give the payment of the money with interest to the insurance company, and that Hunter was a free agent because his contract had been breached by the club.

During the 1974 regular season, Catfish had put together another outstanding year, going 25-12 with 23 complete games and a league leading 2.49 ERA. The 28-year-old right-hander had also pitched a perfect game and would soon pick up the American League's Cy Young Award.

On October 4, the day before the start of the American League Championship Series, Finley agreed to pay $50,000 to Hunter. In the A's locker room and in the presence of MacPhail, who was there to serve as a witness to the transaction, Finley offered the money to the pitcher. Miller recalled:

> Hunter, who could take care of himself very well, when confronted with this in the locker room by his boss and the league president and a $50,000 check, said (I wasn't there but I was told that Hunter simply said), "This won't do it, Mr. Finley. The contract calls for the payment of this money to an insurance company. That was an important part of our contract to have this on a deferred basis and this doesn't fix the problem. It was part of the contract. If I had wanted the whole $100,000 in salary, then we wouldn't have had a deferred payment agreement. In addition, your check does not include interest due because of the non-payment of the $50,000 to date."[10]

Kuhn was asked by Miller and the Players Association to declare Hunter a free agent, but the commissioner was not willing to take that unprecedented step. He believed that such a move would be too extreme a remedy, especially since Finley had offered to pay Hunter the money.

The Players Association appealed Kuhn's decision, believing that the commissioner did not hold the power to set aside the terms of a contract. The process for settling a dispute such as this between a player and an owner had been agreed to in the 1970 collective bargaining agreement.

Hence, Gaherin, Miller, and arbitrator Peter Seitz, who had been selected jointly by the MLBPA and the PRC, sat as the panel to hear the appeal. Both sides presented their arguments at the November 26 hearing. Seitz and Miller voted in favor of Hunter in the 2–1 decision, which was officially announced on December 16. Hunter became baseball's first bona fide free agent.

The final paragraph of Seitz's 40-page decision summed up his findings:

> Mr. Finley's refusal to accept the insurance company as the "person, firm or corporation" designated by Mr. Hunter to which compensation should be paid, as deferred compensation, constituted a violation of the Special Covenant and justified its termination by Mr. Hunter.[11]

It was a major victory for the players and a stunning setback for the owners. However, the gates to free agency had not been flung wide open by the decision:

> ... this case has no general implication for other players, or the reserve clause in general. The issue is simply the failure of Charles O. Finley, owner and operator of the A's, to carry out payments to Hunter in the way his contract required.[12]

Both MacPhail and Kuhn were shocked by Seitz's decision. The American League president said, "We agreed that Finley had been wrong and should be assessed some kind of penalty but we never anticipated that Hunter would be declared a free agent. This was a case in which the penalty hardly fit the crime."[13]

Kuhn's response was in a similar vein:

> To forfeit the contract over a few days' delay in paying the $50,000 was like giving a life sentence to a pickpocket. Hunter's contract was of enormous value to the Oakland club. It should not have been forfeited unless Oakland was guilty of serious wrongdoing. Finley clearly was a pickpocket, trying to hold the $50,000 in his own account for as long as possible, but so far as I know, that was the worst of it.[14]

Miller was amazed by Kuhn's response:

> The $50,000 was to be paid semi-monthly starting on April 15. Instead as October began, Finley had made zero payments. The "delay" was somewhat more than a few days.
> The arbitrator did not fashion the remedy of contract termination and free agency. The remedy was written into the contract long before there was an arbitrator or a union. Once there was a finding that there was this breach, and that really couldn't be disputed, all Seitz could do was make the decision he did.[15]

The American League supported the Oakland A's subsequent appeal even though the Basic Agreement set forth that an arbitrator's decision was final and binding. A California appeals court supported Seitz's decision.

Hunter signed a five-year, $3.75 million contract to play for the New York Yankees in 1975. At the time, the average major league salary was $45,000. Catfish's signing, which was announced on New Year's Eve, represented the birth of a new era in baseball economics. Kuhn labeled the Yankees' move "fiscal insanity."[16]

Perhaps, the decision had served as payback time for Hunter. Finley had loaned Catfish $120,000 in 1969 to buy farmland in North Carolina. The agreement between the two men was that Hunter would repay $20,000 annually at six percent interest. A few months after the agreement was finalized, Finley began to adamantly demand that all the money be repaid immediately since he needed the funds to help with the purchases of basketball and hockey teams. Hunter didn't have the money available, since it had been used to buy the land. After Finley continued to badger him, especially on the days when he was scheduled to pitch, Hunter sold thirty acres of his land in order to silence his insistent boss.

After the White Sox signed Dick Allen in February to a $250,000 contract for the 1975 season, Finley expressed his opinion about escalating salaries:

> There's an old saying that pigs get fat and hogs go to market. Well, some of the players these days aren't even pigs or hogs—they're gluttons. We have to keep salaries within reason. If we just rolled over and gave them what they wanted we'd price ourselves out of business.[17]

The Athletics' owner was much more charitable after Oakland's top reliever Rollie Fingers won his arbitration case against the A's. After the arbitrator awarded Fingers a $90,000 contract, which was $15,000 more than the Athletics had offered him, Finley called the pitcher's agent, Jerry Kapstein, and congratulated him. Kapstein was amazed by the call:

> Mr. Finley called me this morning to congratulate Rollie and me on our victory.... He was very gracious and I would have to say it is most unusual when an owner can call you like that. As for the contract, I guess you could say it was a landmark case for a relief pitcher.[18]

On March 6, 1975, former commissioner A. B. Happy Chandler spoke about the current status of the reserve clause and need for change:

> Baseball is operating from Justice Holmes' interpretation of baseball ... as not being a business. But that was in 1922. Baseball is a tremendous business now and is subject to trust and antitrust laws. The reserve clause needs to be amended to fit the 1970s, but it would be against the interests of the owners and players to have the whole thing thrown out.[19]

In 1975 two other players sought to take control of their contract situations via the free-agent route. Pitchers Andy Messersmith of the

Los Angeles Dodgers and Dave McNally of the Montreal Expos were unhappy with the conditions in their 1975 contracts and refused to sign new agreements. Messersmith, the ace of the Dodgers' staff with a 20-6 record and a 2.59 ERA in 1974, wanted a no-trade clause included in a new contract. When the Dodgers refused, he played the '75 season under the conditions of the contract from the previous year. In late summer, the Dodgers raised their salary offer to Messersmith and were discussing a three-year deal worth $540,000, but they made it clear that a no-trade clause would not be included in the pact.

Following the 1974 season, McNally, with his 16-10 record, was sent to Montreal by the Baltimore Orioles as part of a major trade between the two clubs. The trade required McNally's approval since he came under the ten-and-five rule. When he spoke with the Expos and asked for a two-year contract at $125,000 per season, the Montreal club agreed to do it. But the Expos changed their position after the deal was finalized and offered McNally $115,000, which was the same amount he had made with the Orioles in 1974. He refused to sign with the Expos, and the club employed the renewal clause. McNally developed arm trouble during the spring and struggled to a 3-6 record with a 5.26 ERA. As he recalled, "My arm was shot at the time anyway. After two months, I decided that I'd enough and went home."[20]

After the 1975 season, both Messersmith and McNally were without new contracts for the 1976 campaign. The clubs were assuming that the renewal approach would work again. In October the Players Association filed a grievance, asking the commissioner to declare both Messersmith and McNally free agents. Kuhn refused to grant the request, and the Players Association made another appeal to Seitz.

The owners' committee did not believe the grievance procedure applied to situations related to the reserve clause. They took the issue to Judge John Oliver of the United States District Court. He advised the PRC to follow through with the arbitration hearings and return to him if that decision was not to their satisfaction. Both the PRC and the Players Association had the power to dismiss Seitz, and the owners' group considered doing that. They remembered his ruling in the Hunter case, and some didn't want to risk a repeat of that decision. Others guessed that Seitz would go easier on management the second time around because of the earlier ruling and the owners' strong negative response to it. In the end, the PRC voted to retain Seitz, with Montreal's John McHale casting the only vote to fire the arbitrator.

The arguments were presented to the three-man arbitration panel which consisted again of Gaherin, Miller, and Seitz. After hearing the testimony, Seitz suggested that the two parties try to settle the matter through negotiation. MacPhail, who made one of the presentations for the American League, remembered considering that option before it was rejected:

> So we in the PRC had another chance, but the thought of negotiat-
> ing with Miller with Seitz standing in the wings was not appealing
> to most of our members. Nor did we think that in a relatively short
> time frame we could produce an agreement acceptable to both par-
> ties. I think I would have given it a try but I don't remember argu-
> ing the issue very strongly. Ed Fitzgerald [chairman of the PRC] and
> most of the committee members were strongly opposed.[21]

On December 23, 1975, Seitz declared Messersmith and McNally free agents. The vote was 2–1, with Seitz casting the deciding ballot. The seminal ruling meant that beginning with the 1976 season a player who had a one-year contract would be eligible for free agency after that season. No longer would clubs be able to renew a player's contract when he chose not to sign again with the club.

The PRC responded by firing Seitz. Although an arbitrator's decision was supposed to be final and binding, management returned to Judge Oliver and appealed the decision in the federal court in Kansas City. They could have taken the appeal to a federal court in any major league city, and they chose Kansas City because of its conservative leanings. The law firm hired by the Players Association assigned a young lawyer from its firm, who was without any special interest or experience in baseball, to argue its case. The lawyer was Donald Fehr.

On February 3, 1976, Oliver upheld the arbitration panel's ruling. The owners' committee was not finished yet, and they took their case to the Eighth United States Circuit Court of Appeals in Kansas City. At the time, MacPhail said:

> The clubs are taking the appeal because they feel very strongly that
> the arbitration panel did not have jurisdiction to deal with the reserve
> system and every avenue should be pursued to establish this fact....
> Despite the decision to appeal, the clubs wish to emphasize their
> determination to continue serious bargaining.[22]

On March 3, the PRC lost its appeal. While the situation involving the two pitchers was taking top billing, another labor-management battle was heating up. Both sides were trying to craft a new Basic Agreement to replace the one which had expired on December 31, 1975. The reserve clause appeared to be the most crucial and divisive matter on the table, but issues regarding pensions, minimum salaries, and other benefits were there as well.

In late July 1975 the players proposed a change in the reserve system which would allow them to test the open market after a yet-to-be-decided period of service with their club. The owners responded, saying that any change in the reserve system would produce chaos.

The members of the PRC during the negotiations were committee chairman Edmund Fitzgerald of the Milwaukee Brewers, league presidents MacPhail and Chub Feeney, Robert Howsam of the Cincinnati Reds, McHale of Montreal, and Calvin Griffith of the Minnesota Twins. Gaherin was the committee's lead negotiator. Kuhn made special note of Fitzgerald's leadership:

> Ed viewed the baseball world with none of the biases that had previously hampered our labor relations. His outlook was completely practical and fair-minded. To the chagrin of some of the more traditional types, he saw no problem in modifying the reserve system if fairness required it. His views closely coincided with my own, which led to an easy and cordial alliance.[23]

Since 1972 some 20 players had played a season without having signed a new contract. Messersmith and McNally were only the latest to have done so. Gaherin foresaw the death of the reserve clause, and he urged the owners to negotiate a change before it was imposed on them, saying, "You don't test the crown jewels.... The deal you make for yourself, no matter how onerous and unpleasant, is better than the deal someone makes for you."[24]

Fitzgerald believed that baseball missed a golden opportunity to mold its future labor relations approach at the annual winter meetings in 1975 in New Orleans, Louisiana. He told the owners:

> The reserve system is doomed in the long haul.... We'd like permission to begin negotiating a revised reserve system beginning this fall. Maybe the reserve system can stand the test, and if it does, fine.... But if it doesn't it fails in a catastrophic mode. Baseball cannot afford that catastrophe. Marvin [Miller] can afford to lose a hundred times as long as he wins once. If we begin to negotiate, we could work out changes in the reserve system that would allow us to gradually adjust over a period of time. The clubs could get used to working with it. We could be comfortable with it. But if we lose in arbitration, we're going to be in trouble from day one. We need to negotiate while we're in a power position.[25]

MacPhail was in agreement with Fitzgerald, as was Griffith, the executive vice president of the Minnesota Twins. But few others were, and the reaction came fast and furious:

> Griffith was appalled by what followed. Fitzgerald was lambasted by owner after owner. Gussie Busch, Bob Howsam, Horace Stoneham—all stepped up for a whack: "We can't give in to the players.... It's been tested by time.... Ridiculous.... Goddammit, Marvin Miller can't tell us what to do."
>
> "What the hell are they doing?" Griffith asked himself. "This is knowledge and vision being laid down. The moment is ripe and this has been perfectly stated."
>
> It made no difference. The first and loudest voices stampeded opinion, as always. The Brewers' chairman might be PRC chief but he was still a baseball newcomer: a "civilian," as some GMs sneered. What did he know?[26]

Fitzgerald commented about his disappointment with the owners' reactions, saying, "It's hard to describe the depths of my disgust following this episode. My eventual departure from baseball was sealed on that date. Lee [MacPhail] had a stronger stomach than I did."[27]

On January 15, 1976, the owners made their first proposal to alter the reserve system. They proposed that a player with eight years in the majors and the last three with the same club could demand to be traded. If the player wasn't traded within a year he would become a free agent. The PRC altered the proposal on February 11, changing the required major league service time from eight years to nine.

Ten days later, the Players Association weighed in with a plan of its own. The idea was to have free agency go into effect after six years in the majors or nine seasons in professional baseball.

On February 23, a shock wave rumbled through baseball. MacPhail and Feeney announced the PRC's position that since there was no Basic Agreement and with the differences between the two sides being so great, it would not be possible to open the 1976 spring training as scheduled on March 1. MacPhail said:

> "We feel the best, quickest and surest way to get an agreement is to negotiate full speed ahead now, get the thing over and behind us and then play baseball.... The idea of playing baseball and negotiating and having it drag on is not desirable."
>
> Asked if they [the owners] would be willing to jeopardize the season, MacPhail replied, "If we have to. We'll go as long as it takes to get a satisfactory agreement."[28]

The PRC's position was an attempt to scare the players about the start of the season in the hope that they would bring pressure on the Players Association to limit their demands.

Bill Veeck, the P. T. Barnum of baseball who as owner of the St. Louis Browns in 1951 had sent 3'6" Eddie Gaedel to the plate wearing number "⅛" to bat against Bob Cain of the Detroit Tigers, announced that he would open the Chicago White Sox site in Sarasota, Florida, as scheduled on March 1, for players on the club's roster. He called the PRC's action a mistake, believing that it was a violation of club rights. Veeck had a battle to fight and uncontrolled salaries were the enemy. He said, "It isn't the high price of stars that is expensive, it's the high price of mediocrity."[29]

Before the first of March, a number of owners had "persuaded" Veeck not to go against the PRC's directive. He had his gates open on the first, but only 25 nonroster players, including seven who had major league experience, were at his club's camp-in-exile. Legally, the 62-year-old Veeck, who was just beginning his second tour of duty as the White Sox owner, wasn't breaking the PRC's lockout decree, but many of the magnates believed that he was doing so, nevertheless. Some remembered Comiskey Park as the site of resistance during the 1972 strike when then owner Arthur Allyn bucked the leagues' guidelines and attempted to entice his players to come back by opening the stadium for them to prepare for the season.

Players headed to playgrounds, college campuses, and other open land to get themselves ready for a season that might not occur. Some of the White Sox' regulars started to exercise at Manatee Junior College, which was a few miles from the club's training base. Soon, however, the eager big leaguers were chased from the field by a woman's softball team. On March 12, the players throughout the majors left the substitute practice fields to wait out the lockout.

During the lockout, the two sides continued to negotiate. The owners returned to the "eight years of service position," but they rejected the players' proposals on the reserve system. That led to the players withdrawing from the negotiations on March 5.

The following day, Miller suggested that Kuhn could rescue the owners by ordering them to open spring training camps. He reminded the magnates that since they had lost their appeal in the Messersmith-McNally case, any player was now able to become a free agent by playing one year without a contract. For the first time, the legal system was behind the players. Miller added:

> Mr. Kuhn says he represents players, fans and clubs, but he has a very honorable job and it is to represent the owners and no one else. His

job is to bail out the owners when they are in trouble and there's nothing wrong with that. The owners' strike is okay in his view as long as it succeeds in making players grovel. But since it isn't succeeding, he may order his bosses to open camps and get them out of the corner they painted themselves into.[30]

Phillies' owner Robert R. M. (Ruly) Carpenter III also sensed that the owners needed to find a way out of the situation they were in, saying, "It's very obvious that the handwriting is on the wall.... Management will have to come down in its demands."[31]

In mid-March the owners offered their "best and final" proposal, including a plan for limited free agency. Miller rejected the proposal and expressed his opinion that the Players Association's executive board would do likewise.

With negotiations appearing to be dead in the water and the prospect for starting the 1976 season on time looking dim, Kuhn, in a surprise move on St. Patrick's Day, March 17, ordered the 24 clubs to open their spring training camps as soon as possible. The shutdown had lasted 17 days. Kuhn had no intention of jeopardizing the season, and he wanted the players ready for the opening pitch. His action confused the owners and angered some of those who had gone against him before. In 1975 Kuhn had met with resistance when he stood for reelection. Finley, Jerry Hoffberger of the Orioles, and Brad Corbett of the Texas Rangers had been unhappy with Kuhn's performance in office and unsuccessfully tried to block his approval for a second term.

Whether or not Kuhn had listened to Miller's earlier suggestion, he took the action Marvin had put forward.

Three days after the commissioner removed the locks on the gates to spring training, the owners were told by their negotiators that some chains had been put on Kuhn. The PRC was worried that Kuhn might use his "in the best interest of baseball" power to block any agreement that altered the reserve clause. The negotiators had Kuhn sign a letter that stated that he would not stand in the way of a change in the reserve system. With that obstacle out of the way, the road to an agreement looked a bit less bumpy.

The season began on time. McNally had retired from the game and never tested his newly-won free agency. Messersmith received bids from a number of teams and signed with the Yankees on March 31. A day later, on April Fool's Day, he claimed that his agent did not have the authority to make a deal for him, and he did not want to play in New York. Kuhn called a meeting with Messersmith and his agent, together with representatives of the Yankees, the PRC and the MLBPA, to try to resolve the strange situation. Messersmith didn't make it to the first day's gathering, but he was there for the talks the following day. The Yankees decided to drop their claim to the pitcher, and Messersmith was free again. On April 3, he signed with the Atlanta Braves, and he pitched for them the next two seasons.

The collective bargaining sessions continued but not much progress was made and, in mid–May, the working group was paired down to five participants. Miller remembered those sessions:

> For the next two months, the five of us—Gaherin, Lee MacPhail, Chub Feeney, Dick Moss, and I—met at the Biltmore Hotel nearly every day, and often into the night. No players were present during the meetings (the season was in progress), but Dick and I did consult with key members of the executive board as we went along. It was, thankfully, the first time any real progress was made.[32]

Settlement was reached on July 12, the eve of the 1976 All-Star Game in Philadelphia. The owners ratified the four-year agreement one week later and the players ratified it shortly thereafter. Baseball's festivities were part of the many celebrations of the 200th anniversary of the nation's independence. The players had gained a large measure of freedom; some owners worried about what it meant for them for the future.

As a result of the historic fourth Basic Agreement, the players gained the right to free agency after six major league seasons. Since the players had already won free agency at the end of a contract through the precedent set by Seitz's ruling in the Messersmith-McNally case in December 1975, the "after six years" condition was a compromise on the freedom they had already gained. The agreement instituted an annual reentry draft procedure that allowed those players to auction their services to the highest bidder. There was also a provision that a club owner would receive an extra pick in the annual amateur draft as compensation for losing a veteran player. The agreement raised the minimum salary to $18,000 in 1976 and to $21,000 by 1979. There were increases in other players' benefits including a raise in the owners' annual pension contribution to $8.3 million.

Miller credited MacPhail's contributions as being significant in the final resolution of the agreement. Marvin, who had sat across the table from Lee, said:

> Lee MacPhail, I have to say, played a major role in the negotiations. He had a rational view of free agency, saying, "We're trying to swim against the social current. We've got to change." MacPhail understood the nuts and bolts of the game as well as anyone, and he took

great pains to draft proposal language before the meetings. The downside, however, was that he was very attached to his own writing. When we tried to reword the language, he reacted with the sensitivity of a poet who had just had a metaphor changed by an editor.[33]

While some owners were beginning to dream about ways to build their clubs through free agency, some had already been concerned about having their teams rent asunder by it. Finley was one of them. As the June 15, 1976, trading deadline approached, the Oakland owner believed that three of his players who had been instrumental in the Athletics' five American League West titles and three World Championships from 1971 through 1975 would be eligible for free agency after the end of the season if the new agreement, which had not yet been finalized, included a change in the reserve clause. Finley was sure that there would be such a change but, even if there wasn't, Seitz's ruling couldn't be overlooked.

Finley had already started to remake the A's by trading left-handed pitcher Ken Holtzman, slugger Reggie Jackson, and minor leaguer Bill Van Bommell to Baltimore on April 2 for Don Baylor, Paul Mitchell, and Mike Torrez. He followed that by selling pitchers Vida Blue and Rollie Fingers and outfielder-first baseman Joe Rudi, rather than risk losing them through free agency. Fingers and Rudi were dealt to the Boston Red Sox for $1 million apiece, and Blue went to the Yankees for $1.5 million.

Ironically, Kuhn was almost within shouting distance of Finley when he heard about the sales. The Athletics' owner had his office in Chicago, and the commissioner was attending a night game between the White Sox and Orioles in Comiskey Park. At approximately 9:00 P.M., Kuhn instructed his administrator Johnny Johnson to contact the players and tell them not to suit up for their new teams. The Red Sox were playing in Oakland at the time and Johnson intercepted Fingers and Rudi before they could make the short walk to the visitor's clubhouse. Blue was preparing to leave Oakland to join the Yankees, but Kuhn's administrator got to him before he departed.

The commissioner telephoned Finley:

> Charlie, I'm at Comiskey and just heard from Johnny [Johnson] about your sales. I don't like the look of these sales at all. I'm putting everything on hold until I decide whether or not to stop them. I've also advised the Red Sox and the Yankees.
>
> [Finley replied] Commissioner, it's none of your damn business. You can't stop me from selling my players. Guys have been selling players forever and no commissioner has ever stopped them.[34]

Kuhn scheduled a meeting with Finley for an hour later in the coffee shop of the Pick-Congress Hotel near Charlie's insurance office. Finley justified the sales to Kuhn:

> Commissioner, I can't sign these guys. They don't want to play for ol' Charlie. They want to chase those big bucks in New York. If I sell them now, I can at least get something back. If I can't they walk out on me at the end of the season and I've got nothing. Now, if I get money for them, I can sign some amateurs and build the team again, just the way I did to create three straight World Series winners.[35]

Bowie got the last word that night, saying:

> Charlie, you've made your points, you've given me something to think about and I'm going to have to do just that. I can't tell you anything tonight. But I'm freezing those players right now until I decide how to handle this.[36]

An angry Finley, who had led the palace revolt against Kuhn in the summer of 1975, continued to justify his move in the press:

> Selling players for cash has been going on for decades. People have short memories. Connie Mack, in two different decades, sold players for cash, many more than this. And people also forget that Babe Ruth was sold for cash.[37]

Kuhn spoke with the Executive Council the day after the sales, and MacPhail and Feeney both were against blocking the deals. MacPhail didn't believe that Finley had broken any specific rules, and an ongoing legal battle with Charlie over the matter would be bad for the game.

After a hearing with Miller and representatives of the Red Sox and the Yankees, Kuhn prepared to make his decision. The next day, on June 18, he blocked the sales. In the decision, Kuhn wrote:

> Shorn of much of its finest talent in exchange for cash, the Oakland Club, which has been a divisional champion for the last five years, has little chance to compete effectively in its division. Whether other players will be available to restore the Club by using the cash involved is altogether speculative although Mr. Finley vigorously argues his ability to do so. While I am of course aware that there have been cash sales of player contracts in the past, there has been no instance in my judgment which had the potential for harm to our game as do these assignments, particularly in the unsettled circumstances of Baseball's reserve system and in the highly competitive circumstances we find in today's sports and entertainment world....

I think the Commissioner's power is clear and binding and its exercise vital to the best interests of the game and accordingly the assignments here involved are disapproved.

The players will remain on the active list of the Oakland Club and may be in uniform and participate in Oakland's games.[38]

The legal battles which MacPhail had feared took place. Finley's lawyers filed a $10 million lawsuit in Chicago Federal Court ten days after Kuhn's decision was announced. The matter was presented and argued during a 15-day trial which ended January 13, 1977. On March 17, the first anniversary of Kuhn taking the locks off spring training, Judge Frank McGarr ruled that the commissioner had the authority to tie Finley's hands. Finley's lawyers took the case to the U.S. Court of Appeals and, on April 7, 1978, that court affirmed Judge McGarr's ruling.

The storm which had been brewing for years, and had been churning more intensely since the Hunter and Messersmith-McNally rulings, struck land with the 1976 Basic Agreement. The provisions of the agreement have had a long-term affect on the game.

As an example, on March 10, 1976, at a major-league meeting at New York's Plaza Hotel, Walter O'Malley, who had been president of the Dodgers since 1950 when they resided in Brooklyn, had told his fellow owners that his club would refuse to sign free agents, and he implored them to commit to the same course of action. It was not long before it became clear that his plea had fallen on deaf ears.

Unlike Finley, who had attempted to protect himself from the expected ravages of free agency, some of the other owners envisioned the Basic Agreement as an opportunity to strengthen their clubs through a new approach. The increasing amount of money coming from television revenue presented an opportunity for an owner to spend some of the new wealth on free agents who would lead the club to the postseason and eventually to an elusive World Championship. Carefully crafted trades began to take a back seat to wild-bidding contests for the available free agents.

St. Louis Cardinals' general manager Bing Devine, with history in mind, spoke pessimistically about baseball's future:

You've seen the beginning of a new era....

Next year [1977] is the big question now. Almost every club will have people playing out their options. So in one year you'll have this great mass of free agents. And after that, you'll have a whole new game.

It's been coming since the war.... You had thousands of guys who came home from the war wanting to play baseball, and all those towns wanting to have minor-league teams. Then television came along and the trend got reversed. You soon had fewer minor leagues. Then you had the amateur draft and you no longer could go out and sign anybody you wanted.

Finally, there were fewer players at the minor-league level; there were more college men in a hurry; there was more money at the top; basketball, golf and football were flooded with money. In baseball, we should have seen it coming and prepared for the transition.[39]

CHAPTER SEVEN

Strike Two: 1981—Fifty Days Without the Game

Major League Baseball's crippling 50-day strike in 1981—baseball's first stoppage with the season in progress—was largely the result of a number of economic changes in the game in the years immediately preceding the shutdown. There were continued salary struggles between owners and players, a tenuous balance between income and expenses for management, and negotiations which had led to an agreement on a number of issues in 1980 but not the most difficult one which focused on baseball's new reality—free agency and compensation for players lost by clubs as a result of it.

In 1979 major league baseball drew 43,550,396 fans to its ballparks, which was a high-water mark for the game. The following year there was a slight decrease in the number of people going through the turnstiles, but attendance figures still topped 43 million.

Revenue from national and local television contracts in 1980 represented 30 percent of baseball's $500 million income. Each club took home $1.8 million from the profits which came from televising the World Series, the All-Star Game, and selected weekday and weekend games. Beyond that, teams had their own local television contracts that added money to their coffers. The amount of that income was uneven and usually depended on whether a club was located in a small or large market.

Attendance and income had both grown, but so had expenses. As commissioner Bowie Kuhn reported:

> The industry, which had experienced a series of essentially break-even years through 1979, had a loss of $19 million in 1980, by far the largest in its history. And in my state-of-baseball address at our annual meetings in December 1980 I forecast that 1981 had every prospect of being worse.[1]

Player salaries were the major reason for the rise in the clubs' operating expenses. With the advent of free agency, which had come as part of the 1976 Basic Agreement, salaries had skyrocketed. In 1971 player salaries averaged $34,000; in 1976 they had risen to $52,300; and by 1980 they had reached $143,756. A few players had signed million-dollar contracts and $10 million club payrolls had become commonplace.

Duke Snider, who played the majority of his career with the Dodgers while they were in Brooklyn and Los Angeles, had retired in 1964. Snider held what could only be described as an "old-timer's" view of the millionaires. The eighteen-year veteran and future Hall of Famer said, "Man, if I made $1 million, I would come in at six in the morning, sweep the stands, wash the uniforms, clean out the offices, manage the team and play the games."[2]

Twenty-three players filed for free agency in 1976, the first year of its existence, albeit far fewer than many owners had feared. Some magnates had expressed the opinion that nearly every player would take advantage of the new opportunity. Two hundred players tried free agency during the first four seasons of its availability, with many of them signing with other clubs.

Some of the most notable free-agent signers were Reggie Jackson who left the Baltimore Orioles in 1976 and inked a five-year, $2.66 million contract with the New York Yankees; Pete Rose who left the Cincinnati Reds two years later and signed a four-year, $3.2 million deal with the Philadelphia Phillies; and Nolan Ryan who departed the California Angels in 1979 and received a three-year, $3.5 million contract to pitch for the Houston Astros.

On March 10, 1977, Sparky Anderson, manager of the Reds who had won the World Championship the previous two seasons, commented about the recent changes that had overtaken the game:

> It's all kind of crazy, and it all started with a fellow named Catfish Hunter. He showed how foolish some owners can be. Catfish went home to Ahoskie, North Carolina, and did nothing but sit there, holding court. The owners came to him with fortunes. This is how the madness began.[3]

At the 1978 winter meetings in Orlando, Florida, Kuhn lamented:

> I am not very happy when I see stars like Luis Tiant and Tommy John signed by the world champion New York Yankees. The Yankees are fully within their legal rights, but this trend fulfills a prophesy [sic] some of us made that the star free agents would tend to sign

with the best teams. It's inevitable that this process will lead to a group of elite teams controlling the sport. Already, five teams have signed 53 percent of the free agents during the first three years of the new system.[4]

Yankee owner George Steinbrenner, responding to Kuhn's remarks, shot back at the commissioner, saying, "I don't agree with free agency, but it wasn't my leadership that created it."[5]

By 1980, with changing economic realities serving as a backdrop to negotiations, the owners and the players were back at the bargaining table in an effort to hammer out baseball's fifth Basic Agreement. Each side had begun its work at its respective annual meetings in early December 1979 in anticipation of the expiration of the fourth Basic Agreement on December 31 of that year.

Marvin Miller spoke about the tenor of player-management relations from the time of the signing of the 1976 Basic Agreement until the start of the new round of negotiations:

> The time between the '76 agreement, which was the first one on free agency, and the opening of negotiations in '79 was not a period of three years of peace. It was a period of constant belly-aching in the press and constant threats that they [the owners] were going to take on the union and change this whole system. For three years, there really was not a moment of peace. You know sometimes you get a honeymoon after an agreement, but there was no honeymoon after the '76 agreement. They started in immediately. By the time we opened the negotiations for the 1980 agreement [in 1979], they were making all kinds of proposals about salary structure and other things, but the real concentration was on getting a major league player when you lost a player to free agency.[6]

The Player Relations Committee (PRC) and the Players Association (MLBPA) were expecting difficult and heated discussions which could very well lead to a strike before or during the 1980 season. John Gaherin, the PRC's lead negotiator in previous talks, had been fired in 1978 and was replaced by Ray Grebey whose background included a lengthy career in industrial relations with the General Electric Company.

Lee MacPhail and Chub Feeney, the league presidents, were members of the PRC. They were joined by Milwaukee's Ed Fitzgerald, the committee chair, Minnesota's Clark Griffith, Kansas City's Joe Burke, Cincinnati's Bob Howsam, Montreal's John McHale, and Pittsburgh's Dan Galbreath. At the time, Major League Baseball's Executive Council was made up of American League executives MacPhail, John Fetzer

(Detroit), Fitzgerald, Ewing Kauffman (Kansas City), and Haywood Sullivan (Boston). The National League's representatives were Feeney, Galbreath, Howsam, Bob Lurie (San Francisco), and Peter O'Malley (Los Angeles).

Both sides were gearing up for the worst. The players were putting together a strike fund, and the owners had purchased $50 million of strike insurance from Lloyd's of London. In 1979 the management of the 26 clubs had arranged to set aside 2 percent of their income to begin a mutual assistance fund which would eventually total $7 million.

The owners also legislated a fine of up to $500,000 against any club whose conduct was determined to be detrimental to the collective bargaining process. A secret five-man panel was put in place to make those judgments should it be necessary—and it was! General manager Harry Dalton of the Milwaukee Brewers, was hit with a fine for a comment he made at one point about the progress of the negotiations.

The PRC brought two new demands to the table. First, they wanted to establish a cap on salaries that stipulated the maximum annual salary for players with less than six years of major league experience. The owners also wanted to put in place what they considered to be a more equitable form of compensation for a player who was lost to another club through free agency. As agreed to in the 1976 agreement, a major league club received an amateur draft choice when it lost a player through free agency, and for the owners that hadn't proved to be an equitable arrangement. The PRC wanted another approach which would allow the club losing a player to be able to select a replacement from anyone not on the 15-player protected list of the team that signed the free agent.

For their part, the players were seeking to improve their benefits package in the new agreement. The MLBPA was not prepared to accept either of the owners' proposals even though Miller recognized the shortcomings of existing compensation agreement:

> The amateur draft choice was not too significant in baseball. It was not like football and basketball where you are talking about somebody who was almost certain to be a valuable addition. There is a lot of conjecture about a baseball amateur draft choice. You are talking about some kids who have played in high school for a very short season because of climate. You can't get a real good scouting report on many of the high school prospects.[7]

On January 14, after seven negotiating sessions between the two sides, Miller said that the opening of the regular season, which was scheduled for April 9, was in serious jeopardy. He urged the PRC to join him and the Players Association in negotiating in a more earnest manner. Miller believed the owners expected the players to be willing to open the 1980 regular season without a new contract in place since they had done so in 1976. Miller reminded the PRC that the situation had been different in '76 since the players were holding the trump card because of arbitrator Peter Seitz's decision in the Messersmith-McNally case, which had made it possible for every player to become a free agent at the end of that campaign. He said:

> They [the owners] have to be straightened out.... I get concerned when I think the other side is acting in a way not based on fact but on a dream. That's dangerous. Assuming that nothing will happen is a fool's dream and therefore an incorrect strategy....
> If I were the owners I wouldn't count on that [the players being willing to begin the season without an agreement].... I don't have any doubt about how the members [of the MLBPA] will react. They've progressed well past the point where you can take them for patsies, which the owners apparently do. They're far too sophisticated for that.[8]

As the talks continued, issues regarding improved player benefits appeared to be solvable; those regarding any form of salary cap or a change in the approach to free-agent compensation did not.

Miller believed that the owners didn't really want compensation. In his opinion, they wanted to dismantle free agency in its infancy:

> When you consider the compensation question without looking at all the hokum, what they were saying is, "We don't want free agency, we have seen what it can do. It costs us money. We want to change free agency into a trade." That's exactly what they were talking about. All the rest was malarkey. We lose a player to the Yankees, we get to pick a like player from the Yankees. How is that different from a trade? The mechanics are a little different, but basically it's the same. So, they really wanted to end free agency.[9]

In mid–March, the PRC dropped its proposal for a maximum annual salary for players with less than six years of major league experience and put its focus and energy into working out a new compensation plan. It was an approach that fell on deaf ears. Players feared that such a plan would reduce salaries, limit their freedom of movement, and dissipate their bargaining power.

As the end of the month approached and with the prospect of major league baseball opening the regular season on time growing dim, the PRC called upon the Federal Mediation and Conciliation Services to assist with the stalemate. Deputy Director Ken Moffett, the Services' top mediator, joined the talks.

On April 1, the players voted to strike, thus wiping out the remaining 92 spring training games. However, the players were prepared to begin the regular season on time, but they said that they reserved the right to walk out again if an agreement was not reached by midnight May 22.

In 1972 baseball had experienced its first strike, and that work stoppage had affected the regular championship season. There had also been a pair of lockouts by the owners (in 1973 and 1976) which had prevented spring training camps from opening on time. The shutdown in 1980 was the game's fourth work stoppage, but since it didn't change the conduct of the regular season, it is not generally listed among the game's four strikes.

The season began on time, and the negotiations continued in an effort to reach an agreement before the players' deadline.

Miller spoke about a strange request from Grebey after the resumption of talks:

> We had resolved most issues, but not the owners' demand to end free agency. I had proposed that we have a study for the next year on the issue of compensating a club for the loss of a free agent and offered them the right to reopen the contract if the study committee produced no results. Grebey came back to me and said he didn't want that. What he'd like to have is the right to implement their [compensation] proposal if there were no agreement. I said, "That's silly. If we're going to give you that right, why wouldn't we do it now?" He said that he needed this to go back to his people to say at least they got something. I said, "Well, it isn't going to be anything, because if we are going to put it in an agreement that you might have the right to implement this, obviously we are going to have the right to strike if we disagree with it. And so you don't have anything. It's just on paper." He said, "Well, we'll be able to go back to the owners and say at least we have this much movement." I said, "It's no movement at all."
>
> If they said they needed this to sell the agreement, and I knew that "this" was nothing, that meant to me that they would have to be painting a far different picture about what "this" is.
>
> So, finally I said, "O.K. as long as you understand that we're going to put the part about the strike in the agreement. We'll have the study committee. If that produces a recommendation that both sides can live with, fine. If it doesn't, you would then have the option of putting in this proposal of yours or something more favorable to the players. And if you did that, we would have the right to open the agreement and strike."

Grebey told the owners a pack of lies—that they had finally won compensation. It's in the agreement that they would have the right to implement their plan, but the union could strike—and the "but" got lost.[10]

On May 21, the night before the scheduled strike, many went to bed expecting to wake up to a world without major league baseball. Sportswriter Red Smith was one of them:

Barring a sudden and improbable turnabout by the baseball hierarchy, major league baseball will grind to a halt tomorrow. Probably this will gratify some of the men who own teams, for there seems no reason to doubt that some of them are determined to invite a strike and test the players and their union....
They have already brought off what may be a greater accomplishment. By a master stroke of propaganda, they have turned the public against the players whose skills draw fans to the parks, defacing the property they sell.[11]

Smith went on to give an example of why he thought the owners' approach to compensation for a free agent was difficult to rationalize:

So you're a star salesman for Ford who for six years has peddled cars at a great rate, making stacks for your employer. After six years, contract expired and all obligations discharged, you offer your services elsewhere. Buick offers $1 million a year. Chrysler proposes setting you up with a beer distributorship on the side. Cadillac would get you started as an owner and breeder of thoroughbreds. But if you go with them, Cadillac must send a sales manager to Ford.
Nowhere in any democratic society does such a situation exist, except in professional sports teams. Nowhere else do employers own their employees and demand compensation when they lose one.[12]

The negotiators, with Kuhn joining them, worked deep into the night in an effort to avoid another work stoppage during the regular season. Less than ten hours before the slate of 13 games would have been wiped away, agreement was reached between the owners and the players and, even though the agreement awaited ratification, the 1980 season went on without missing a beat.

Kuhn commented about baseball's "little miracle:"

There was a tendency all around to believe that both the Players Association and the clubs were willing to have a strike ... but I never viewed it that way. I never believed the rhetoric fairly indicated the views of these people. When it got close to the wire, it was very obvious they wanted to settle. The proof of the pudding was what they did in the last few days. I don't mean to sound naïve, but both sides perceived the strike as bad for the game and the fans, as something to be avoided. There is no other way to explain the little miracle that was wrought.[13]

There were a number of important elements in baseball's fifth Basic Agreement. The amount of money designated to go into the pension fund, which had been $8.3 million in the 1976 agreement, was almost doubled when it was raised to $15.5 million in the new plan. Management's original offer had been $14.4 million. The minimum salary was upped to $30,000 and it was to be increased to $35,000 in 1982. Players also benefited from an improved method for drafting free agents.

Through collective bargaining, the players had made great strides; the owners looked ahead and hoped that a new compensation plan for the players lost to free agency, which was to be worked out before the 1981 season, would benefit them.

Grebey stated in his press release that "In 1981, the clubs' proposal for compensation becomes a part of the basic agreement and it cannot be removed without agreement of the two sides."[14] Miller hastened to add that Grebey had only told part of the story and had not mentioned the possibility of a players' strike.

Some players were skeptical about the future. The Mets' Elliott Maddox, himself a free agent in 1977, was one of them:

Then there'll be a strike next year.... We've just postponed it for a year.

What makes anybody think the owners will change their minds about demanding compensation for free agents? What makes anybody think the players will accept it?[15]

A Joint Study Committee comprised of two general managers and two players was formed to study the compensation question and, hopefully, come up with a workable solution to the vexing problem. The committee was instructed to make its recommendations no later than January 1, 1981. Dalton and Frank Cashen of the Mets, both general managers, represented the American and National Leagues respectively, and Sal Bando of the Brewers and Bob Boone of the Phillies represented the players. The committee faced a formidable task:

If changes are recommended and the two sides reach agreement on them, they will become part of the basic agreement between the owners and players that replaces the one that expired last Dec. 31.

If, however, the sides cannot reach agreement, the owners have a right, between Feb. 15 and 20, 1981, to implement unilaterally their compensation proposal or a variation "not less favorable to the players."

Once the owners do that, though, the players would have the right to reopen the basic agreement on the free-agent issue and strike by June 1, 1981.[16]

The future of the 1981 season rested on a single issue and that did not provide much wiggle room for either side. MacPhail said:

In retrospect, the clubs would probably have been better off to have resolved things one way or the other before finishing the agreement in 1980. It postponed strike day for a year. First, in 1980, there were other issues that could have been used in seeking a compromise solution. It is very dangerous to have a negotiation reduced to a one-issue crisis.[17]

Fitzgerald agreed with MacPhail:

We were left with a single bargaining issue and that is not a desirable strategic position in a labor negotiation. We had an insurance policy against the strike, and still the owners wouldn't stand and fight.[18]

During the Joint Study Committee's work, neither side was willing to move off the different positions the owners and players had presented in the earlier negotiations. The owners wanted to craft a plan by which a club losing a "ranking player" to free agency would be able to choose an unprotected player from the roster of the signing team. In order to be considered a "ranking player" he would have to meet two criteria. First, the player would have to be selected by at least eight teams in the reentry draft. Second, he would have had to be among the top 50 percent of major leaguers in a certain performance category the previous season. If he was a starting pitcher, he would have to have made a certain number of starts. If he was a reliever he would have to have made a certain number of appearances out of the bullpen. Other players would be judged by the number of plate appearances. The number of players the signing team could protect would depend on the free agent's performance the previous season.

The Players Association had floated a couple of their ideas. One was for the owners to establish a money pool from which a team losing a free agent would be compensated, the amount of money to be determined by the clubs. They also said that any compensation system involving the exchange of players should involve only a predetermined number of players each year, perhaps five. Additionally, they presented a proposal that would allow potential free agents to be traded more easily before they became free agents.

After the study committee's January 1 deadline passed, the foursome continued to meet during the early days of the month. However, they could not break the impasse, and the ball was back in Grebey's and Miller's court.

According to Miller, it soon became clear that Grebey had painted himself into a corner with the owners. He had told them of the "agreement" to implement their compensation plan if the study committee failed to produce an acceptable proposal. However, he had glossed over the certainty of a players' strike if the owners instituted their compensation plan.

On February 19, 1981, as stipulated in the 1980 Basic Agreement, the owners chose to implement the compensation plan. Also, according to the agreement, the MLBPA was required to notify the owners of a strike date by March 1 and if they chose not to strike at that time they would forfeit their right to strike during the remaining years of the four-year agreement. On February 25, the 26 player representatives, meeting in Tampa, Florida, voted unanimously to reopen the basic agreement on the free agency issue and set May 29 as the strike date. That date was chosen since it would threaten cancellation of the games scheduled for Memorial Day weekend.

The day before the players set the strike date, the numbers were posted on 1981's salary-arbitration scoreboard. A record 98 players had filed, but only 21 went to arbitration. Eleven players won their cases and 10 decisions went to the clubs. Detroit's Steve Kemp was the biggest winner. The Tigers had offered him $360,000 and he was awarded his asking price of $600,000. Among the losers were two Oakland A's—Tony Armas and Mike Norris. Armas had earned $37,000 in 1980 while leading the Athletics with 109 RBI. He asked for a $500,000 salary, but the arbitrator awarded him the club's $210,000 offer. Norris, who won 22 games while working for $40,000, asked for a $450,000 salary and was awarded $300,000. Even the losers appeared to be winners in the arbitration game!

Although Kemp's victory represented a sizable award, it did not match the Chicago Cubs' Bruce Sutter's a year earlier. The 27-year-old Cubs' reliever, who had made his major league debut on May 9, 1976, made 62 appearance with 37 saves and had a 6-6 record with a 2.22 ERA in 1979. He captured the National League's Cy Young Award that year and, at the hearing, his representatives argued that he should be paid the $700,000 he was asking for the 1980 season. Chicago proposed $350,000 which, at the time, was considered a high salary for a player with barely four years of service. The arbitrator ruled in favor of Sutter. The decision stunned management and prompted the Reds' executive Dick Wagner to . say that the award was "like an atom bomb to our industry. It will have a rippling effect throughout the leagues."[19]

The arbitration process had led to the creation of another type of baseball job. Talbot M. "Tal" Smith had represented the Athletics in the Armas and Norris arbitration hearings in 1981. Smith had been general manager and president of the Astros from 1975 through 1980. He and John McMullen, Houston's new owner, had serious disagreements about running the club, and Smith was fired shortly after the Astros lost the 1980 National League Championship Series to the Phillies, three games to two.

Smith had a pair of losing arbitration experiences a year before the victories for the Athletics. The wins had further whetted his appetite, and he formed Tal Smith Enterprises to provide his services and those of a small group of legal and statistical experts to other clubs. He had long been concerned about spiraling salaries, and he set out to try to save owners from potential fiscal collapse. In 1982 six major league teams retained him to go into battle for them that year against players seeking salaries beyond what the clubs were willing to offer.

During the 1982 arbitration season, Tal Smith Enterprises won seven of their eight cases. Soon they had been retained by 13 clubs, which was half of the major league teams.

With a possible player walkout on May 29, 1981, Steinbrenner believed that the owners were "'more unified and more prepared for a strike' than at any other time since he has been affiliated with baseball.... 'I don't think a strike is going to help anybody. I wouldn't blame the American public for getting turned off.'"[20]

In 1980 the Phillies had captured their first World Series but, by the following spring, their owner had been turned off. He had had enough. On March 7, Robert R. M. (Ruly) Carpenter III announced during a tearful meeting with his players in their spring training locker room in Clearwater, Florida, that he was selling the team and getting out of the baseball business. Ruly's family, who were part of the Delaware duPonts, had owned the club since November 1943, when his father, Robert R. M. (Bob) Carpenter, Jr., bought the bankrupt team.

For some time the 40-year-old Carpenter, who had been president of the club since 1973, had been concerned about the rising tide of players' salaries, the bickering with the Players Association, arguments with other owners about their approaches to free agency and other management issues. He said the final straw came in November, after the most recent period of free agency, when he read in a newspaper that Claudell Washington had signed with the Atlanta Braves. Washington, an outfielder, had played for the Cubs and the Mets in 1980. He was in 79 games with New York, hit .275 with 10 home runs and 42 RBI, while striking out 63 times. Carpenter spoke about the signing:

> It was the morning after the free agent draft.... I read that the first player signed and paid was Claudell Washington, the outfielder from the Mets. I read that the Atlanta Braves had signed him for $700,000 a year. What did I think? You couldn't print what I thought....
>
> We're not entirely blameless.... We signed Pete Rose for a hell of a lot of money, but he was worth it. We inherited a couple of big contracts through trades that we had to eat, like Rawley Eastwick's. But the only free agents we signed in the market were Rose and Richie Hebner, and we won four division titles in five years....
>
> The Claudell Washington thing made no sense. And, after the horrible battle we had with the players last spring, I almost got down on my hands and knees. We almost saw an industry grind to a screeching halt. But I don't blame the players. It's just that a few of my peers don't think the same way I do.[21]

George Vecsey, writing in the *New York Times*, examined some of the prevailing views about the financial future of professional sports:

> Network television advertising will keep some franchises from falling apart.
>
> Many teams are banking their futures on added income from cable and subscription television. In fact, most teams will be involved in cable management in the next five years.
>
> Several club owners could run out of money before selling their clubs, leading to the dispersal of players, further transfer of franchises and embarrassing lawsuits from players with broken longterm contracts.
>
> New ownership will bring huge sums of money into sports, because of tax writeoffs that can reach 70 percent of losses and because of the rising value of franchises.
>
> Current salaries and team losses are often less than they seem because of deferred payment and inflation.[22]

Discussions between the PRC and the MLBPA continued throughout the spring, but there was little movement towards an agreement on the compensation question. Moffett was called back to the negotiations in April in an effort to shore up the sagging talks. He would at one point remark, "These are the most bizarre negotiations I've been involved in during 22 years as a mediator.... The issues are resolvable, but there's no negotiating."[23]

Miller changed the focus of the discussions by claiming that statements by the commissioner and certain owners about the deteriorating financial conditions of the game had made the topic a bargaining issue. Kuhn had said that if the owners were going to survive financially they would have to find "oil wells under second base" or be rescued "by some other miracle."[24]

Miller asked the clubs for their financial statements for the years 1978 through 1980, believing the facts would show that most of the franchises were making a profit rather than losing money. On May 13, after the PRC refused to produce the requested documents, Miller and the MLBPA filed a charge of "refusal to bargain" with the National Labor Relations Board (NLRB). Under existing law, an employer who, in collective bargaining claims an inability to pay, must document it. Failure to provide the relevant information is considered "refusal to bargain." The NLRB ruled in favor of the MLBPA, and their lawyers took the matter before Federal District Court Judge Henry Werker of New York City.

The NLRB was seeking an injunction to prevent the owners from implementing their compensation plan until they decided the "refusal to bargain" complaint. On May 28, the two sides agreed to postpone the strike until Judge Werker decided the matter before him.

Werker ruled on June 10, following a two-day hearing which began on June 3 in Rochester, New York. He rejected the NLRB's request for an injunction. Had he approved the injunction, a players' strike and the owners' implementation of the compensation plan would both have been postponed for a year, giving additional time for the two parties to reach a compromise solution. Werker concluded his opinion with the words, "PLAY BALL!!! SO ORDERED."[25] The words had an ironic twist. After the ruling, nothing stood in the way of a strike which began when 650 major leaguers walked off the job, leading to the postponement of the games scheduled for June 12.

Miller wrote about Werker's decision:

> So Werker assumed (because the owners had told him so) that the Players Association had engineered the NLRB action because we were afraid to strike.
>
> Even more preposterous was his opinion that free-agent compensation—the only issue in the negotiations—was *not* an economic issue. Millions of owners' dollars and players' salaries were at stake, but Werker found that *compensation* was not an economic issue.[26]

When the talks resumed, Miller removed himself from the negotiations. He wanted to make the point that the difficulties between the two sides were the result of tough issues and not because of his presence at the bargaining table. Some owners had charged that Miller was the major obstacle standing in the way of a negotiated settlement.

Miller reasoned:

> I decided that I would take myself out of the negotiations to demonstrate what should have been self-evident: the dispute was about free agency, not personality. During the two weeks I was away from the talks, Don Fehr was in charge. I told him to let the players do most of the talking. There were some old-fashioned shouting matches during my absence and no progress was made. In the end, some of the owners, who were most anxious to see me out of the talks, were calling for me to come back and saying that my presence was necessary for a settlement.[27]

The players Miller alluded to were Doug DeCinces and Mark Belanger of the Orioles, Steve Rogers of the Montreal Expos, and Boone. Donald Fehr, who had gotten his feet wet in baseball while working for the law firm hired by the Players Association during Major League Baseball's 1976 appeal of Seitz's ruling in the Messersmith-McNally case in federal court in Kansas City, had become counsel for the MLBPA.

As the talks continued, the focus moved to some form of compensation pool. Through a designated process, players would be put in the pool and any team who had lost a free agent could choose from it. The approach would not penalize a signing team by forcing it to give up one of its players to the club losing the player. Miller had proposed the idea even before the strike, but it hadn't gotten very far. The pool concept offered some hope for the negotiations, which weren't going anywhere fast.

A minority of owners were upset with Kuhn, believing that he should be using the powers of his office to do more to bring about the end of the players' walkout. Three in particular, all American League owners—Eddie Chiles (Texas Rangers), Steinbrenner, and Edward Bennett Williams (Orioles)—were the most outspoken. Five days into the strike, Chiles asked for a meeting with the commissioner. Steinbrenner and Williams accompanied him to Kuhn's office to meet with the commissioner and MacPhail. Chiles gave Kuhn a harsh tongue-lashing:

> You're sitting here in your office doing nothing.... If you can't figure out anything to do, you could at least put your desk out on the sidewalk and talk to the fans. It's up to you to do something! But as far

as I can see, you're not doing a damned thing. I won't tolerate that. You and MacPhail work for me! I pay your salaries. You're like any other employees I've got. I tell you what to do and you're supposed to do it.[28]

Kuhn also began to hear from members of Congress who wanted a restart to the season. Ted Kennedy of Massachusetts and Wyche Fowler of Georgia were among the group who were in touch with the commissioner, urging him to use his position to end the walkout.

Kuhn was no Kenesaw Mountain Landis who had ruled the game with an iron hand. The current commissioner's words about the situation had become almost meaningless and his actions nearly powerless. During his appearance before Werker, he had distanced himself from the PRC and they had done the same with him.

Miller was also picking up heat from some owners.

I had owners tell me in the period after the strike began that we did not live up to the agreement. They said, "There it is, we had the right to implement this compensation plan."

I said, "Turn the page, we had the right to strike." Grebey had not told them about that part of the agreement.[29]

On June 15, the owners began collecting on the $50 million strike insurance policy. The policy would pay the magnates $100,000 per game for 500 games. The money, however, would not flow forever. Some owners were seeking binding arbitration in an attempt to get major league baseball going again. Other owners resisted that approach.

Some players began to speak out about the ongoing work stoppage. Milwaukee Brewers' outfielder Paul Molitor commented that the strike needed to be settled before the July 13 All-Star Game if the season was to be saved, saying, "We'll need at least 10 days to reach playing condition, and that would leave only two months of the season."[30]

On July 8, Moffett, as mediator, offered a compromise compensation proposal that addressed the number of free agents who qualified as "premier" (ranking) players. It was a complex plan that involved the use of a number of criteria to determine the exact compensation a team would receive.

Moffett's proposal ignited a surge of optimism, and the Players Association voted to approve it. However, the owners rejected the idea.

On Saturday, July 10, Kuhn cancelled the All-Star Game. There was, however, activity in Anaheim Stadium and San Diego's Jack Murphy Stadium that weekend. It would be live baseball instead of the many fantasy games and replays of earlier contests which had been on the radio and television in a number of areas. In Anaheim, on Friday night, a pair of real clubs from the Class-A California League went to battle in the Stadium and fans, who would also be entertained by a post-game fireworks show, welcomed them. The California Angels' Redwood Pioneers faced San Diego's Reno Padres in the first game of a "home-and-home" series. The Padres beat the Pioneers, 2–1, before 9,556 paying customers. The next evening, 37,665 were on hand in San Diego for the Class-A rematch.

Secretary of Labor Raymond Donovan joined the talks on July 15. With the move, the federal government became involved at a level above the intervention of the Federal Mediation and Conciliation Services. The President wanted to do what he could to get the games going again. Ronald Reagan was a baseball fan and, after all, he had once pitched his way to victory as Grover Cleveland Alexander in the 1952 Warner Brothers film, *The Winning Team*.

A few days later, the negotiations were moved to Washington, D.C., so that they would be out of the "fish-bowl atmosphere" of New York City. Representatives continued to talk for the next five days, with a press blackout of the proceedings.

In early July there had been signs of a change in the PRC's leadership, and Miller spoke about how it eventually affected the negotiations:

> I don't remember whether or not I heard it from a newspaper person. Grebey was losing credibility with the owners. Lee [MacPhail] telephoned me and we met at the Helmsley Palace Hotel. Ordinarily, I wouldn't do this, i.e., meet alone with a management representative, but I told the Players Association about it and went. We had a frank talk. Nothing was settled, but I realized from the conversation that it was more than a rumor that Grebey was out. Later, I called Lee and we began the constructive work towards a settlement.[31]

Grebey was not formally removed and, on July 16, the PRC issued a press release which gave him the proverbial "vote of confidence." In reality, however, MacPhail was at the PRC's helm.

MacPhail remembered the critical July 27 meeting with Miller:

> By now, the issue of the players' service time for free agency, salary arbitration, and pension purposes had come up. Would the players get service time for the period of the strike? When the meeting was over, I had a pretty good idea of just how far Miller might be willing to go in attempting to reach a decision. I reported this to the PRC and to Bowie.[32]

The owners met on July 29, the 49th day of the strike, and expressed their strong desire that either the two sides reach an agreement or that the matter go to binding arbitration. Their strike insurance was scheduled to run out on August 8, and the season would be lost if the games weren't resumed soon. For the magnates, the strike had gone on long enough. They had lost over $70 million in revenue. The players had also suffered, losing about $4 million a week, representing more than $28 million in lost income.

Representatives of the PRC and the MLBPA met on the afternoon of July 30 in the National League office. MacPhail and Grebey represented the PRC, and Miller and Fehr were there to speak for the players.

The four negotiators worked through the afternoon and into the night, moving from the National League headquarters to the law offices of Wilke Farr & Gallagher. That was thought to be a sign that they were near an agreement. It took until 5:00 A.M. for them to put the finishing touches on the 22-page document.

At approximately 6:00 A.M. on July 31, in the Crystal Ballroom of New York's Doral Inn, the announcement was made that an agreement had been reached, and the 50-day strike was over—a strike that had cost 713 games. Major league baseball was set to resume with the All-Star Game in Cleveland on August 9, and the regular season would start again the following day.

All that had happened on the field since opening day counted as the first half of the campaign; what transpired beginning on August 10 was to be the second half of a split championship season. The Yankees, with a two-game lead—which was the largest in the majors' four divisions— were the American League East's first-half champs and the Athletics claimed the West. In the National League, the Phillies and the Los Angeles Dodgers sat at the top of their respective divisions.

For the time being, the agreement resolved most of the issues. A compromise on the compensation question provided that teams signing free agents could protect 24 players and those not signing free agents could protect 26 players. The remainder of their players would go into a compensation pool. Since nonsigning clubs stood to lose players, there was not much excitement for this plan on the part of the owners.

A maximum of nine free agents per year were subject to compensation from the pool. Those "premier" players would have to rank in baseball's top 20 percent of players as determined by a formula. Teams that lost one of the nine got to pick from the pool. A team that lost a player in the pool would be compensated with $150,000. Clubs losing lesser free agents would continue to be compensated with a pick in the amateur draft.

The fifth Basic Agreement was extended through 1984. The players received credit for service time during the strike, and the minimum salary was raised again and it was projected to reach $40,000 during the final year of the contract.

As in most strikes, everyone suffered in the short run. Owners lost an estimated $72 million in revenue, which was offset by $44 million of strike insurance. The players missed $28 million worth of paychecks. In the long run, the players' salaries would continue to spiral upward and clubs' payrolls would have to meet the new demand.

MacPhail, who was given much of the credit for the final agreement, remembered a comment made by Belanger at the news conference when the end of the strike was announced. Belanger said, "Lee, we can never let this happen again."[33]

The cover of the August 10 issue of *Sports Illustrated* was almost a repeat of the cover that had appeared on April 13. The previous season's MVPs, George Brett and Mike Schmidt, were pictured. The earlier words "HOTSHOTS AT THE HOT CORNER" had been replaced with "HERE WE GO AGAIN." At the top of the cover, "SPECIAL BASE-BALL ISSUE" now included the word: "(CONT.)."[34]

The split season necessitated an extra round of postseason play—a Division Playoff in each of the four divisions to precede the League Championship Series and the World Series. In a best-of-five series, the Expos, winners of the second half in the National League East, defeated the Phillies. The Dodgers topped the Astros in the West. In the American League, the Yankees beat the Brewers, and the Athletics took the Kansas City Royals. The Reds were the biggest victims of the split championship season. They posted the best overall record in the National League West and didn't get a ticket to the postseason.

CHAPTER EIGHT

Strike Three: 1985—
Out for Two Days

A number of important personnel changes had taken place in base-ball before another round of union and labor negotiations began in antic-ipation of the expiration of the fifth Basic Agreement on December 31, 1984.

On November 1, 1982, at a major league meeting in Chicago, base-ball commissioner Bowie Kuhn failed in his bid to gain a third seven-year term. He was scheduled to leave office in August 1983, and a three-fourths vote of the owners in each league was needed for him to be given another term. Some who opposed Kuhn's reelection were upset by what had appeared to be a much too soft approach to the players' union, such as when he opened the spring training gates in 1976 after the owners had locked the players out. Other of Kuhn's opponents were wary of his plan for the reorganization of the Commissioner's Office.

Throughout the summer of 1982, Kuhn and his backers worked to line up the votes necessary to keep him in office. His major support came from the American League's magnates, while a number of those in the other circuit were committed to defeat his reelection bid. In the end the National Leaguers won the day.

The Junior Circuit's owners voted 11–3 in favor of giving Kuhn a third term, but only seven of the 12 owners in the Senior Circuit had risen in his support. Because of the voting rules in affect at the time, the 69 per-cent favorable vote was not high enough to save his job.

A group of Kuhn's supporters made plans to block the election of a successor and have the Executive Council keep him in office, in the hope that time would erode the opposition. However, others feared that such a move might end up in court, which would, no doubt, prove to be detri-mental for the game. Lee MacPhail, a long time coworker and supporter of Kuhn, was one of those who urged the Executive Council not to take that approach, believing that baseball's rules should prevail.

Bud Selig was selected to chair the Search Committee. Kuhn's name continued to be listed among those who were mentioned for the post. White House Chief of Staff James Baker, Yale University president and professor of Renaissance Literature A. Bartlett Giamatti, and Peter Ueberroth, who was in charge of the 1984 Summer Olympics in Los Angeles, appeared to be the leading candidates. The fact that Kuhn was still being considered was a positive sign for owners such as the Montreal Expos' Charles Bronfman and the Los Angeles Dodger's Peter O'Malley; it was an abomination for the New York Mets' Nelson Doubleday, the Houston Astros' John McMullen, and others.

Kuhn recognized that he was waging a losing battle and, in Boston on August 2, 1983, he announced that he would not seek another term. At the beginning of Kuhn's 230-word statement to the owners, he said, "I have advised Bud Selig as Chairman of the Search Committee that I am withdrawing my name from any further consideration by his committee. This decision is final, irrevocable and emphatic. I will not review it or reconsider it now or at any time in the future."[1]

Kuhn was asked to remain in office until a successor was chosen and in December the owners extended his contract until March 1, 1984. On March 3, Ueberroth was unanimously elected baseball's sixth commissioner. At the time of his election, the 47-year-old Ueberroth was committed to work with the Summer Olympics until October 1. He announced that he would not accept election to the baseball post unless there was a qualified person running it until he was available to take over. A number of people were suggested, including MacPhail, but, in the end, the commissioner-elect said he would only accept the position if Kuhn remained during the interim.

Although Kuhn had not been chosen for a third term, he gained a partial victory. His plans for electing a commissioner, for protecting him legally, for reorganizing the Commissioner's Office and for increasing the commissioner's power were all approved by the owners. Future commissioners would be elected by a simple majority of the owners with the stipulation that there be a minimum of five votes from each league. The commissioner would be protected from litigation by the clubs. Ueberroth was designated baseball's CEO with all administrative departments reporting to him. The level of fines possible for him to mete out was increased from $5,000 to $250,000.

The Player Relations Committee (PRC) had also undergone changes. Ray Grebey had been fired by the owners and MacPhail, who had completed his second five-year term in the American League office at the end of 1983, became full-time president of the PRC and their lead negotiator on January 1, 1984.

O'Malley commented about having MacPhail as the PRC head:

> When Lee MacPhail chaired the Owners' Player Relations Committee, I was very optimistic that for the first time we would begin a frank, honest dialogue with the Players Association. Lee's reputation was excellent and the Players Association trusted him.[2]

The National League's president Chub Feeney and Bobby Brown, who had replaced MacPhail as American League president, were PRC members. They were joined by Milwaukee's Selig, named PRC chairman, and Baltimore's Edward Bennett Williams as the two Junior Circuit's representatives. McMullen and O'Malley represented the National League. Barry Rona was the PRC's legal counsel and Lou Hoynes and Jim Garner were attorneys for the respective leagues. Before negotiations on the new agreement began, the PRC hired George Morris, who had recently retired from the General Motors Corporation where he had been in charge of labor relations, to provide assistance during the talks.

A change in the leadership of the MLBPA boded well for the upcoming round of negotiations. Marvin Miller had retired and Ken Moffett, formerly of the Federal Mediation and Conciliation Services, had been elected in January 1983 to replace the union's legendary leader.

MacPhail and Moffett had enjoyed a good working relationship during the 1981 negotiations. During the summer of 1983, they began discussions about developing an effective Joint Drug Program for the major leagues. Moffett had been concerned about baseball and drugs for some time. In 1980, he had said that "as many as 40 percent of major league players might be drug abusers."[3]

MacPhail was concerned about drug abuse, but he also had another critical item on his agenda. He believed that if the two sides could work in a supportive and creative manner to craft a plan to address the growing problem of drugs in baseball, they might also be able to bring a more cooperative spirit to the upcoming talks dealing with the game's troublesome economic situation.

When the drug discussions began, MacPhail and Moffett discovered areas of disagreement. The players wanted to limit testing to cocaine; MacPhail preferred that the testing also include alcohol, amphetamines, and marijuana. The players wanted voluntary testing; the owners wanted a tough mandatory policy.

Although the two sides made progress toward a workable program, the leader of the Players Association was gone before a final plan was approved. Moffett, who had alienated some of the players with what seemed to be a soft approach toward the owners, was fired suddenly on November 22, 1983, and Miller was appointed the MLBPA's interim director. Sixteen days later, on December 8, Donald Fehr was named the Players Association's acting director. Miller was retained as a consultant to the MLBPA.

The negotiating scene had changed. MacPhail was still there, but now he would be working with Fehr who, in his *acting* status, was on trial with the players and had to avoid falling into the "owners trap" that had ensnared Moffett.

MacPhail was pleased that Fehr wanted to continue developing a drug program. On June 21, 1984, the owners approved a compromise plan that the players had ratified on May 23.

The plan provided for a three-man board of physicians (Joint Drug Doctors) who would review cases of suspected drug abuse that had been brought to them by the clubs. The main focus was on players who used cocaine. Other drugs were beyond the scope of the new program, but the commissioner retained the right to respond to a player caught abusing alcohol, amphetamines, or marijuana. The Players Association retained the right to file a grievance in such cases.

If a player was sent for drug treatment he would receive full pay for 30 days, half pay for the next 30 days and then be paid $40,000, the major league minimum, until he returned to active status.

By the time the Joint Drug Program was approved, MacPhail, as president of the PRC, had finalized a decision in a different but familiar area—free-agent compensation.

After the 1983 season, the Toronto Blue Jays had selected left-handed pitcher Tom Underwood, a Type-A free agent (who had been 1-4 with the New York Yankees and 3-2 with Oakland Athletics in 1983) from the A's. As the 1981 Basic Agreement stipulated, the Athletics were compensated with a player from the free-agent pool, and they took Yankees' pitcher Tim Belcher, who was not on the club's 26-player protected list. New York had selected Belcher on January 17, 1984, in the secondary phase of the amateur draft, and they had signed him on February 2, for a $120,000 bonus. Oakland's choice was an interesting one since the 21-year-old right-hander had not yet begun his professional career.

On February 15, the Yankees protested the Athletics' selection to the PRC, claiming that they never had an opportunity to put the pitcher on the team's protected list. MacPhail ruled in Oakland's favor, saying,

[It would] be inappropriate for the parties to retroactively alter the clear language of the agreement. If changes are in order, they should be negotiated by the two parties [the PRC and the MLBPA] for the future.

Unfortunately for the Yankees ... the basic agreement does not provide that the players' contracts acquired after the protected lists were submitted were not eligible for selection.[4]

The PRC and the MLBPA held a number of preliminary meetings before the end of 1984. With baseball possibly facing another strike, the owners considered purchasing strike insurance again but, because of their experience in 1981, the cost of the policy from Lloyd's of London was extremely high. In insurance circles, baseball's magnates were "poor risks." There was also sentiment among some owners that the promise of strike insurance had not been a beneficial influence on the negotiations that preceded the 50-day strike in 1981.

In preparation for the bargaining process, MacPhail organized and conducted a series of regional meetings for the owners and club personnel of from five to seven clubs. He wanted to keep the lines of communication open between the PRC and the clubs' executives which, according to many, was a shortcoming during the 1981 talks. MacPhail was accompanied to each meeting by Brown or Feeney, a counsel for one of the leagues, and other members of the PRC. The purpose of the gatherings was to hear what the clubs' basic issues were as management was developing its positions for the upcoming negotiations.

It became clear that compensation for a player lost through free agency, which had been the most difficult issue in 1981, was still at the top of the owners' list. Miller recalled:

I should tell you that when the negotiations for the 1985 contract opened in 1984, the first proposal the owners made was to get rid of the pool compensation which was there for their benefit. They'd had enough. On the first day of the negotiations, they made a proposal to take that out of the contract.[5]

For the owners, player salaries also demanded attention. The clubs claimed that they were taking a financial hit. Payroll figures for the 24 major league teams in 1976 had averaged $1.3 million per year with the Philadelphia Phillies topping the list at $1,978,000. The figures represented base salaries, deferred salaries, and prorated signing bonuses. The average for the 26 clubs in 1985 had ballooned to $10.7 million. The Yankees led the way with a $14,129,881 payroll.

The owners wanted to put a cap on escalating salaries which had resulted from free agency and salary arbitration. They were seeking to cap the salary of players through an average payroll plan as well as limit salary arbitration awards to a 100 percent increase.

In 1984, the average player salary was reported to be $363,000 with 20 players earning $1 million dollars or more. A year later, 16 more players would join the millionaires club.

The PRC sought to expand the League Championship Series (LCS) from five to seven games, which would bring in additional revenue. They offered the players a share of the income from the first four games rather than from the first three games, as was currently the case under the five-game format. Management also wanted to be able to call up players from the minors in September without crediting them with service time.

The Players Association's major goal was to have the owners contribute one-third of the national television revenues to the Pension Fund. The amounts designated by the owners in the previous agreements had approximated that percentage, but the players wanted a fixed one-third. Major League Baseball had signed a lucrative $1.125 billion, six-year contract with ABC and NBC, and the players wanted a guaranteed percentage of the windfall.

The MLBPA also had the minimum salary on its agenda, along with a change in the procedure for paying a terminated player.

On February 8, 1985, the Players Association proposed changes in the free agent process. They wanted free agents eligible to be signed by any club, while also requiring the players' former teams to make them bona fide offers based on fair market value or lose the rights not only to negotiate with them but also to receive compensation when they signed elsewhere. They also proposed eliminating the five-year waiting period to be a repeat free agent.

It was clear from the start that negotiations would be challenging, and another strike was possible if an agreement was not ratified before the start of the 1985 campaign.

MacPhail met with the players' representatives in New York on February 27, and he asked them for their help through the difficult times. He commented about the meeting:

> The owners agreed unanimously that the situation was bad and was getting worse.... If anything further happened that would be adverse to baseball's economics, it could be disastrous. The players have as much at stake as the clubs. We have to look at the whole basic system we're working under.

> We're not playing any games. This is no delaying action. This is no public-relations ploy to get a better deal. We're concerned about the welfare of the game, the financial structure of the game. We asked them to sit down together with us and work out joint solutions. We can't go in and cure everything by cutting back what players get. We'll have to take a look at costs and revenues from all sources. It's not a position that anyone is pleased to have to come to.[6]

In early 1985, the PRC made a major tactical move in an effort to help the tone of the talks and, perhaps, bring about an early agreement. They offered to make financial records available to the MLBPA. In 1981, after Miller had asked the clubs for their financial statements for the years 1978 through 1980 and they had refused, he and the Players Association filed a charge of "refusal to bargain" with the National Labor Relations Board. That action led to slowing down the talks while the issue went before a judge. MacPhail hoped to prevent that from happening again, and he believed that knowledge of the figures would help the players and the fans understand the owners' financial plight.

At the major league owners' meeting on February 26, the PRC requested permission to use the clubs' financial information in the negotiations and received approval to do so. Ueberroth, now on board as the full-time commissioner, expressed his agreement with the approach.

MacPhail recalled some of the new commissioner's other actions:

> There were some other Peter-type surprises at the meeting. He simply announced that there would be no more regional meetings; no meetings of the PRC's Executive Council; that Barry [Rona] and I—with the advice of the league presidents and counsel—would have the authority to do whatever we thought best. I was not really in accord with this. On the surface that made our job easier but I still believed firmly in having the clubs be well-advised and with us each important step of the way.[7]

Ueberroth, who exhibited a willingness to take unpopular stands during his time in office, would soon meet resistance from some owners with respect to opening their financial records to the MLBPA. He was beginning to get a sense of the demands of the position, and said:

> I don't think that you can be afraid of this job.... I'm looking at some other things that might not be very attractive to some owners, either. The issue of superstations may be one of them. But you've got to do what you think is right....
>   As I said.... I didn't demand anything [about opening the books]. But, if it became a key item in slowing down the process of negotiating, I wanted the owners to know I would act.[8]

The mention of superstations was a reminder of an action Ueberroth had taken in January when he concluded five-year agreements with the Atlanta Braves and the Yankees on a television revenue-sharing plan under which the two teams would make annual payments to the other clubs for the right to extend cable television coverage of their games beyond their local markets. Atlanta's WTBS and New York's WPIX, which had been broadcasting to many areas of the country, had caused owners of the other clubs to react to the Yankees' and Braves' games competing with their own. The Braves would pay a total of $30 million over the five-year period, and the money would go into the Major League Central Fund for equal distribution to the 26 clubs ($230,000 a year), including the Braves. That amount worked out to about 20 cents a year for each of the Braves' 33 million cable households. Although the amount of the money to be paid by the Yankees was not announced, it was understood that the two agreements were based on identical formulas having to do with the number of households reached by the superstations. Ueberroth announced that he was continuing his negotiations with the Chicago Cubs, whose games were carried on WGN, and the Mets, who had a working relationship with WOR, to broadcast their games to wider audiences.

The labor negotiations stalled while Fehr and others in the union sifted through the mass of the clubs' financial information that had been provided by the owners. Fehr anticipated that it would take a month to six weeks for the MLBPA to study the material and go over it with all 650 major league players.

Initially, Fehr received figures representing Major League Baseball. They indicated that only once in the past nine years had the clubs as a whole been in the black, and that was in 1978 when they showed a $4,566 profit. The owners reported that 18 of the 26 clubs suffered losses in 1983, with 10 teams losing more than $3 million apiece.

Fehr and the Players Association were not convinced by the statistics. He noted that the material the PRC had supplied indicated that the clubs' stated expenses had totaled $588 million in 1983, with just over $200 million going to pay players' salaries. That amount coupled with the $220 million which went into the players' benefit plan left $168 million unaccounted for.

In order to get a better sense of the owners' situation, Fehr requested information about 28 items from each club including radio contracts, licensing agreements, concession agreements, parking agreements, minor league financial obligations, and other areas of operation.

MacPhail was critical of the other side's approach to the financial information, commenting:

Peter Ueberroth—Baseball's sixth commissioner. (National Baseball Hall of Fame Library, Cooperstown, N.Y.)

A lot of clubs are frustrated that the Players Association doesn't seem to be looking with an open mind at the financial figures we have given them…. They remember the Players Association pledging that if we had problems, bring the problems to them and they would help find solutions. They don't see that happening at this point. We're having a very difficult time convincing the players there is a problem.[9]

During spring training, Fehr and his staff moved from camp to camp, keeping the players informed about the progress of the talks.

Initially, there were 37 different items under consideration in the negotiations. Some of those were quickly agreed upon and others were dropped. However, the major ones—a one-third contribution by the owners to the players' Pension Fund, a salary cap and the seven-game LCS (League Championship Series)—were causing difficulty.

The owners were not about to accept a "one-third rule." The Players Association was not convinced that the owners were suffering financially and were adamantly against a salary cap which would limit the amount of money a club had available to pay its players.

The first of the major issues was settled on April 3, when both sides approved an expanded, revenue-producing LCS format. After 16 years of a five-game LCS, the new seven-game series in each league would provide an additional $9 million in television revenue. The MLBPA asked for one-third of that amount, but the owners balked at the request. The two sides agreed to handle that detail as part of the final collective bargaining agreement. If one was not reached by September 16, the money would be placed in an interest-bearing escrow account.

Television revenue was playing an important part in baseball's income, as well as in some of its decisions. The new five-year television contract with ABC and NBC, which began with the 1984 season, brought 126 million dollars into the game's coffers the first year. In 1989, which was the final year of the agreement, baseball was scheduled to receive $231 million. On May 29, 1985, it was announced that ABC had exercised a clause in the television contract that called for each of the World Series games to be played at night in "prime time."

The PRC was committed to gaining some control over spiraling salaries. They believed that this was critical not only for the owners but for the future of the game as well. They originally considered an approach that they later decided would have been too inflexible. The plan created brackets based on years of major league service, and a player's salary would be an amount somewhere between the upper and lower levels of each bracket. Management then offered another approach for consideration which involved the establishment of an "Annual Payroll Level" ($10.7 million for 1985). It offered a way for the clubs to police themselves and established rules and procedures for governing the economic operation of each club.

MacPhail commented about the complex "Annual Payroll Level" plan that did not find favor with either the MLBPA or Ueberroth:

> There were no limitations on what a team could give its own players even if it put it further over the level, but teams over the level could not acquire players (free agents or acquisitions by trade) if it put them further over the level. Teams over the level, if the rule was adopted, would be given time to adjust to the level. The level would be adjusted annually and changed in response to increased attendance or the gross income of baseball overall.[10]

The proposal found favor with neither the players nor Fehr. For the players it would take away the gains in free agency made over the past 10 years. "It's difficult to imagine a more reactionary proposal, said Fehr. Telling the players at this stage that they won't have a free market isn't calculated to get an agreement."[11]

The regular season began without an agreement or a strike. Negotiations continued, but progress was minimal. It had been seven months since the talks began and MacPhail was beginning to lose the hope that he had brought into the process:

> The reason I took this job was I thought I might be able to promote a little better feeling between the clubs and the Players Association. Obviously, we'd had problems in the past, and I thought that it was important for baseball that we try to get a better relationship between the two. I don't seem to be making much progress in that.[12]

The Joint Drug Program had been a logical start, but it had come up short. On May 7, 1985, Ueberroth ordered all major league personnel except the unionized players to submit to drug testing and urged the players to join in the program as well. Minor leaguers, since they were not members of the MLBPA, would also be under Ueberroth's tough new mandatory testing program. The commissioner commented, "We will include everyone from the owners on down.... Drug use is a problem in sport, in society, and baseball has to clean it up."[13]

At the time, baseball was mired in a number of highly publicized drug-related incidents. The Athletics' Mike Norris had been arrested, the California Angels' Daryl Sconiers had undergone treatment for drug abuse and the San Diego Padres' Alan Wiggins was in treatment for the second time. There was also an ongoing federal grand jury meeting in Pittsburgh to examine the possible involvement of major league ballplayers with illegal drugs.

The commissioner spoke to the MLBPA about including players in the program. Fehr said that he and the players were satisfied with the Joint Drug Program and didn't see the need for a change. Ueberroth tried to assure the Players Association that they would be the only ones with information regarding any player who tested positive for cocaine or other illegal drugs. He also told them that he was concerned about the players and didn't see himself as a policeman. He said, "There are laws in society to punish people.... I don't see my main role as commissioner to punish people. I think I'm different from my predecessor in that way."[14]

Ueberroth was unable to convince the players to go along with his new approach. The Joint Drug Program, which MacPhail, Moffett, and Fehr had helped develop and establish, was disbanded at the owners meetings in October 1985.

In early July the financial figures that had been supplied by 24 of the 26 major league clubs were examined by an accounting firm hired by the MLBPA. Their findings would be critical to the further progress of the talks. When the results were in, the two sides stood millions of dollars apart. The owners had said that they had lost $43 million in 1984, but their accountants narrowed the losses to $27 million. The Players Association's accountants said that their examination of the figures showed that the owners *made* $9.3 million that year.

A breakthrough came on July 11, when the two sides agreed that they would try to negotiate a new collective bargaining agreement without having the players acknowledge that the owners were experiencing significant financial problems. Fehr said:

> Whether or not we agree with them on their financial situation ... we still have to negotiate an agreement. We have to get back to the nuts and bolts, go back to the basics, down the line, one by one, and see what we can reach an agreement on. We'll do that starting next Thursday, at which point we will be staring a strike date in the face.[15]

One day before the July 16th All-Star Game, the executive board of the MLBPA, meeting in Chicago, set August 6 as the strike date. Shane Rawley, the player representative for the Phillies, announced, "We mean business ... and the sooner we get this over the better. The date is set, and if there's no agreement by then, adios."[16]

On July 27, it was announced that some progress had been made when the negotiators reached or neared agreement on approximately 20 noneconomic issues. The hard work, however, still lay ahead.

Both sides commented about the prospect of a future role for Ueberroth in the negotiations. MacPhail stated, "Frankly, we would prefer to work things out among us, assuming they can be worked out.... Ueberroth has been operating independently of us [the owners]. He certainly has not been on our side in a lot of areas."[17]

Since Fehr viewed the commissioner as the employee of the owners, he saw no reason to welcome him to the table.

Dave Anderson, writing in the *New York Times*, saw Ueberroth walking the proverbial tightrope:

> If the new commissioner were to mediate a settlement without a strike, he again would emerge as a folk hero, as he did after the artistic and financial success of the Los Angeles Olympics last year. But if a long strike occurs, he would be considered as hollow and helpless as his predecessor, Bowie Kuhn, was during the 1981 baseball strike.[18]

On July 29, MacPhail, anticipating a strike on August 6, issued a confidential PRC memorandum to all major league chief executives that described the strike regulations for the clubs. Category A included those areas that impacted the competitive aspects of the game and Category B mentioned the noncompetitive items. MacPhail instructed that the regulations in the competitive category "be strictly adhered to by the Clubs—to the letter of the law."[19]

With reference to the competitive area, the memo outlined the clubs' responsibilities to the players should a strike take place:

> The payment of salaries to players on your active roster must be discontinued after August 5th and no advances or loans to players may be made. No contract negotiations should be conducted with Major League players during the strike.
>
> If players are on the road at the commencement of the strike, they should be left where they are. No further transportation, allowances or hotel accommodations should be provided. Meal and tip allowances should not be paid for periods beyond August 5th.
>
> No equipment (including bats, balls, uniforms, etc.) should be furnished players for workouts or exercise; and no training, exercise or player facilities should be furnished to players for workouts or exercise; and no training, exercise or player facilities should be provided or arranged for.[20]

Items discussed in the second category, the non-competitive area in which the clubs were given some freedom to make their own decisions, included ticket policies, plans for nonplaying employees and plans for the resumption of the season should the strike be short-lived.

In early August, the Players Association agreed to give up the one-third demand regarding the Pension Fund, and they accepted an increase to $33 million annually with an additional $6 million raise in 1989. The amount had been $15.5 million in the 1980 Basic Agreement and $33 million represented a sizable increase.

Four days before the strike, Ueberroth weighed in with a series of proposals. He hoped that both sides would be interested in accepting one or more of them as a way to avoid another work stoppage. He proposed that the free-agent system include the right of first refusal for the free agent's team. Ueberroth also suggested that players gain free agency after four years instead of six in return for eliminating salary arbitration. Under his plan, there would also be an escalating minimum salary in their first four years. Neither the owners nor the players expressed interest in the eleventh-hour package of proposals.

On Sunday, August 4, two players reached personal milestones to thrill a baseball world braced for yet another strike. In New York, Tom Seaver, the Chicago White Sox 40-year-old right-hander, beat the Yankees, 4–1, to register his 300th career win. While negotiators were discussing whether or not to eliminate the free agent compensation pool, Seaver was toiling for the White Sox as a result of it. The Mets had left Seaver unprotected after the 1983 campaign and the future Hall of Fame pitcher was taken by Chicago after they lost a high-ranking free agent.

The second milestone was reached on the West Coast when the Angels' Rod Carew delivered his 3000th hit in a game against the Minnesota Twins. Should there be a strike, the Cincinnati Reds' Pete Rose, who was closing in on Ty Cobb's career hits record, would have to wait to set the new mark of 4192.

True to their word, the players struck on August 6. Once again, the season would have to wait. Three of the four divisions were featuring tight races. New Yorkers were dreaming of a subway series between the Mets, who were in first place in the National League East and the Yankees, who sat in second in the American League East. The Dodgers and Angels, both of whom were at the top of their divisions, were imagining an all–California Fall Classic. Major League Baseball was on a pace to set an all-time attendance record.

The next day, after the forty-third formal bargaining session, Ueberroth announced that a tentative understanding had been reached, that the strike was over and the games would begin again. The agreement was later ratified.

It was clear to many that there was a small window of opportunity to reach an agreement before a short work stoppage turned into a long, extended one. An unidentified management source said:

> If you get past three days or so in a strike ... the parties begin to get locked into positions. The next opportunity for any kind of meaningful compromise is a long way down the road. Once the strike started, we felt the best chance for a settlement was two or three days after it began. If, in fact, we could get a respectful compromise, we should do it. By Tuesday, we knew pretty much where a deal was.[21]

Ueberroth had been instrumental in getting the talks going again, although he was not a part of them. Looking back, he said:

> They had quit bargaining.... They only had days to go. There were no offers on the table. The players had not made an offer since 1984, and the owners' offer was clearly not adequate, and it had been sharply rejected. There were no meetings scheduled. For the commissioner to sit back would not be correct.[22]

The breakthrough came at the start of the 10:00 A.M. meeting on August 7 at MacPhail's upper East Side apartment. Fehr and Rona met privately while seven other negotiators waited in separate rooms.

Rona told Fehr that the owners were willing to drop their demand for the 100 percent cap on the salary a player could receive in salary arbitration. The players had already agreed to having the eligibility requirement for free agency raised from two years to three years in 1987, the third year of the five-year agreement. From that point of compromise, the two sides moved smoothly to the final agreement.

The owners had gained some ground in the sixth Basic Agreement. They did not secure a salary cap structure but, after 1987, they would gain an additional year before a player became eligible for salary arbitration. Also on the owners' side, television revenue from the expanded LCS would provide an estimated $9 million of additional income for the clubs to divide.

The new agreement scrapped the short-lived pool compensation approach for the loss of free agents which had been created in 1981. In its place was a new draft compensation procedure.

Along with the increased contribution to the Pension Fund, the players' minimum salary was raised to $60,000. There would be regular annual increases, elevating the minimum to $68,000 by the end of the five-year agreement. Also, free agents would thereafter be permitted to negotiate with any club rather than with a maximum of 14 as was previously the case.

After the agreement was reached, MacPhail said:

> It was a great feeling. We had not solved baseball's financial problems, but for the first time in our labor history we had made some gains for baseball; we had avoided a major strike; had hopefully made some progress in our relationship with the union; and had five years ahead (the longest agreement yet negotiated) without worrying about negotiating a new Basic Agreement.[23]

True to his militant style, Miller voiced disappointment with the outcome:

> When the 1985 negotiations ended, the players accepted the defeat; eligibility for salary arbitration was increased from two to three years of service (something which was a direct cause of the lockout in 1990, as the union attempted to get back this 1985 concession). And for the first time, they agreed to accept less than one-third of the national television and radio revenue for the pension plan. Management agreed to contribute $33 million in 1985, 1986, 1987, and 1988 and $39 million in 1989—a healthy increase, but many millions less than the players would have gotten had they maintained the one-third formula we had established in each pension agreement until then.[24]

The players returned to the field on August 8, and the two days of postponed games were rescheduled. There was agreement between the two sides about how the players would be paid for the games that had been postponed during the strike. If a game was rescheduled as a separate date, the players would receive their entire pay for that day. However, if the game was replayed as part of a doubleheader, the players would receive half pay. Whereas some might consider that item minutia, it was probably heady stuff for the negotiators!

CHAPTER NINE

No Strikes, but Three Collusion Decisions and a Lockout

On October 16, 1985, as Lee MacPhail prepared to leave as president of the Player Relations Committee (PRC), concluding more than 30 years of a Hall of Fame career in baseball, he proffered his thoughts about the economic future of the game.

In a memorandum to the major league club owners, MacPhail expressed his growing concern about the trend toward long-term player contracts. He informed the clubs that they currently owed a total of 45 to 50 million dollars under guaranteed contracts to players who had been released. He posited a correlation between increases in disability time and the lengths of contracts.

MacPhail also shared an analysis that the performance of many hitters and pitchers had declined after they signed long-term agreements. He had drawn his statistics from research done by the PRC which showed, among other things, that the combined batting average of 104 hitters who had inked contracts for three or more years had declined during the successive years of those contracts. The players had averaged .280 before signing and in the following three seasons the numbers were .272, .264, and .261.[1]

Pitchers had not eluded the pattern. The study charted the performances of 56 pitchers who had signed long-term contracts. By the end of the third season, only 40 of them were still active in the major leagues. The pitchers' average ERA was 3.30 at the time they signed with their clubs and, in the three successive seasons, they had risen to 3.36, 3.58, and 3.73. By the end of the third year, 58.3 percent of the hurlers' ERAs were higher than their pre-multi-year-contract level.

Bud Selig, the chairman of the PRC, understood MacPhail's concern:

When he wrote the letter in 1985, he saw what guaranteed contracts were doing to the industry. Here was a man who had spent his whole life in baseball. Shouldn't he be able to articulate and express that to his colleagues? He knew that you have to view things in terms of what is in the best interest of baseball. He was one of the people who taught me that.

As it turned out, he was right. History proved him to be brilliant.[2]

On October 22, at the owners' meeting during the World Series in St. Louis (which was just before the free-agency election period was to begin), MacPhail distributed the memorandum and summarized it. Later, when commissioner Peter Ueberroth realized that many owners had not read MacPhail's appeal to reason and self discipline, he had additional copies made and distributed, and he urged them to study it. After the October meeting, Ueberroth wrote a letter to the few owners who were not able to attend the meeting and included the gist of MacPhail's thoughts and comments in it. He acknowledged that he supported the ideas although he could not force any owner to act on them.

Whether it was MacPhail's words or the result of more conspiratorial forces, Major League Baseball's executives soon set out on a path that would lead to perhaps their darkest labor relation days—and certainly their most costly—COLLUSION.

That was not MacPhail's intent when he penned his now notorious memo:

I didn't mean for it to end up as an issue of collusion. I was basing my letter on studies which had been done to show that long-term contracts were not producing good results. Later, at a meeting of the owners, Peter [Ueberroth] asked if they had read the letter. Few had, so he made copies for them to read.[3]

Marvin Miller, who had worked closely with MacPhail during the 1981 and 1985 labor-management negotiations, was angered by the memo:

The only time I was upset with Lee was when he became involved in what would become the collusion situation. We had just concluded the 1985 Basic Agreement and Lee was out there urging the owners not to sign free agents.[4]

On January 31, 1986, the Players Association filed a grievance against the 26 major league clubs claiming that they "have been acting in concert with each other with respect to individuals who became free agents under Article XVIII [of the Basic Agreement] after the 1985 season."[5]

Paragraph H of Article XVIII is titled "Individual Nature of Rights" and reads:

> The utilization or non-utilization of rights under this Article XVIII is an individual matter to be determined solely by each Player and each Club for his or its own benefit. Players shall not act in concert with other Players and Clubs shall not act in concert with other Clubs.[6]

Ironically, the owners had proposed this particular language during the 1976 negotiations as protection for them from joint actions by players similar to the one taken by Los Angeles Dodger pitchers Don Drysdale and Sandy Koufax in 1966.

In their grievance, the MLBPA charged that the owners had conspired against them through collusion in their dealings with the 1985 class of free agents.

Following the 1984 season, 26 of the 46 free agents had signed with a new team, and 16 of the 26 major league clubs had signed at least one player from another club. That scenario changed dramatically following the 1985 campaign. Prior to the beginning of the 1986 spring training only four of the 62 free agents had changed teams. Nine others, who had not reached a contract agreement with their current clubs, signed later with new teams. During the entire "free-agent season," the Boston Red Sox' Carlton Fisk was the only free agent who had received a bona fide offer from another club (from George Steinbrenner of the New York Yankees) before his 1985 team indicated that they were no longer interested in signing him.

The Detroit Tigers' Kirk Gibson had elicited significant interest from the Kansas City Royals shortly after the 1985 season. However, Kansas City's interest in Detroit's left-handed hitting outfielder had mysteriously cooled about the time of the owners' meetings in St. Louis in October and in Tarpon Springs, Florida, in November. The Royals never pursued Gibson after that.

The hearings to determine whether or not the owners had colluded ran from July 25, 1986, through May 20, 1987. Against the backdrop of a season without action in the free-agent market, each side presented its case during 32 days of testimony before the panel, comprised of arbitrator Thomas Tuttle Roberts, the MLBPA's executive director Donald Fehr, and the PRC's executive director Barry Rona. Roberts had been in the field of arbitration since 1958 and had been a baseball arbitrator since 1974. Roberts' work had taken him beyond baseball, and, during the collusion hearings, he became president-elect of the National Academy of Arbitrators and was scheduled to begin a one-year term in office in May 1988.

The Players Association argued that the owners had been intent on destroying free agency ever since Peter Seitz's 1975 decision in the Messersmith-McNally case. According to the MLBPA's position, the pattern exhibited in 1985 represented a boycott of free agents in which all 26 major league clubs participated with the intent of reaching the goal of ending free agency. The Players Association reviewed the history of free agency and showed that in most years the clubs had shown an interest in journeyman players as well as baseball's stars. They sought to make the case that no club would turn its back on free agency unless it was confident that all of the other clubs would do likewise. It was their contention that:

> Their [the owners] conduct demonstrated a conviction and belief that none of the other clubs would interfere in the negotiations with their own players until and unless they announced they no longer desired to retain the services of the player. Nor are we speaking here of only "significant" free agents. Each and every free agent had the same experience, i.e., no offers until their former clubs stated they were no longer interested. This is precisely the result forbidden by Article XVIII (H).[7]

The PRC argued that the owners had certainly not colluded after the 1985 season, and their approach had not been an effort to destroy free agency. They testified that the owners had made a commitment to follow Ueberroth's recommendations that the clubs show fiscal responsibility for their own good and for the good of the game.

Management reminded the panel that, from the beginning of free agency, not all teams had been active to the same degree. Some clubs had never signed a free agent and a number of others had only occasionally participated in the market. The most active clubs—the Atlanta Braves, California Angels, Yankees, San Diego Padres, and Texas Rangers—had often engaged in spirited bidding for free agents.

The owners showed how the acquisition of free agents as a means of improving a club had diminished gradually from the late 1970s. The clubs, they contended, considered the 1985 pool of players to be weaker than in previous years. Many teams had been burned trying to build through free agency, and the cost of signing those players, especially to long-term contracts, had risen dramatically. Most clubs had chosen to make a commitment to improve their farm systems and to rebuild by relying on development of minor league players. It was also a more economically sound approach since those players commanded smaller salaries than the veterans they replaced.

In the PRC's Post-Hearing Brief, filed on August 31, 1987, it was stated:

In other words, by 1985, it was clear that the free agent market of the 1970's was over and that a more sober and rational market was taking its place. The Clubs believe that the evidence of this natural progression is so strong that there is nothing truly surprising about the level of activity in the 1985 market.[8]

In the midst of the 11-month hearing, the owners, upset with Roberts' recent unrelated ruling that drug-testing clauses could not be inserted in player contracts without the consent of the MLBPA, attempted to remove him. But on September 11, 1986, Roberts was reinstated for the remainder of the collusion case when Richard Bloch, another arbitrator, ruled he could not be dismissed in the middle of a case.

Management presented evidence to show that many free agents, even though they had not signed with another club, gained financially as their teams sought to retain rather than lose them to a competitor. It was stated that:

This market, after all, valued [the Angels'] Donnie Moore—a relief pitcher with one outstanding season and many poor ones—at $1 million a year for three years. This market offered Carlton Fisk—a 38-year-old without a position—a choice of two or three-year contracts with different Clubs at a salary approaching $1 million. And this market rewarded Kirk Gibson—a good but hardly great player, who never hit .300 or 30 home runs over a season—with a guaranteed $4 million for a three-year commitment to play baseball. These signings hardly justify the inference that the Clubs agreed to restrict the market for free agents. They certainly provide no basis for a far reaching award of damages or injunctive relief.[9]

The major league owners suffered a major setback on September 21, 1987. Roberts, after poring over 5,674 pages of verbatim transcript and examining 288 exhibits, ruled in favor of the Players Association in baseball's first collusion case.

In one section of Roberts' 16-page ruling, which was announced in New York, he commented about MacPhail's memorandum:

The retiring Director of the Player Relations Committee, Leland S. MacPhail, distributed a memorandum (dated October 16, 1985) that had as its message the undesirability of long-term contracts because the players signed to such agreements frequently do not thereafter perform to the level of their ability or suffer injuries that force them to leave baseball while still enjoying the salary benefits of the contracts. MacPhail declared, "We must stop day dreaming that one free agent signing will bring a pennant. Somehow we must get our operations back to the point where a normal year for an average team at least results in a break-even situation, so that the Clubs are not led to make rash moves in the vain hope that they may bring a pennant and a resulting change in their financial position. This requires resistance to fan and media pressure and is not easy."[10]

Rona naturally disagreed with Roberts' ruling and asked, "What is it that we have to do different to be in compliance with the arbitrator's decision. I asked that question of the arbitrator today. The arbitrator was not in a position to answer that at this session."[11]

The ruling had been made, and it was a moral victory for the players. Later it became a financial victory as well. What remained was for Roberts and representatives of the MLBPA and the PRC to devise an appropriate remedy for the owners' collusion.

In January 1988, Roberts ruled that seven of the players in the 1985 case were free agents again (so called "new-look free agents"), giving them until March 1 to renegotiate with other teams without relinquishing their existing contracts. At the time of the announcement, only 14 of the original 62 free agents in 1985 were bound to major league teams. Roberts did not offer new-look free agency to seven of the 14 since they had been free agents again since 1985.

Gibson, one of the "new-look" seven, signed with the Los Angeles Dodgers and would soon spark them to victory in game one of the 1988 World Series when he limped to the plate and powered a dramatic ninth-inning home run off the Oakland Athletics' Dennis Eckersley. The Dodgers went on to beat the A's four games to one to capture the World Championship.

The other six granted "new-look" free agency were Juan Beniquez of the Toronto Blue Jays, Tom Brookens of the Tigers, Fisk of the Chicago White Sox, Joe Niekro of the Minnesota Twins, and Butch Wynegar and Moore of the Angels.

Roberts' ruling came a bit late in the careers of all but Brookens and Fisk. Beniquez, Niekro, Moore, and Wynegar all played with their current clubs in 1988 and retired after the season. Brookens was with Detroit in '88 and moved on to play for the Yankees in 1989 and then with Cleveland the following year before retiring. Fisk stayed with the White Sox the rest of his playing career which ended in 1993.

Roberts' findings were not the end of the collusion issue. During the 1988 season, an arbitration panel chaired by George Nicolau deliberated Collusion II on behalf of the 1986 crop of 76 free agents. Although they were considered better players than those who had been involved in the 1985 case, they experienced the same lack of interest from the clubs as had befallen the previous year's group. The Player Association's brief cited the clubs' lack of interest with regard to four categories of free agents. Among those mentioned in the brief were:

> The first was Jack Morris and the "January 8 Eight." The second group were those players who were non-tendered free agents who were not voluntarily eligible for free agency, but became such when their 1986 team did not tender them a contract by December 20. The Detroit Tigers' Darrell Evans was the premier player in that group. The Players Association's brief addressed the intentions of the Tigers and the other clubs who had used the approach, saying it "was a method of defeating the player's salary arbitration rights and avoiding the maximum cut rules which would apply if the player was tendered a contract."[12]

The "January 8 Eight" was a group of free agents who had not signed contracts for the 1987 season with their teams of the previous season by the January 8 deadline, and they were not free to negotiate with their clubs until May 1. Each of them would be ineligible to play until that date unless another team signed him.

The eight players became the focus of a subplot within the collusion issue. After the January 8 deadline, the PRC wanted the teams to be able to continue negotiations with their players while they were waiting for them to become eligible to sign and play on or after May 1. The MLBPA filed a grievance about the PRC's position because it felt that the continued presence of the player's former club would inhibit other teams from negotiating with them.

On February 9, 1987, Nicolau ruled that a club "may not engage in negotiations leading to an employment relationship" with a "January 8" free agent before May 1.[13]

Of the eight, five—Doyle Alexander (Atlanta), Bob Boone (California), Rich Gedman (Boston), Ron Guidry (Yankees), and Tim Raines (Montreal)—signed with their 1986 clubs on or after May 1. Andre Dawson exchanged a Montreal Expos' uniform for one with the Chicago Cubs, and Lance Parrish left the Tigers and joined the Philadelphia Phillies. Bob Horner traveled from Atlanta, Georgia, to Yakult, Japan, where he played with the Swallows.

Morris' story was different. Detroit had offered him salary arbitration on December 7. The right-handed pitcher, who had played all ten years of his major league career with the Tigers and had posted a career-best 21-8 record and a 3.27 ERA in 1986, had until December 19 to accept or reject the offer. On December 10, Dick Moss, Morris's agent and a former counsel for the Players Association, announced that the pitcher would visit four clubs in an attempt to make a deal, of his design, with one of them. Morris's list indicated his preferences in descending order of interest—the Twins, Angels, Phillies, and Yankees. On December 19, after none of the four clubs took Morris up on his contract figures, he chose to accept the Tigers' offer of salary arbitration. They filed at $1.35 million and Morris asked for $1.85 million. The arbitrator ruled in Morris's favor.

The third group of free agents were those players who did not receive offers from a club other then their own and chose to sign a new contract prior to the January 8 deadline so that they could go to spring training and begin the regular season with their teams.

The final group were those free agents who had been signed by another club, but only after their 1986 team had decided not to sign them.

Management countered, as it had done during the collusion hearings in the 1985 case, that they had not colluded and that there had, in fact, been increased activity in the 1986 market. However, they added that the economic realities of the game required that the clubs act prudently in the selection of free agents.

On August 31, 1988, after 39 days of hearings spread over seven months, Nicolau handed down his ruling and, for the second time, found the clubs guilty of collusion. Regarding the Players Association's allegations, Nicolau said:

> In my opinion, the evidence as a whole convincingly establishes that everyone knew that there was to be no bidding before January 8 for free agents coveted by their former clubs. It was also known that "other clubs" were not expected to sign such free agents after January 8....
>
> In any other year, there may be a great deal of bidding between former clubs and other clubs; in another year, substantially less. But the abrupt cessation of activity in 1985 and the repetition of that pattern, with only minor post–January 8 deviations in 1986, cannot be attributed to the free play of market forces....
>
> In my opinion, their [the Clubs'] conduct with respect to the 1986 free agents was in deliberate contravention of Club obligations as embodied in Article XVIII (H), for which an appropriate remedy is fully justified.[14]

Nicolau's report cited a number of instances where some owners and executives had contacted one another regarding a specific player. Nicolau found that American League president Bobby Brown and club owners Jerry Reinsdorf of the White Sox and Selig of the Milwaukee Brewers had telephoned Bill Giles, president of the Phillies, trying to dissuade him from signing Parrish.

The Detroit catcher's situation was intriguing. He had become a free agent on November 6, 1986, and, according to the MLBPA, "was unquestionably *the* American League catcher of the 1980's."[15] Parrish's salary in 1986, the option year of a five-year contract, was $850,000.

In 1985, Detroit had discussed with Tom Reich, Parrish's agent, the possibility of giving the Tigers' catcher a lifetime contract patterned after the one that George Brett had signed with the Royals. Those discussions ended soon after the owners' pivotal October meeting in St. Louis.

Parrish had missed the last two months of the 1986 campaign because of back problems but, to that point, he had put together a strong season (22 home runs and 62 RBI in 327 at bats). He had announced that he was interested in leaving Detroit, but no team other than the Tigers had made him an offer prior to the January 8 deadline. Before that date, Detroit had initially offered him a one-year $850,000 contract, and then made successive offers of $1 million and $1.2 million. The final offer would have placed his salary among the top three catchers in the game and only the fourth to exceed the $1-million level. After Parrish refused to sign a contract, the Tigers said that they still wanted to negotiate with him and sign him on or after May 1, when they would be permitted to do so. Detroit advised all other clubs of their continued interest in Parrish and the amount of the final offer they had made to him.

The Phillies were in need of a front-line catcher. During the collusion testimony, club president Bill Giles offered his rationale for not having made an offer to Parrish before the January 8 deadline, saying:

> [it] was his belief, "despite the rules," that teams shouldn't go after each other's players. As Giles put it, he thought "a man of Parrish's quality and longevity in Detroit" shouldn't leave and that the Tigers should have "every opportunity to sign him"; that signing a player when the former club is still interested is a "little bit" like stealing, while trading for that player, even when he doesn't want to leave his club, is not stealing and "just part of the game."[16]

After the January 8 deadline, Giles became convinced that Parrish wanted to leave Detroit and his interest in signing him to a Philadelphia contract intensified. On a personal level, Giles worried about doing so because Jim Campbell, the Tigers' president, was a close personal friend.

As Giles' interest increased so did the telephone calls:

He was telephoned by American League President [Bobby] Brown, who reminded him that the Tigers still wanted Parrish and that he, Dr. Brown, didn't want to lose one of his star players to the National League. He was then called by two American League owners, the Brewers' Bud Selig and the White Sox' Jerry Reindorf, fellow members of the PRC Board of Directors. Both asked if he was going to make an offer to Parrish and, when told he was considering it, urged that he keep his "fiscal responsibilities" in mind.[17]

In late January, Giles met with Parrish and Reich and told them that he was "catching heat from all over everywhere."[18] Nevertheless, Giles made Parrish an offer of $800,000 with an additional $200,000 if he remained free of disabling injury prior to the All-Star Game.

Then a strange thing happened. On February 13, William Webb, the Phillies' counsel, sent Reich a release which Parrish would have to sign as a condition of the deal. Webb had already shared the content of the release with the National League counsel.

Parrish would not be able to sign with Philadelphia unless

he agreed to waive all rights he might have to bring any claims not only against the Phillies but against all other clubs and any other conceivable entity in Major League Baseball including, specifically, the PRC and the Commissioner; *and* in addition the MLBPA must agree to waive any rights it might have to process such a claim; *and* the MLBPA must agree not to use evidence of the Phillies' conduct in regard to Parrish in order to prove baseball-wide collusion against free agents.[19]

Parrish refused to sign the document unless it related only to the Phillies. The MLBPA filed a grievance, seeking to have the arbitration panel declare the waiver/release invalid.

On February 19, Giles gave a statement, which Webb had helped prepare, saying that Philadelphia had broken off negotiations with Parrish and Reich because the parties had been:

Unable to agree on satisfactory contract language that would release the Phillies and the rest of Major League Baseball from recent threats of legal action relating to negotiations with free agents such as Lance Parrish....[20]

Hours before the next day's arbitration hearing, the Phillies withdrew the restrictions placed on the Players Association and the case was settled. Parrish signed a contract and became the property of the Phillies.

In October, Nicolau ruled that 14 of the 79 players in the 1986 case were free agents and could negotiate with other teams. As part of the collusion decision, the arbitration panel responded to the owners' position that there had not been an agreement to restrict free-agent movement in the situation involving Parrish:

> The Chairman does not share that view. Giles was severely encumbered. It was not just the obvious external pressure; the unsolicited calls from the head of the league from which Parrish might depart and calls from owners in that league with whom he met regularly on labor relations matters. Giles was well aware, even without those not so subtle messages, that breaking ranks by signing a player still wanted by his former club, something not done in 1985 and not yet done in 1986, could unleash unwanted forces, that his bid could lead to another or to escalating bids for other players and undo what he and his fellow owners had set out to accomplish.[21]

The owners' actions in the collusion cases, whether intended or coincidental, were not their only attempts to regain control over players' salaries. While Nicolau was weighing a third collusion case against the magnates with regard to the 1987 group of free agents, they launched a lockout which postponed the opening of spring training camps in 1990.

The prospect of a lockout had been mentioned as early as December 1988. At the time the owners were trying to get lockout clauses in players' contracts. There were two types of lockout language being discussed. The first, and most extreme, would free the clubs of any salary obligations should there be a lockout. The other, and less extreme, would leave the question about pay during a lockout to an arbitrator.

If a new agreement to replace the one due to expire on December 31, 1989, was not agreed upon by the spring, the magnates preferred to have a work stoppage then, rather than have the players strike later in the season. As one owner said, "By August, the players have 80 percent of their income and the owners have 20 percent of theirs."[22]

The point of the comment was that the owners didn't want to risk losing the radio and television income generated by the postseason. That income had continued to grow even though Ueberroth, during the negotiations for the existing Basic Agreement, had warned that future television contracts would not be as lucrative as they had been. The contract in 1985 was a six-year deal worth $1.125 billion. CBS had recently signed a new four-year contract with Major League Baseball for $1.06 billion. It was estimated that, once the income from the cable contracts was added to that amount, each club would receive an annual $15-million package, which was over twice the amount they were currently receiving.

During the labor negotiations for a new agreement, the owners put a revenue-sharing proposal on the table. They wanted to give the players a fixed 48 percent of the revenue from ticket sales and radio and television rights for salaries and benefits. Those sources represented 82 percent of the owners' total revenue.

The PRC, now under the leadership of Charles P. (Chuck) O'Connor who had replaced Rona after he resigned as executive director in November 1988, also wanted a "pay for performance" salary scale which provided that salaries for players who had been in the majors from one to six years would be based on service time and a scale in four position groups. Salary arbitration, guaranteed salaries, multi-year contracts, and a limit of 20 percent on pay cuts would all be eliminated if this proposal was accepted. In the view of the owners, salaries had gotten further out of hand. Prior to the 1990 season, no player had a salary which averaged $3 million for a season. During the upcoming campaign, nine players would be playing for $3 million or more a year.

A third proposal would make players with six or more years of service free agents. A team's payroll, however, would determine the team's ability to sign free agents. If a team's payroll was higher than a proposed limit they could sign their own free agents but not those from other teams.

From previous collective bargaining battles, the owners must have known that the three areas which they had proposed—a fixed percentage of revenue for player salaries and benefits, a "pay for performance" approach to salaries, and tying team payrolls to free agent signings—were pipe dreams. It was difficult to imagine the Players Association agreeing to any of them. However, down the line they may serve as bargaining chips in the discussions of other less difficult proposals for the players to accept.

The MLBPA sat on the other side of the table under Fehr's leadership. They sought to reduce salary arbitration from three to two years of major league service; to return to 25-man rosters from the 24-player limit which had existed for several seasons; to increase the minimum salary from $68,000 to an amount between $100,000 and $125,000; to eliminate the five-year waiting period for repeat free agency; and to receive approximately one-third of the revenue from the new television contract for the benefits plan. The players also wanted some kind of powerful protection to guard against a repeat of the recent collusion practices by the owners.

Many of the proposals were unacceptable to Major League Baseball. The players remained, as always, opposed to a revenue-sharing plan and, as long as that was being considered, progress in the talks was minimal.

In February, with a lockout a foregone conclusion, baseball commissioner Francis T. (Fay) Vincent, Jr., who had succeeded A. Bartlett Giamatti following his sudden death in September 1989, suggested that the revenue-sharing plan be taken off the table and placed in the hands of a committee to study at length. He believed that action would open the way for some movement in the collective bargaining. Vincent would become much more involved in the negotiations between the two sides than any of his predecessors had been.

Vincent, a lawyer by way of Williams College and Yale Law School, had come to a post in Major League Baseball after serving as president and CEO of Columbia Pictures from 1978 to 1983. He became chairman in 1983 after Coca-Cola bought Columbia, and he stayed with the company until 1989. Giamatti, who was a noted academician and lover of the game, Vincent hired Giamatti to oversee the business affairs of the Commissioner's Office.

When Fehr was asked to comment about Vincent's involvement, he said:

> I'll take input from anybody I can find. I don't think this commissioner has made any pretense of who he works for. As he has explained to us, it's pretty hard to hide the fact that he's in their meetings and he isn't in ours. That coming from a commissioner of baseball is a refreshing thing.[23]

The owners' hope to include some form of revenue sharing in the seventh Basic Agreement was not to be realized. The idea of it was, again, totally untenable to the Players Association, and the PRC removed it from the negotiations on February 22.

O'Connor and Steve Greenberg, the deputy commissioner, would play major roles down the stretch for the PRC, and Fehr and Gene Orza, the union's associate general counsel, would be lead negotiators for the Players Association as the discussions moved toward resolution. Together, they would work out the eventual agreement that led to opening of the gates to spring training.

The announcement of the settlement and the end of the 32-day lockout was made by Vincent at 1:15 A.M. on March 19. The seventh Basic Agreement, which was intended to ensure labor peace for another four years, provided a change in the three-year minimum for salary arbitration. The new agreement added the top 17 percent of players with service time between two and three years to those eligible for arbitration.

The players' minimum salary was increased to $100,000 and the minimum minor league salary was raised from $22,700 to $25,000. The owners' contribution to the pension fund was increased to an average of $55 million. Although the players did not get their desired change in the roster size from 24 to 25 players for 1990, it was slated to become 25 in 1991.

The National League's two-team expansion was to be announced within 90 days, with the names of the teams to be announced at a later date. With regard to collusion, the owners would be charged triple damages if they were found to conspire against free agents in the future. Finally, either side was given the right to reopen the four-year contract on major issues after three years.

Major league executives expressed differing points of view about the lockout and the effect it had on negotiations. Marge Schott, the owner of the Cincinnati Reds, was critical of the move, saying:

> I wish they hadn't done that.... Maybe the players wouldn't have gone on strike. Sometimes I don't think they would have, not with all the money they're making. Of course, we'll never know.[24]

Al Harazin, senior vice president of the New York Mets, thought that the lockout had produced the desired results:

> It's all a matter of leverage.... You don't want to be at the mercy of the other side during the season. From that point of view, not wanting the other side to pull a strike halfway through the season, as happened in the past—from that point of view, the lockout was successful.[25]

Not long after the start of the regular season, Nicolau returned with another collusion ruling. In June, 1990, he handed down his second decision against the owners—and baseball's third—when he ruled that the owners had operated in a concerted effort against free agents after the 1987 season. Management's approach, which involved a "salary offer data bank," had been different the third time around, but it was still contrary to the intent of the Basic Agreements.

Murray Chass, in the *New York Times*, described the new style of bank:

> The bank in question has no money, but it has lots of information about money, money offered to free agents. It is the free-agent information bank of the Player Relations Committee, and it is the latest source of controversy between the clubs and the players over the owners' approach to free agents in recent years.[26]

The PRC said that it had established the information bank as a way to avoid the collusion situations such as had occurred with the 1985 and 1986 groups of free agents. For the owners, it served as an improved method for deciding the best offer to make to a free agent. In an effort to justify the approach, they argued that if a team knows what others are willing to pay a free agent, that information could lead to a more attractive offer since the team isn't just bidding on speculation. Also, when agents don't tell a club how much other teams have offered one of his players, the bank approach enables the club to have the necessary information in order to craft a fair and appropriate deal.

Fehr disagreed with the PRC's position, saying, "I cannot conceive that it's pro-competitive.... I have to believe it would have an anti-competitive effect and that's why we asked the arbitrator to enjoin it."[27]

Nicolau's understanding of the information bank's purpose was more in line with the players' view:

> Against that backdrop [Roberts' ruling], the bank's message was plain—if we must go out into the market and bid, then let's quietly cooperate by telling each other what the bids are. If we do that, prices won't get out of line and no club will be hurt too much.[28]

On September 17, 1990, Nicolau ruled that the clubs must pay the players $102.5 million for lost salary for the 1987 and 1988 seasons. Of the total amount, $38 million was for lost salary in 1987 and $64.5 million was for 1988. The number of players who would receive money had yet to be determined.

Fehr was pleased with the ruling:

> This decision represents a substantial win for the players.... When coupled with arbitrator Tom Roberts' decision, total damages awarded to players in collusion cases now stand at $113 million, and counting. There will be much more to come when the remaining damages are determined, including the lost salary for 1989 and '90, interest and other damages. Protest as they will, the owners can no longer downplay either the significance or the effect of their intentionally wrongful conduct.[29]

There was much more money to come! When the final figures were in, the owners agreed to pay the players $280 million—$10.77 million per club—for salary lost from 1986 through 1990 because of collusion that had diminished the free agents' market value. The first payment of $120 million would be made January 2, 1991, with four additional payments of $40 million each (plus accrued interest) to be made during the next 15 months.

On December 17, 1990, the PRC and the MLBPA revealed a new approach to collective bargaining which would hopefully lessen the bitterness and ineffectiveness which had marked the recent negotiations. The two sides announced the formation of a joint committee that would include the "regulars" as members, but would also draw upon the resources of experts from outside baseball to help address the game's economic issues. Selig and Fehr would serve as cochairmen of the committee. Paul Volker, who had served as chairman of the Federal Reserve Board in the administrations of Jimmy Carter and Ronald Reagan, was one of the people who was mentioned as an "outside" member of the committee.

Fehr said:

> We wanted to constitute a committee with people who have unquestioned status and unquestioned experience and are not beholden to the people who appoint them or to anyone else in baseball.[30]

The committee would be asked to produce a report prior to the expiration of the seventh Basic Agreement on December 31, 1994. An optimistic O'Connor said, "We would like to think that when it is done, it will provide to the parties something they had not had; a common economic language."[31] Only time would tell if the committee would help lead negotiators to the promised land of agreement.

CHAPTER TEN

Strike Four: 1994—
The Big Out

In 1991 Richard (Dick) Ravitch took over for Chuck O'Connor as president and chief negotiator of the Player Relations Committee (PRC). Ravitch, who was raised on New York's Upper East Side and later made a personal fortune running his family's construction business, was new to the business of baseball. After working in construction, a change of jobs took him to New York's Metropolitan Transportation Authority where he eventually became its chairman. While in that position he found himself in the middle of a highly volatile 11-day Transportation Workers Union strike. Following the settlement of the walkout, Ravitch received praise from both mayor Edward Koch and the union for his work during the impasse. In 1989, he briefly entered the political arena, losing handily to Koch in the city's Democratic mayoral primary.

Ravitch was positioned to guide the PRC through the next round of negotiations with the MLBPA. The 1990 Basic Agreement provided that either the PRC or the MLBPA could vote to reopen labor negotiations in December 1992, and Ravitch quickly pushed the owners to do so. He thought that by reopening the Basic Agreement, management would benefit by negotiating changes that would give them more control over the players and their salaries. The New York Mets' Fred Wilpon and the Baltimore Orioles' Larry Lucchino were two of the most vocal owners opposing Ravitch's proposed plan.

While the owners were trying to decide whether or not to take Ravitch's advice in an effort to immediately moderate player salaries, a number of clubs were again taking sizable financial plunges into the newly appealing free-agent market. Left-handed pitcher John Smiley, who had posted a 16-9 record with a 3.21 ERA in 1992 with the Minnesota Twins, signed a four-year contract for $18.4 million with the Cincinnati Reds.

Right-hander Doug Drabek (15-11 and a 2.77 ERA) and slugger Barry
Bonds (.311, 34 home runs and 103 RBI) both departed Pittsburgh via
free agency. Drabek agreed to a four-year, $19.5 million contract with the
Houston Astros, and Bonds took a gargantuan $43.75 million over six
years to play for the Giants in San Francisco. Jose Guzman, a right-
handed hurler (16-11 and a 3.66 ERA), left the Texas Rangers and received
a $14.3 million deal to pitch for the Chicago Cubs.

On December 7, 1992, the owners took a pair of important votes. First,
in anticipation of spring training, they decided that a three-quarters vote
rather than a simple majority would be needed to close the camps in a lockout action. In the second vote, Ravitch got what he wanted when the owners agreed by a narrow 15–13 margin to reopen the 1990 Basic Agreement.
The two-vote margin of victory indicated the great divide that existed
between the owners, for whom anything approximating unanimity was rare.

With the narrow victory in his pocket, Ravitch asked the Players
Association to begin negotiations toward signing a new basic Agreement
before the start of the 1993 spring training.

The first meeting between representatives of the two parties took
place on January 6, 1993. A week later, Ravitch, after announcing that he
would recommend to the owners that they not lock the players out of
spring training camps, asked the MLBPA to consider moving up the expiration date of the seventh Basic Agreement from December 31 to November 1. The reasoning behind Ravitch's request, which had little chance of
gaining the Players Association's approval, was:

> The operative provisions of the contract take effect in two months
> after the World Series.... If the contract didn't expire by Nov. 1, there
> would be no way of altering the economics of the 1994 season.[1]

Players' salaries weighed heavy on the owners' minds. During the
past 20 years they had risen 20 fold. While the number of players earning over $1 million in 1993 was down seven from 269 the previous year,
over four seasons the number of $3-million-or-more men had grown from
1 to 32 to 69 to 100. The average salary of 10 clubs was less than it had
been in 1992, but 16 had their average salary rise, including five—Baltimore, Houston, Philadelphia, Seattle, and Texas—that surpassed the $1
million level for the first time.

Many owners believed that salary arbitration continued to be the
biggest cause of spiraling players' salaries. Before trying to eliminate arbitration in the new round of collective bargaining, clubs were taking an
aggressive approach toward signing their own players who were eligible

for salary arbitration. They offered the players more acceptable increases in an effort to sign them before they went to an arbitration hearing.

During the previous three years, an average of 155 players had filed for arbitration. That number dropped to 118 in 1993. When the final arbitration figures were in, they showed that 100 players who had filed reached a negotiated settlement before going to a hearing. Of the 18 arbitration decisions, the clubs won 12 cases and the players were victorious in six. The overall record for arbitration since it was first negotiated in the third Basic Agreement in 1973 stood at 199 decisions for the clubs and 156 for the players.

The owners had an approach in mind to mollify their economic woes. On February 7, they voted unanimously to link revenue sharing on their part with a cap on the players' salaries. It was clear that the implementation of any revenue-sharing plan would be contingent on the union accepting a salary cap.

Fehr reacted skeptically to the owners' plan and spoke about another way of understanding "linkage":

> Just because they said so doesn't make it so.... Maybe one day they'll explain to us what the linkage is. I'm glad they did it [reached an agreement]. I'm sure they got an enhanced feeling of solidarity. I hope they feel better. But the real linkage is the big-market owners won't share with the small-market owners unless players give them back the money. That's the only linkage we've heard about.[2]

Bud Selig, the acting commissioner, was optimistic about the owners' action:

> We're saying today that there is a linkage between these two things.... It's often been said by the Players Association, let them solve their own problems first. Let them go to revenue sharing. The clubs took a step today to acknowledge there is a direct linkage.[3]

Selig had become acting commissioner after Fay Vincent was forced from office by the magnates in September 1992. On September 4 of that year, 18 of the 27 owners who voted (the Reds' Marge Schott did not vote) asked Vincent to resign. Selig was among the group of owners voting for Vincent's resignation.

Some who voted against Vincent wanted to take a hard-line position with the Players Association in the upcoming negotiations, and they didn't believe that Vincent would support that move. Others who opposed him were upset that the $190 million in expansion fees from the new

National League franchises in Miami and Denver were not divided equally between the leagues. Instead of taking that approach, the commissioner decided that the American League clubs would receive only 22 percent of the expansion money while each of their 14 teams would lose three players in the expansion draft. The rub was that since the National League was operating at the time with only 12 teams, with each losing three players, the Junior Circuit would supply 54 percent of the personnel for the new Senior Circuit clubs and would receive only slightly more than one-fifth of the expansion fees. Vincent went on to say that in the future the leagues would split expansion fees equally, but that didn't help the American Leaguers in the near term. A third force, the Tribune Company, owner of the Chicago Cubs, was especially angry with the commissioner because of his attempts to reduce the impact of superstation broadcasts.

On September 7, after a long and contentious battle with some of the owners, Vincent, not wanting to turn the situation into a long legal battle, bowed to the will of the majority and announced his resignation. Vincent, who had taken office after the tragic and sudden death of Bart Giamatti in 1989, said:

> I cannot govern as Commissioner without the consent of the owners to be governed.... I do not believe that consent is now available to me. Simply put, I've concluded that resignation—not litigation—should be my final act as Commissioner "in the best interests" of baseball.[4]

The owners' concerns about escalating salaries had been an ongoing issue. Congress's concern about baseball's 71-year exemption from Federal antitrust laws, which had not been on the front burner for a while, was again becoming a hot issue.

On March 31, 1993, Florida Representative Michael Bilirikis introduced legislation in the U.S. House that would repeal baseball's antitrust exemption. Bilirikis cited the multimillion-dollar salaries of some players and the almost $600 million in revenue which had come into the game's coffers in 1991 from national broadcasting contracts. Two months later, Jim Bunning, a former major league pitcher and current Republican Congressman from Kentucky, thought he saw a connection between the impending investigation and All-Star Game tickets for the midsummer classic in Baltimore. Bunning smelled "bribe" when the leagues offered to sell the hard-to-get ducats to members of the House and Senate. The future Hall of Famer said, "Legislation to repeal the antitrust exemption is starting to move in Congress now.... And Major League Baseball is trying to curry favor with members."[5]

Also leading to the owners' sense of urgency in righting the game's financial ship was the fact that in June a new and drastically reduced major league television contract, effective for the 1994 season, was put in place. Peter Ueberroth's forecast about reduced revenues from television, which had not come true as early as the former commissioner had predicted, had finally become an economic reality of the game at a time when baseball's television ratings had also fallen significantly. CBS, which had held the contract previously and had bid a modest $120 million a year to renew it (which was down from an annual $265 million in the expiring four-year, $1.06 billion contract), was not a player in the new agreement. ABC and NBC were approved by Major League Baseball in a new six-year joint venture with an economic downside.

The joint venture, which was called The Baseball Network (TBN), would change how the game was sold. Under previous agreements, television networks paid Major League Baseball (MLB) a rights fee for televising regular and postseason games. Under the new arrangement, ABC and NBC would not pay any money to MLB but would share advertising and sponsorship revenues with them. In the case of postseason games, the revenues would increase with the length of the series. This prompted some to suggest that owners or players might have a financial reason to extend the series. That had not been an issue prior to the new agreement since players only received money through the fourth game of each series.

Before management and labor could address a new labor contract, they had to decide whether or not to realign the two leagues, each of which now had 14 teams as a result of the National League's expansion. The addition of two new clubs had been a part of the 1990 Basic Agreement, and the Colorado Rockies and the Florida Marlins came into existence and had begun play in 1993. That season the American and National Leagues each had two seven-team divisions. When a final agreement on realignment was reached in January 1994, the leagues each had three divisions and a new playoff format. There were five teams in its East and Central divisions and four clubs in the West.

Realignment had ramifications for the postseason and television. The union had to approve the new playoff format that would add another series in each league—a League Division Series (LDS)—to precede the League Championship (LCS) and the World Series. The owners believed that the new arrangement would help maintain fan interest down the stretch as a number of teams would be vying for the postseason's wild-card spot which would go to the nondivision-winning club with the best record.

Besides changing how baseball was sold, the new television contract also changed how the game would be viewed. Beginning in 1994, ABC and NBC planned to televise all of the postseason games in prime time. Day games would become a thing of the past on The Baseball Network. Also, the country would be divided into four sections for the five-game wild-card round (LDS) and into two sections for the seven-game LCS. Most of the postseason games prior to the Fall Classic, which had been spectacles for the entire nation to watch, would no longer be available to everyone across the country. The only exceptions would be games six and seven of the LCS, which would have staggered starts.

Although there had been meetings between the PRC and the MLBPA early in 1993 in anticipation of the expiration of the seventh Basic Agreement on December 31, the sessions had not produced much of substance. Besides realignment, the owners had other items to consider.

On June 17, the magnates voted to focus their energies first and foremost on solving a portion of their economic woes by coming up with a plan to share revenues between the richer and poorer clubs. They would begin collective bargaining with the Players Association once that was accomplished.

Ravitch commented about the owners' process and the reasons for the delay in meeting with the players:

> Right after the owners passed the resolution, they said go ahead and put together your plan.... I immediately convened all of the chief financial officers in baseball and broke them up into committees. And we worked at great length. Then I got the owners to pass a resolution to agree to share financial information with each other—a major step forward—and we put together a great deal of information....
>
> It is complicated and time-consuming, but I think that everybody felt that if we tried to resolve this before everybody was ready, it would be silly.... So we just took a few more weeks.[6]

The players were talking among themselves, waiting for the "salary cap" shoe to drop. There was some suspicion within the union that the owners' decision to withhold talks with the players was part of a well-orchestrated plan. Fehr wrote about it in a July 23 "status of negotiations" memo:

> This behavior is certainly consistent with, if it is not in deliberate furtherance of, a strategy to delay the negotiations long enough to get past any possibility of a strike at the end of the 1993 season.[7]

Fehr went on to say in the memo that, because of the delay in negotiations, the MLBPA was considering the possibility of a late-season work stoppage.

Historically, management in-fighting had made it difficult for the owners to project a unified stance in negotiations with the MLBPA, and the rocky issue of revenue sharing didn't promise a smooth ride for the owners.

A visionary Andy MacPhail, general manager of the Minnesota Twins who were a small market club and had captured the World Championship in 1987 and 1991, called for a cooperative spirit among the owners. He was bothered by the entire process and the manner in which baseball was conducting itself. MacPhail, calling for reason, said:

> The unfortunate aspect of it is that the clubs have perpetually lost in collective-bargaining agreements because we have never been unified.... The fact that we haven't been unified isn't because we're stupid or that we're egomaniacs, but because we have very different, diverse self interests, as opposed to the players....
>
> It will be much easier for baseball to deal with its immediate problems if we will for once stop carving up every issue that confronts us with how it affects our individual club.... We think way too short-term. We're going to have to start looking at things long-term and how they affect the game of baseball and start to put our own individual needs second.[8]

The owners failed to forge an agreement on revenue sharing after 30 hours of meetings over two days in August in Kohler, Wisconsin. The two sides seated at the table were not management and labor but the owners of the richer clubs and their poorer counterparts. A group of the ten richer clubs—Baltimore, Boston, California, Colorado, Florida, both New York teams, St. Louis, Texas, and Toronto—offered the greatest resistance to plans aimed at providing a way for the "haves" to economically help the "have nots." At the conclusion of the meetings, Ravitch, speaking about the next steps toward reaching an agreement, reported:

> Though I'm obviously disappointed we didn't obtain closure on a plan today, I believe an enormous amount of progress has been made.... I hope in the very near future I will be able to tell you there is a total agreement between the clubs on how to redistribute revenue among themselves and meet the obligation to players under the new economic system we will propose to them.[9]

Although they didn't reach an accord on a revenue-sharing plan, the owners did pledge to the union that they would not lock out the players during the 1994 spring training and they would not change the work rules, including salary arbitration, for the coming season. In response to their pledge, the owners sought a promise from the other side that they would not strike during the remainder of the 1993 campaign. On August 23, Fehr announced that the players would complete the season as scheduled.

While the management-labor negotiations were sputtering, Major League Baseball was rolling along, registering its highest attendance in history. The 70,256,456 fans who passed through the turnstiles surpassed the existing record, which had been set in 1991, by 23.7 percent. Clearly, more people were focused on what was going on the field than what wasn't happening at the bargaining table.

During the off-season, the 28 owners continued to work on a revenue-sharing plan and, on January 18, 1994, they reached unanimous agreement on it. But, as had been noted earlier, its implementation was contingent on the players' accepting a salary cap. Perhaps, even the owners who were opposed to the idea of revenue sharing were willing to buy into it at the time because they believed that there was precious little chance, because of the players' unwillingness to accept a salary cap, that it would ever be implemented. However, if it should be, according to the preliminary guidelines and using the previous year's revenue, one-third of the clubs would have paid money, one-third would have received financial support, and one-third would have neither received nor paid any money.

The owners had been able to agree on revenue sharing, but they hadn't been able to choose a new commissioner. Without the 21 votes needed to decide on a successor to Vincent, Selig would continue as baseball's acting commissioner a while longer. However, the impact of the position was changed as a result of the owners' vote to strip the commissioner of his "in the best interest of baseball" power in labor matters. As it was stated at the time:

> The power of the commissioner to act in the best interest of baseball shall be inapplicable to any matter relating to a subject of collective bargaining between the clubs and the Major League Baseball Players Association.[10]

Before the start of serious negotiations between management and labor in March 1994, the Senate weighed in with another bill in the ongoing battle over baseball's antitrust exemption. With the owners' recent action which had redefined the commissioner's job serving as the focal point, Senator Howard Metzenbaum, Democrat of Ohio, issued the challenge, saying, "Let the baseball owners come and try to explain how destroying the job of the commissioner is in the best interest of the fans."[11]

Bud Selig—The acting commissioner would later become baseball's ninth commissioner. (National Baseball Hall of Fame Library, Cooperstown, N.Y.)

By the time the bill got to the Senate Judiciary Committee it had been revised to apply to only labor relations between major league owners and players. Like previous attempts to change the 1922 Supreme Court decision, this one also failed. On June 23, by a vote of 10 to 7, the Senate Judiciary Committee rejected the bill that would have brought baseball's labor relations under antitrust law. Had the bill been voted out of committee, some in the Senate saw a possible dilemma for at least one member of the body. George Mitchell, Democrat of Maine, was the Senate majority leader and was also considered by many to be the leading candidate to become baseball's next commissioner.

Management's negotiations with the Players Association about the Basic Agreement didn't begin in earnest until March 1994. The talks proceeded slowly. The owners planned to reintroduce a salary-cap proposal, which had been on their agenda in 1985. The plan, if accepted by the union, would impose a ceiling on how much a team could pay its players. Once again, the proposal would certainly not be acceptable to the MLBPA. The owners also sought to eliminate salary arbitration which had been a player's right for 20 years. As a carrot, the owners were willing to lower the number of years for free-agent eligibility from six to four.

The players, on the other hand, had a number of demands, including lowering the threshold for salary arbitration to two years, raising the minimum salary to $175,000 or more, and increasing the level of pension benefits for those major leaguers who had played before 1970.

The negotiating styles of Fehr and Ravitch did not make for smooth sailing. As described in *Sports Illustrated*:

> The futility of the situation is exacerbated by a prickly relationship between the two principal negotiators. In one of the first meetings, Ravitch laid out to Fehr his preferred approach to negotiations: He likes to develop a personal bond with his opposite number to facilitate a deal through backroom bargaining. Fehr was jolted by the idea.

Battle-hardened and adversarial after 17 years of negotiating for the players, he wanted no such coziness, and he would not think of excluding players from the front line. The personal conflict has heightened since. "It's a problem," admits one insider to the negotiations. "It's getting worse."[12]

The 1994 season began without a new Basic Agreement and with the possibility of baseball's fourth strike looming even larger. As negotiations continued between management and labor, the proposal for a salary cap became, predictably, the major stumbling block.

On April 21, lawyers for the owners turned over the first set of economic data to the Players Association. The financial information was the same as the owners had used to formulate their revenue-sharing plan.

The negotiating fights were just beginning, but brawls at the pitcher's mound were in full force—so much so that the players and the executives were getting together to examine what was causing them and what could be done to stop them. More pitchers were throwing inside, more batters were being hit, and the ugly confrontations between hurler and hitter had increased dramatically. Gene Orza, associate general counsel of the Players Association, remarked:

> Obviously, the time has come for some heavy thinking to see what can be done to curtail the incidents…. Somebody's going to get seriously hurt one of these times. I'm concerned about players getting serious back injuries.
>
> We'll have discussions and get the players' input on this question…. It's a question we're concerned about. It's a multifaceted matter; it's not as simple as saying don't charge the mound. There are a whole bunch of concerns to be taken into consideration. We want to do something about it. How to resolve it is another matter. It's a trickier question than anyone wants to acknowledge.[13]

The figures about how many brawls there had been in 1994 weren't released, but they were on the rise. However, other statistics were known, and perhaps they were related to the increase in hitter-pitcher confrontations. In April 1994, a record number of home runs had been hit— 708. A year earlier, *only* 498 balls had "left the yard."

One of management's proposals could not have been aimed at winning friends from the other side of the table. On May 23, the owners proposed a series of give-backs by the players in noneconomic areas. The list of more than 20 items dealt with schedules, termination of pay for released players, a reduction of credited service time from 100 percent to 50 percent while a player is on the disabled list, elimination of service time for players called to the majors in September, and other benefits which players had gained over the past 20 years.

On June 14, a cap was put on the table—the *salary cap*. The basic elements of the 27-page document, which described the cap and other matters, were:

TERM Seven years

PLAYERS' SHARE Fifty percent of gross revenue (no revenue excluded) to cover all money players receive, including salaries, bonuses, termination pay, post-season shares and pension and benefit plan. Gross revenue would include Players Association licensing revenue.

SALARY CAP Clubs can pay no less than 84 percent and no more than 110 percent of average, with average being $1/28$ of 50 percent of gross revenue.

TRANSITION PERIOD Clubs have four years to bring payrolls within the limits of the salary cap, with cap taking full effect in 1999.

GUARANTEE Player compensation in any year will not be less than 1994 compensation (in dollars, not percentage) unless gross revenue falls below 1994 total. [The owners also guaranteed the players $1 billion a year over the seven years.]

FREE AGENCY Players can be free agents after four years in the major leagues (instead of the present six), but clubs will have right of first refusal for five and six year players, meaning they can match offers from other teams.

SALARY ARBITRATION An escalating scale of minimum salaries for players in their first year through their fourth year will replace salary arbitration, with the scale of salaries to be negotiated.[14]

Two days later, the Players Association's executive board met in Chicago to discuss management's proposal. They also considered going on strike during the regular season.

A players' strike was a distinct possibility unless the two sides reached agreement in the not-too-distant future. It was hard to imagine that players would be willing to play out the season without a new Basic Agreement and then face the possibility that the owners would impose the salary cap and other elements of their package at some point during the off season. Management had refused to pledge that it would not take that step. A preemptive strike by the players during the season, while they still had the leverage, appeared to be in their best interest. They would be almost powerless if they chose to strike after management imposed their package. At the Chicago meeting, the players did not set a strike date, but discussions were held about doing so in the near future.

Fehr spoke about the players' feelings about the salary cap which he saw as a way to artificially limit salaries:

> We have never seen a cap which would do anything other than lower salaries.... It would be impossible for me to envision owners proposing a cap that would increase player contracts. The one group that has the most experience with it, the basketball players, can't wait to get rid of the cap. They feel it has lined the owners' pockets at the expense of their fair market value.[15]

Before accepting or voting down the owners' proposal, the Players Association needed time to examine the 50-50 revenue split which management had offered. A quick perusal of the owners' approach suggested that in the end, because of the way that some of the revenue was to be treated in the new agreement, the players might in fact end up receiving a share closer to 40 percent rather than the 50 percent called for in the proposal.

There was something familiar about many of the elements in the owners' proposal. Four days before the 1985 strike, Ueberroth had presented an economic package to both union and management which sounded quite similar to the 1994 effort to bring salaries under control. Items in Ueberroth's plan included: the team's right of first refusal in the free-agent process; free agency after four years instead of six; the elimination of salary arbitration; and an escalating minimum salary for players in their first four years. Neither side was excited about the proposals in 1985; only one side was interested in pursuing them nine years later.

The two sides met in early July to discuss the salary cap. The talks also included yet another reminder of Ueberroth and his time in the commissioner's office as the negotiators also spent time discussing a drug policy for baseball, which had been without one since October 1985. The clubs and the players had both indicated that they would like to see the reinstitution of some form of a joint program.

On July 18, the Players Association flat-out rejected the owners' salary cap proposal. Fehr, speaking for the players, reasoned, "The concept we've received [the salary cap proposal] would destroy free agency, harm competitive balance, principally benefit large-market clubs, reduce incentives to grow the business. We are not about doing any of those things."[16]

The union's representatives put their demands on the table. Management immediately said that the players' proposals to restore eligibility for salary arbitration from three to two years, as it had been before the 1985 agreement, and an increase in the minimum salary from $109,000 to between $175,000 and $200,000 would create more economic hardship · for the game. Management quickly voted down the players' proposals.

On July 28, with the gulf between the two sides widening both economically and philosophically, the union set their strike date—August 12—but they also let it be known that they believed there was still a ray of hope that a strike could be averted.

The players expressed disapproval that management had left the bargaining work to their negotiator and said they wanted the owners to rejoin them in the talks so that they could have more direct dialogue with them. Ravitch reminded the Players Association that he had been chosen to negotiate for the owners and, like large corporations where the Board of Directors don't sit at their bargaining table, the owners didn't need to be at baseball's.

The union did not get the owners to the table, but they did receive a final "message" from them. On August 1, Fehr received a letter stating that management's contribution to the pension and benefit plan, which was due on that date and represented one-seventh of the owners' $57 million annual contribution, would not be paid. The remaining six-sevenths of the money was due on November 1. A look back showed that management had made the payment on August 1, 1985, as that strike approached.

The owners' action raised the anger level of many of the players and had them calling for an immediate work stoppage. Management's rationale for withholding the money was that they were not obligated to pay it because the Basic Agreement had expired. Since they were currently in collective bargaining about how much money would be allotted to the pension and benefit plan in the new Agreement, they reminded the players that they did not know how much the payment would be. They advised the Players Association that the money would be paid, once that figure was agreed upon.

As the championship season and the negotiating struggles edged into August, a strangeness fell over the game. Teams began to talk about the magic number needed to win their division. The Yankees' clinching number was three in the American League East. The Cleveland Indians and the Chicago White Sox were locked in a race to the wire in the AL Central as were the Oakland A's, Seattle Mariners, and the Rangers in the AL West. The Montreal Expos and the Los Angeles Dodgers led their divisions in the National League and the Astros and the Reds were hooked up in a tight race in the NL Central.

Many thought if the players did go out on strike on August 12 that the owners would make every effort to reach an agreement so that, at least, the postseason would be salvaged and they wouldn't lose the 75 percent of their television revenue from those games. Therefore the standings on August 12 would have earlier than usual importance for a number of the clubs.

Personal accomplishments were also in the news as a probable strike approached. San Diego's Tony Gwynn, who was hitting a robust .392, was daring to become baseball's first .400-hitter since 1941 when Ted Williams hit .406. The White Sox' Frank Thomas and the Indians' Albert Belle were battling to accomplish a rare feat not seen since Carl Yastrzemski did it in 1967—winning a Triple Crown.

Fehr and Ravitch hit the talk show circuit together, making appearances on *Nightline*, David Brinkley's show, and other programs. When the two negotiators were off-camera and at the bargaining table, the talks moved away from the basic disagreement—the salary cap—and on to less contentious issues such as a drug program.

Peter Angelos, who had become the owner of the Orioles in 1994, was another voice heard from as the season's possible conclusion was in sight. He viewed the cast-in-stone disagreement between the owners and the players as to whether or not the clubs were making or losing money as the most difficult question of all. Angelos suggested that an independent Presidential commission be given the responsibility of sifting through the clubs' financial records and coming up with a true assessment of gains and losses which both sides could accept as fact. Joint committees of owners and players, even when guided by outside professionals as had been tried in the past, had never produced an assessment which both sides trusted.

As August 12 approached, there was silence from Milwaukee where Selig sat, 1000 miles away from Manhattan. The Executive Council, which was Major League Baseball's ruling body in the absence of a duly-elected commissioner, was equally silent.

Attempts to bring the resources of the federal government into the dispute in an effective way failed. President Bill Clinton said that he was unable to use the power of his office to prevent the strike and his offer of negotiating assistance from Government offices did not generate hope on either side.

Robert Reich, the Secretary of Labor, made a foray into the struggle while attending a game at Fenway Park in Boston on August 7. He asked fans of all ages to write letters urging the players and the owners to continue talking and to send them to him at the Labor Department. He said, "I can assure you if every kid sends it to me, I will make sure it gets to both sides."[17]

But by then there was little hope of avoiding a strike. And if the players walked out, hope of restarting the season, as had been done in 1972, 1981, and 1985, was slim. No eleventh-hour savior rode in with the right message to settle the mess and, with the conclusion of the games on Thursday, August 11, major league baseball's fourth strike was on.

In a pair of articles in the *New York Times*, which appeared only two days apart, George Vecsey wrote about the nostalgia of the game and then the disappointing reality of what, for him, it had become. First, he described the afternoon of the eleventh of August when New York met Toronto in venerable Yankee Stadium:

> It was one of the sweetest ways to spend a summer afternoon that Americans have ever devised, and the kids must have been thrilled when the game went into extra innings, hoping for lots of doubles and outs at the plate and lineup changes, and maybe the Yanks and Blue Jays would play forever, with the shadows creeping over the field, holding off the strike, but ultimately the Yankees lost, 8–7, in the 13th inning, and maybe the season was over, too.[18]

On the second day of the shutdown, Vecsey wrote:

> Here's the best thing we can do about this baseball strike: We can permit ourselves another day or two to wallow in self-pity, a lost weekend of the soul. And then we can get on with our lives.
> I personally plan not to dwell on vanished baseball in the coming weeks and months and maybe even years. They got themselves into it; let them get themselves out of it.[19]

Soon after the walkout began, management and labor accepted an offer of assistance from the Federal Mediation and Conciliation Services. The two sides held confidential meetings with a mediation team in the hope that they could reach an agreement so that the regular season could start again as it had in earlier work stoppages. That did not happen in 1994. The new, expanded postseason, with its promise of added excitement for the fans and additional income for players and owners, also became a victim of the strike.

For the record, the Expos posted the season's best record with a 74-40 mark, which gave them a six-game lead over the Atlanta Braves in the National League East. Cincinnati topped the Central Division by one-half game over the Astros, and Los Angeles held a three and a half game advantage over the Giants in the West. The New York Yankees took the American League East with a 70-43 record, six and a half games in front of Baltimore, and the White Sox captured the Central Division, finishing one game in front of the Indians. The Rangers edged the Athletics by a game in the West. Atlanta and Cleveland had won baseball's first pair of wild-card tickets to the non existent postseason.

Interestingly, in a year when there had been considerable discussion about richer and poorer clubs, it was noted that the Expos, with the majors' best record, had baseball's second lowest payroll and the Detroit Tigers, with the second highest payroll, finished in the basement in the American League East.

Major League Baseball had set an attendance record in 1993 when 70,256,456 people came to the games in the 30 ballparks. In 1994, approximately 70 percent of the schedule was played and the 50,010,016 fans who came through the turnstiles represented another record in the making.

With the season behind them, many expected that during the off-season management and labor would reach agreement on the tough issues that had brought major league baseball to a standstill in 1994. The vision of the 1995 season, culminating in the crowning of a World Champion, presented a hopeful winter dream.

CHAPTER ELEVEN

Baseball Returns Without a New Basic Agreement

On August 14, 1994, nearly two weeks after the start of the strike, 12 club owners and executives and half a dozen players sat down, face-to-face, in the Astor Room of the Hotel Inter-Continental in Manhattan to hold their first meeting since the work stoppage began. The players had gotten owners back at the table, something they had hoped to do earlier but hadn't been able to make happen. The day-long meeting, which included a number of caucuses by each side, accomplished little, other than getting management and labor talking again.

A few days prior to the meeting, the MLBPA had issued a report on the clubs' finances which they had commissioned Roger Noll, a Stanford University economist, to produce. Noll was not new to the scene, having analyzed the clubs' financial data for the Players Association during the 1985 contract negotiations. His finding in that report disputed the owners' claims of financial hardship caused by rising player salaries.

The 1994 Noll report, which was based on figures supplied by the clubs, said that the owners' financial problems were primarily caused by excessive general and administrative costs and not by the amount of money going to pay their players. The report also looked ahead and found fault with baseball's new television arrangement, The Baseball Network (TBN), and predicted that the owners would be in for more financial hard times because of the reduced revenue projected to come from the joint venture with ABC and NBC.

The 65-page report covered a wide range of issues and drew conclusions which the union expected management to either challenge or disregard. Among them were:

> The clubs' 1994 profit-and-loss projections, which said that 19 clubs would lose money, are inaccurate because their revenue projections

are wrong. Baseball's financial statements persistently understate the actual financial performance of all teams and the claim of widespread financial disaster in the sport is pure fiction...

Total player compensation in professional baseball, contrary to widespread belief, is not increasing faster than revenues and can't reasonably be said to be causing a decline in the financial status of the sport.

A salary cap "is not only unwarranted but pernicious." [Noll contended that a salary cap would increase profits of large- and medium-market teams but reduce profits of teams in small markets.][1]

In September and October there was a flurry of activity, but none of it was on the field of play and very little involved conversations between management and labor. On September 14, the owners voted 26–2 to cancel the remainder of the 1994 regular season and the postseason. Baltimore Orioles' owner Peter Angelos, who had been outspoken against some of management's positions during the negotiations, was one of the parties not voting for or signing the resolution. He agreed with canceling the season, but was against placing the blame on the Players Association. Marge Schott, the Cincinnati Reds' owner who had had little to say since the start of the strike, also did not support the move. The strike, which was 32 days old at the time of the owners' decision, thereby became a work stoppage of at least 52 days, surpassing 1981's 50-day record.

The baseball world would have to wait for the first-ever League Division Series (LDS), and the pair of freshman league presidents, Gene Budig (American League) and Leonard Coleman (National League) would not be crowning their first champs until at least 1995. The World Series was canceled for the first time since 1904 when New York Giants' manager John McGraw had refused to let his National League champions go to battle against the Boston Pilgrims of the upstart American League.

Claire Smith, writing in the *New York Times*, said:

The abyss that [Donald] Fehr and others long feared baseball flirted with in each of the game's eight work stoppages finally swallowed the game yesterday. Labor discord managed to do what the Kaiser, Hitler and the Great Depression could not: bring the national pastime to the ground in ignominious defeat and disgrace. That fate was made official yesterday when Bud Selig, the acting commissioner, canceled the rest of the 1994 season....

Who, what and how, not when, are now the pertinent questions. As is why. Why could 700 players and 28 owners not set aside issues of power, greed and ego long enough to divide a multibillion-dollar pie? Why is it that this unending feud was allowed to do the unbelievable and give the game its own sorry date that will live in infamy?[2]

At the time of the season's cancellation, a double bill was taking place in Congress, and, once again, the antitrust issue was being batted around. In the Senate, Howard Metzenbaum, Democrat of Ohio, and Orrin Hatch, Republican of Utah, were hoping to pass a floor amendment tacked onto other legislation that would remove part of baseball's antitrust exemption if the owners unilaterally imposed new labor conditions. In the House, Judiciary Committee chairman Jack Brooks, Democrat of Texas, had scheduled a hearing for September 22 to discuss the antitrust exemption in the Economic and Commercial Law subcommittee.

Brooks was intent on addressing the issue because, as the law currently stood, baseball players couldn't sue over illegal restraints of trade because the owners were allowed to practice illegal restraints of trade. He wanted that situation changed, and endorsed legislative initiatives that would repeal the game's antitrust exemption in areas of labor relations at the major league level.

Players and owners testified before the subcommittee, with each side presenting its view of the antitrust exemption. In the end, the House Judiciary Committee voted to eliminate baseball's exemption from antitrust laws if the owners imposed a salary cap on the players. Metzenbaum's and Hatch's effort in the Senate was unsuccessful.

Writing for the *New York Times*, Jim Bunning, a Republican Representative from Kentucky and former major league pitcher and an early leader of the MLBPA, described what he thought was the downside of the exemption:

> The antitrust exemption gives the owners every incentive to try to break the union. In turn, because the exemption makes it impossible to challenge unfair labor practices under the law, it forces the players to play hardball in labor negotiations.[3]

Lee MacPhail, former two-term president of the American League and later president of the Player Relations Committee (PRC), presented the position that the exemption was necessary for the game:

> Baseball is in a different position from that of football and basketball. While those two sports take their players from college, baseball must develop its players through the minor leagues. College football and basketball programs receive huge financial support from their institutions; baseball farm clubs, by contrast, depend on their major league affiliates. Next to players' salaries, this is the most expensive part of most major league operations. The major league clubs pay the salaries (and signing bonuses) of their minor league players, managers,

coaches and trainers. They provide uniforms and equipment. Few minor league clubs could exist without these subsidies.

If the antitrust exemption were repealed, major league teams would be likely to lose control of their minor league players. If the minor league clubs could not continue, the caliber of play in the majors would be seriously damaged. Even more important, hundreds of cities would lose professional baseball—and minor league baseball truly contributes to the quality of life in many parts of the country.[4]

The strike was taking money out of the pockets of many associated with the game. Some employees of Major League Baseball and a number of those who worked for individual clubs were laid off. Concessionaires and those who sold merchandise and memorabilia at the ballparks were without jobs. The Players Association filed default notices on the part of 18 players who had been recalled from minor to major league teams the week before the strike began or during the first week of September when the clubs expanded their rosters from 25 to 40 players. Those players were not being paid either their minor or major league salaries. Gene Orza, the Players Association's associate general counsel, argued that those players should be declared free agents under the provisions of the Uniform Player's Contract.

On October 5, management put the next bone of contention on the table—an off-season freeze. What they wanted was to push back the free-agent filing period and other off-season dates and rules until November 15. The timing of the free-agency season was an important issue for the owners, and a delay would allow them the opportunity to revise their salary cap proposal based on an estimated $600 million of lost revenue because of the season's shutdown.

An agreement on the delay request was not reached between the two parties, and free-agency filings took place at the usual time. Another debatable issue arose because of the filings. By October 25, 111 players had filed and 11 of them, including Jim Abbott of the New York Yankees and Jack McDowell of the Chicago White Sox, needed some or all the 52 strike days to reach free-agent eligibility. The debate between the union and management centered on whether, as the players believed, time on a club's active roster was counted as service time, or, as the owners argued, service time can only accumulate when the game is being played! The matter most directly affected the 11 players whose eligibility for free agency was in question, but, in point of fact, every major leaguers' service time was at stake.

President Bill Clinton had not had an impact on the negotiations prior to the strike; perhaps his administration could be an effective force with the work stoppage in full swing. On October 14, Secretary of Labor Robert Reich brought 70-year-old Bill Usery, Jr., who was considered by many to be the nation's leading mediator, onto the going-nowhere, getting-angrier collective bargaining scene. Hopefully, with his skills, he would be able to bring the warring parties back to the table and help them reach an agreement to end professional sports' longest strike. Perhaps, Usery would come to the meeting between the Hatfields and the McCoys armed with the wisdom of Solomon.

Five days later in Washington, representatives of the two sides met together in a formal session for the first time in 40 days. It was a getting-to-know-you gathering, and there was a faint ray of hope emanating from some of the reports from the meeting. As reported in the *New York Times*:

> If the words their chief labor executive [Richard Ravitch] spoke today were not simply rhetoric, major league baseball club owners may be backing away from their "three-imp" plan: impose a freeze on free-agent signings, declare an impasse in negotiations for a new labor agreement and implement the salary cap they covet.[5]

Before the more serious talks began on November 10, a new element entered the mix. On November 1, plans were unveiled for the late twentieth century's version of the Federal League.

Bob Mrazek, a former five-term Congressman from Long Island, John Bryant, a Congressman from Dallas, Dick Moss, formerly a counsel for the MLBPA and also a player agent—most notably for Jack Morris during the owners' collusion in 1986, and Andrew Zimbalist, an economist at Smith College, announced the formation of the United Baseball League (UBL). Curt Flood was named the league's vice president and was to be a member of the management company which would oversee the league's operation.

The founders of the new league aimed at building a working partnership between the clubs and the players. The players would receive 35 percent of a team's pretax profits and a 10 percent equity share in all teams collectively.

The UBL was projected to kickoff its inaugural season in 1996, with eight teams from the United States, one from Mexico, and one from Canada playing a 154-game schedule. It was expected that half of the players on the opening-season's rosters would have forsaken the major leagues for the UBL. International expansion in the Far East the following year was part of the founders' grand design.

Flood, speaking about the opportunity offered by the fledgling enterprise, said:

America deserves an alternative league. I just wish there was one when I played. Too often, the fans have been subject to the whims and abuses that occur when a handful own and monopolize an industry.[6]

The UBL offered a dream for the future; Major League Baseball was providing a present nightmare. Usery called management and labor back together for meetings beginning November 10, in Rye Brook, New York. The owners had met Usery's request that they choose a chairman. They appointed Boston Red Sox' CEO John Harrington to the post, with Richard Ravitch, who would soon resign effective the end of December, taking a diminished role on the owners' negotiating committee. It was a reminder of 1981 when Ray Grebey was removed as lead negotiator for the Player Relations Committee, and MacPhail moved to the head of the table. Two other owners began to play more active roles in the Rye Brook talks—Atlanta's Stan Kasten and Philadelphia's David Montgomery.

Usery had another request of the owners—that they take the salary cap off the table. Management began to move away from the goal of having a salary cap, and started to focus on the payroll tax, which had been revised from the one that had been offered on June 14. In the revised version the owners removed the previously included $1-billion-a-year guarantee for salaries. They also reintroduced the idea of a salary scale for players during their first four years of major league service in lieu of salary arbitration. For the Players Association, one was no more acceptable than the other, since a salary cap or a payroll tax would limit the amount of money available for players' salaries.

The payroll tax plan, which was somewhat similar to one that had been proposed unsuccessfully by the PRC in 1985, would not be fully implemented for four years. It would be based on a "threshold" for each season depending on the economic factors for that year. It appeared that the initial threshold would be in the neighborhood of $34 million. Any team with a payroll under that amount would not be subject to a tax. For each $500,000 up to $5 million that a club exceeded the tax threshold, it would pay a 1 percent tax. Beyond that level, the club would be assessed an additional 1 percent tax for each $250,000 increment. The aggregate tax—to be known as a "luxury tax"—would be the sum of all the 1 percent penalties applied to *the club's entire payroll*. Had there been an uninterrupted season in 1994 and based on the salary figures for that year, the tax plan, if it had been in place, would have produced $193 million in taxes from 18 clubs. The Yankees would have been the largest contributor, paying $31 million.

The addition of one player could have a significant effect on a team that was at or near the threshold. If the team had a $33 million payroll, it would be under the threshold and not liable for any payroll tax. However, if it acquired a player whose salary was $5 million, its total payroll would become $38 million, which would put the team $4 million over the threshold. Under the proposed guidelines of the plan, the team would have to pay an 8 percent tax on its *entire payroll amount [38 million]* which would amount to $3.04 million. The total coast of the new $5-million acquisition would have become $8.04 million! The Players Association viewed that scenario as being extremely restrictive!

If "payroll tax" was the buzz phrase during the talks that began in Rye Brook, other words became the focal point after the negotiators moved their discussions to Leesburg, Virginia, outside of Washington, D.C. They were "replacement players."

Some owners were committed to beginning the 1995 spring training and the regular season on time even if an agreement was not reached and the striking players would not go back to work. They were talking about using other players to replace those on the major league rosters. Colorado Rockies' owner Jerry McMorris was one of those who proposed the idea. Harrington, responding to McMorris' view, said:

> If we have to do that, it will be with a great deal of reluctance.... What Jerry is saying is in the minds of all the baseball owners. We want to make a commitment to the fans that we're going to play the 1995 season with some caliber of professional baseball player.
>
> We believe it will be entertaining and we believe that's what the fans want. Our preference is to put major league players out there, but if they're unwilling to play, then we'll have to go with someone else who's willing to play. It's something we don't want to do, and we're working in every respect away from that.[7]

In 1987 the National Football League had hired and used replacement players for a three-week period in October after the regulars walked out on September 28. They were striking because the owners were unwilling to include free agency in a new collective bargaining agreement.

Peter Widdrington, Toronto's owner, announced that the Blue Jays and strike-breaking baseball players wouldn't mix in Canada, since Ontario law barred replacement workers from taking the jobs of strikers. If the club went the replacement route, they were considering playing their home games at their spring training ballpark in Dunedin, Florida.

Angelos, who had a long career as a labor lawyer, was vehemently opposed to using replacement players and was considering not allowing the Orioles to play their regular season schedule. The club would be in a difficult situation if the season were to open without the regulars since Cal Ripken's unbelievable consecutive-game streak, which stood at 2009 games, would come to an end.

When it became known that some in management believed that Latin players would defect from the union in large numbers and report to spring training, members of the Players Association lashed out. The Orioles' Raphael Palmeiro, a Cuban native, fired back at the owners, saying, "That's ridiculous. I think that's a racist statement. They're degrading the Latin players. Latin players are going to do what the other players do. Let me tell you, if anybody crosses that line, it's not going to be a Latin player."[8]

In early December, "implementation" became another key word. Management had threatened to unilaterally implement their salary cap proposal if a new agreement was not reached, and implementation time was drawing near. Usery was successful in persuading the owners' negotiating committee to hold off on their action in order to give the MLBPA an opportunity to present a proposal of their own.

On December 10, the Players Association came back to management with their ideas for breaking the log jam and ending the four-month-old strike. Their plan called for a flat tax of about 5 percent on club payrolls (which was later stated to be 5.02 percent), a contribution of at least $30 million of their money to an industry growth fund of $60 million (half of which was to come from management), and giving players input in crucial matters such as expansion and television contracts. The union's stated goal was to form a partnership with management in order to generate greater revenue to help pay player salaries and to produce increased profits for the clubs.

A number of ideas were proposed for an industry growth fund which would involve the two sides working together to create new revenues by promotional and community service activities, licensing ventures, advertising and marketing projects, the development of new and emerging media technologies, and other opportunities which might arise. A committee of four players, four owners, and staff members from both management and the union would administer the funds.

After the presentation of the union's payroll tax plan, differences between the approaches of the two sides remained. The Players Association's tax was based on a set percentage that would become effective immediately upon the signing of a new Basic Agreement. Management's proposal involved a limitless tax on teams that were over the threshold and would be phased in and not be fully implemented until the fourth year. The players' plan would generate $58 million which was the same amount the owners' approach would provide for the low-revenue clubs through the revenue-sharing plan they had adopted in January.

The management committee returned the next day with a new proposal. They had altered their position on the tax question and presented a payroll tax plan that began with a flat 4.64 percent tax. However, it didn't end there. They also wanted to maintain a secondary tax that would be levied on teams whose combined salaries were more than the designated threshold.

The competing proposals created an interesting scenario that illustrated the opposing positions:

> The clubs would maintain the elements of the revenue-sharing plan they adopted last January, moving $58 million to the low-revenue clubs in the way they originally designed. They would then take the $35 million raised by the payroll tax and use $10 million of it each year for their share of the growth fund and distribute the remaining $25 million to clubs based on the ratio between their revenues and their payrolls.
>
> Clubs like the [New York] Mets and the Colorado Rockies would benefit the most because this year they had high revenue and low payrolls. Under the players' plan, the Mets and the Rockies would pay money into the revenue-sharing pool, but under the owners' proposal, those teams would get money back from the tax pool. The clubs would thus be encouraged to make as much money as they want; just don't spend it on salaries.[9]

On December 11, there was some clarity given to the use of replacement players when it was announced that the United States Labor Department had certified the strike. As a result of the action, the Immigration and Naturalization Service would not grant visas to foreign players who might want to replace the striking major leaguers.

Players and owners were unable to come up with an agreement that would satisfy both sides—although for a brief period of time it looked as if they were close to a deal. The last bit of movement came on December 20 when the Players Association raised their flat rate to 5.25 percent and included a new floating tax on revenues, starting at 2.05 percent for 1995. The latter approach was an attempt to satisfy the owners who had proposed a somewhat similar form of taxation. However, nothing came of the proposals and the talks ended without an agreement.

On December 23, Major League Baseball's (MLB) executive council declared that the negotiations in the 133-day-old strike were at an impasse and they were taking unilateral action. Harrington made the announcement:

> Due to the continued existence of this deadlock and the need to pre-
> pare for the 1995 season, the executive council voted today to exer-
> cise Major League Baseball's right under Federal Labor Law to
> implement the clubs' final salary cap proposal, effective 12:01 A.M.
> EST Dec. 24, 1994.[10]

Harrington's announcement angered several senior members of Congress and they spoke as if baseball's bouncing ball was back in their court.
Daniel Patrick Moynihan, Democrat of New York, said that he would
introduce legislation titled the "National Pastime Preservation Act" on
January 4, the Senate's first day of the 104th Congress. Sensing the mood
of the Senate, Moynihan gave the bill to end baseball's antitrust exemption in labor issues close to a 100 percent chance of passing. Hatch, who
had earlier sought to end the exemption, said that he would do all in his
power to push the legislation to the Senate floor as quickly as possible.
He reasoned:

> I am fast becoming convinced that the majority of the owners are
> trying to break the players' association.... I don't want to become
> involved in collective bargaining negotiations, but I'm starting to
> believe, like many people, that these negotiations are not being done
> in good faith.[11]

In the House of Representatives, Michael Bilirakis, Republican of
Florida, planned to introduce a bill that would call for the complete repeal
of the game's exemption under the sports broadcasting act.

Another bill was introduced in the House that would require the
owners and players to submit to binding legislation if they didn't reach
agreement by February 1.

Taking Congress's action more seriously than ever, a cadre of owners made their way to Washington to become lobbyists and make visits
to Senators and Representatives in order to impress upon them the historic and current importance of the antitrust exemption for baseball.

While members of Congress were gearing up for the antitrust hearings, there was action beginning at the state level. Richard Brodsky,
Democrat from Westchester County, New York, introduced a bill in the
New York State Assembly that would prevent the Mets and Yankees from
playing with replacement players in Shea and Yankee Stadiums. A similar bill which would affect the Orioles had been introduced by the Baltimore (Maryland) City Council.

On January 5, the owners' negotiating committee sent a letter signed
by Harrington to the players. For Fehr, the letter was propaganda. The

union's leader was mainly referring to the section in which the committee said:

> At the time of the strike vote, perhaps you were told that: (1) the owners would fold in a couple of weeks; (2) the owners would never let your strike cancel the post-season; and (3) the strike was the only sure way to prevent the clubs from implementing the salary cap.[12]

The letter also accused the union of not having been focused on reaching a settlement in November and December and having spent too much time lobbying in Washington and too little time at the bargaining table.

MLB's executive council, on January 13, anticipating that the two sides would not reach an agreement, approved guidelines for the use of replacement players for the 1995 season which would begin with spring training on February 16. Tentative plans were for the clubs to pay each player at the $115,000 minimum salary for the first-year players. The salary was prorated at $628.42 per day (based on a 183-day season) in case the replacement players weren't needed because of a strike settlement. Should the strike not end by the start of the regular season, each club would carry 32 players with 25 to be declared eligible for each game.

In response to management's action, the Players Association advised all players on the clubs' 40-man rosters not to report to spring training.

General managers and other club officials were busy seeking players to fill our their rosters. Players who had retired or had been released and six-year minor league free agents were the primary source of replacements. Others who had never worn a professional uniform made their way to tryouts camps, carrying both a glove and a dream.

Player agents were not of any help to the clubs in their search for talent since they were certified by the union and didn't want to appear to be helping strikebreakers.

Managers, coaches, and trainers, who were union members, would find themselves in a difficult position should their clubs expect them to work with the replacement players.

On February 1, after 40 days of absenting themselves from the bargaining table, the two sides sat down together to begin talking again. President Clinton had been the major impetus for delivering them from the wilderness of silence. Three days earlier he had given management and labor until February 6 to make substantial headway towards an agreement or the Government would ask Usery to propose a solution.

Harrington and Chuck O'Connor, who had served earlier as the owners' lead negotiator and was now their chief labor lawyer, presented a new

Paul Darcy, a replacement hopeful, leaves an Atlanta Braves tryout at Dekalb College. Darcy displays his contract demands! (*The Atlanta Journal-Constitution*)

luxury tax proposal. The owners would tax payrolls over $35 million in two tiers—75 percent for the portion between $35 and $42 million and 100 percent for the portion beyond $42 million. The two major changes from management's earlier proposals were that a club that went above the threshold would not have its entire payroll taxed and the threshold would not be adjusted annually as had been built into earlier plans. The money coming from the tax would be used for the owners' payment to the players' pension and benefit plan. The Players Association was quick to reject the owners' new proposal.

The National Labor Relations Board (NLRB) joined the action and used its position to convince the owners to rescind the salary cap they had implemented six week earlier. The Board's power came in the form of advising the owners that they would file an unfair labor complaint against them unless they scrapped the salary cap. The cap was removed on February 3.

The NLRB's action set off a "battle of freezes" between the two sides. The Players Association responded by removing the signing freeze that they had put in place after the salary cap was unilaterally imposed by management. Fehr warned the owners that a failure on their part to sign free agents would constitute an act of collusion. The clubs quickly countered by imposing a signing freeze of their own. They delegated their power to sign players to the Player Relations Committee, their labor arm, until the two sides reached a new collective bargaining agreement.

On February 6, which was D-Day—Deadline Day—acting commissioner Bud Selig, who had not taken an active role in the talks, led management's delegation to the White House to meet with Clinton, Vice President Al Gore, Reich, and Usery. The owners' team consisted of Harrington, O'Connor, McMorris, Stuart Meyer who had been the former CEO of the St. Louis Cardinals, Rob Manfred who was with the law firm of Morgan Lewis & Bockius, and Selig. The Players Association was represented by Fehr, Orza, the Pittsburgh Pirates' Jay Bell, the Kansas City Royals' David Cone, the Detroit Tigers' Cecil Fielder, the Atlanta Braves' Tom Glavine, and free agent Scott Sanderson, who had been a member of the White Sox in 1994.

Usery came prepared to offer a proposal, as the President had instructed him to do. First, his plan allowed for the 1995 season to be played under the economic system that was in place in 1994. His approach also offered a compromise in the four major items that labor and management had on the table. Using the Yankees' 1994 salaries as an example, the Federal mediator's luxury tax plan would have had New York paying a $5,335,036 tax. Under management's plan, the Yanks would pay close to $14 million and the Players Association's approach would claim $1.5 million from the club's coffers.

The compromise proposal for the players' minimum salary had an escalating scale from $125,000 to $1 million, based on the length of service. The owners' progressive range for the first four years would reach a top salary of $750,000. The players wanted a $175,000 minimum salary without any prescribed raises.

Usery also presented a plan for salary arbitration that would eliminate it, as of 1996, for players with four or more years of major league service, and eliminate it a year later for anyone else who was eligible (three-year players and 17 percent of two-year players), with those players coming under escalating minimum salaries. Players would be given unrestricted free agency after four years in the majors. Management wanted salary arbitration eliminated, with players who were eligible qualifying for restricted free agency, subject to their former club having the right of first refusal. The Players Association's plan called for the end of salary arbitration in return for unrestricted free agency or its elimination for all but three-year players and eligible two-year players with others qualifying for unrestricted free agency.

The final area of contention involved the length of a new agreement. Usery proposed a length of six years, with the option for either side to reopen it after four years and submit the tax element to binding arbitration. That plan was in between the owners' and players' proposals. Management wanted a seven-year agreement and the players sought four or five.

After it became clear that Usery's proposal was not acceptable, it was then suggested that the parties engage in extensive fact-finding before a blue-ribbon presidential commission. The upcoming season would be played under the 1994 economic rules, and after the season, the two sides could resume negotiations based on the findings of the commission. The union accepted the proposal, but the owners rejected it.

After a long, frustrating summit meeting at the White House, the parties left without any resolution. There were now four proposals on the table—Usery's, management's, the union's, and the suggestion of a fact-finding commission—and not one was acceptable to both sides. The hope for a negotiated settlement in the near future looked bleak; a disappointed President talked about asking Congress to impose binding arbitration on the game; the Republican-controlled Congress appeared reluctant to become involved in a private labor dispute; Usery's role appeared to be in jeopardy; and the possibility of replacement players looked more certain.

Hope for a "regular" regular season now seemed to reside with the Congress or with the NLRB. The Moynihan-Hatch bill, which was aimed at revoking the antitrust exemption as it applied to labor issues, was scheduled to be introduced in the Senate on February 14. A tougher bill, which was sponsored by Patrick Leahy, Democrat of Vermont, and Strom Thurmond, Republican of South Carolina, sought to completely revoke baseball's exemption, and it was on the Senate's docket. The NLRB had charges by the Players Association against the owners to consider, and the Board could end up having a powerful influence on baseball—both on and off the field.

As the major league players began to anticipate spring training without them, there were calls for unity within their ranks. There were warnings issued to those minor leaguers who would decide to follow their careers past the picket lines into the camps. Those who were sitting out the camp would "remember" those who reported. The real game would return some day, and strikebreakers would be branded as turncoats by the union membership. Philadelphia outfielder Lenny Dykstra became a lightning rod for the issue when he said in an ESPN interview that the players needed to rethink their position and suggested that the union take a more compromising position with the owners. He was soon the object of anger from other players.

Management had its own lightning rod in the person of Jerry Reinsdorf. The White Sox owner had been a hard-liner during the negotiations and was unwilling to make concessions to the players. On February 22, he blasted the union in general and Fehr in particular:

> The only hope [for an agreement] is if the players come to the realization that they are being misled by Fehr. My perception is that he is obsessed with the antitrust exemption and that he has no real interest in the welfare of his players. Donald Fehr has a pathological hatred for baseball owners.[13]

During the 1995 spring training, many players who were not on the teams' 40-man rosters were wearing major league uniforms. The clubs did not want to force their roster players to be strikebreakers. That meant that neither the teams' regulars nor their top minor leaguers were in the camps. Other minor leaguers had an important choice to make with regard to their future in the game. Many took the opportunity to show off their talent to the observing brass.

The replacement players were generally drawn from teams below the AAA level. Some clubs were also recycling retired major leaguers into their lineups. The White Sox signed 35-year-old Dennis "Oil Can" Boyd, a free-spirited pitcher in the 1980s who had last played in the majors in 1991 and had retired with a 78-77 record. The team from the north side of Chicago, the Cubs, was committed to go with youth. President and CEO Andy MacPhail and general manager Ed Lynch, both of whom had just come to the Cubs, believed that it would be to the club's long-term advantage to give enthusiastic younger players an opportunity to play and gain experience in a major league environment.

A trio of teams were having particular problems with the prospect of opening the season with replacement players and, perhaps, playing the entire campaign with them. Because of Ontario law, the Toronto Blue Jays were planning to play their regular season home games in Dunedin, Florida. Montreal, which might have had problems because of Quebec's similar regulations against using replacement workers to take the jobs of those who were legally on strike, was exempted and given permission to play in the Canadian city. The Orioles, whose owner was opposed to any use of replacement players, cancelled the first 12 games of their exhibition schedule and were expected to wipe out the remainder of their 32-game slate rather than play against other clubs who had the strikebreakers in their lineups.

The players on the clubs' 40-man rosters and others practiced on their own, attempting to work themselves into playing shape should a sudden agreement be reached. More than 800 of them were still unsigned and over 100 players were listed as free agents. Even with an agreement, there would be much to be done on the financial scene before an opening pitch could be thrown.

On the 200th day of the strike, two teams of five negotiators met each other in Scottsdale, Arizona, to revive the dormant talks. For a while the tone of the discussions was hopeful. During the third day of meetings, Fehr, speaking about a decision to meet a second time that day in even smaller groups, said, "It's an indication that there's some chance for a better dialogue in a smaller group.... There's a mutual interest in continuing the discussions."[14]

Selig added to the optimistic atmosphere, saying, "We delved into issues in a much deeper manner. We got to the heart of the matter on a number of subjects."[15]

However, hope vanished as quickly as it had appeared, and the future of the talks seemed bleak.

With the talks in recess, the NLRB came on the scene. The union had filed an unfair labor practice charge with the Board that was based on the owners having ended salary arbitration and having not followed the directives against collusion regarding free agents as they had been agreed to in the last Basic Agreement. The NLRB was considering whether or not to seek an injunction against the clubs. The Players Association had already made it clear that they would return to work if an injunction was issued that required the clubs to restore the economic terms of the most recent Basic Agreement.

With April 2, the scheduled opening day of the regular season, rapidly approaching, Fred Feinstein, the NLRB's general counsel, sought to speed up the Board's consideration of the union's charges. Once the NLRB got rolling, there was no stopping it. Whereas the talks had slumbered along, the Board's work did not.

On March 26, the NLRB voted 3–2 to seek an injunction against the club owners, and a hearing was set for Friday, March 31, in United States District Court in Manhattan before Federal Judge Sonia Sotomayor. The government's wheels were in motion!

On the day of the NLRB's vote, the owners put a new payroll tax proposal on the table. The plan raised the threshold from $40 million to $44 million, but the plan would place a 50 percent tax on the portion above the threshold. They also made some changes in their stance regarding salary arbitration and free agency. For the first time, the owners proposed a three-person panel to hear and decide arbitration cases, rather than a single person as had been the procedure to that point. The payroll tax plan was still the central issue and the gap between the owners' plan and the current union plan, which had a $54 million threshold and a 25 percent tax, was still too great, and hopes for a last-minute settlement ended.

Sotomayor reviewed the two sides' briefs and came prepared for the March 31 showdown. After a 98-minute hearing and an 18-minute recess, the Federal judge read her 47-minute opinion in which she issued a temporary injunction against Major League Baseball's clubs. In the swift and stern ruling, Sotomayor instructed the clubs to reinstate salary arbitration, to participate in competitive bidding for the available free agents and to follow the anti-collusion guidelines. She also warned against the imposition of any new work rules in the absence of a new Basic Agreement.

The ruling set the stage for the players to return to work if the owners would allow them to return. The owners' first response was to seek an immediate stay of the injunction, but that request was denied. There was some brief discussion among management about locking the players out again, but that path was not taken.

During meetings in Chicago on April 2—the 234th day of the longest strike in professional sports history and the day originally set for the Mets and the Marlins to open the 1995 regular season in Florida—management accepted the players' offer to return to the field of play and opening day was rescheduled for April 26. The clubs were going to play a shortened 144-game schedule.

The owners allowed those on the clubs' 40-man rosters to come to a second edition of spring training, and the replacement players were released from the major league rosters. Those who had already been on a minor league roster and some who were signed for the first time during the strike made their way back to minor league camps. Since the owners were appealing Sotomayor's ruling, they had to be ready to replace the regulars should they win the appeal and the players vote to walk out again.

The strange circumstances of the 1995 spring training were nowhere more evident than in Homestead, Florida, where 29 unsigned players worked out in the majors' twenty-ninth camp. The Homestead operation was organized by the union for the benefit of those players who were not yet under contract for the new season. The early arrivals were only a reliable closer short of being able to field a formidable major league club. Perhaps the closer would appear from among others who would soon make their way to Homestead.

Some players took pay cuts when they signed. For example, Bob Welch, who had made $2.9 million with Oakland in 1994, was re-signed for $225,000 and no performance bonus. Catcher Pat Borders, who had been paid $2.5 million by Toronto a year earlier, signed with the Royals for $310,000. It appeared to be a buyer's market!

The season began without a new labor agreement, but the longest and costliest work stoppage in professional sports history was over. Baseball was still operating under the guidelines of the 1990–93 Basic Agreement. Future negotiations would hopefully lead, in the not-too-distant future, to baseball's eighth Basic Agreement.

Before that, however, Major League Baseball had a more pressing need to reach an agreement with the umpires who had been locked out on January 1 in a contract dispute. During spring training, on opening day and until May 3, replacement umpires were making the calls.

CHAPTER TWELVE

A 1996 Agreement Brings Labor Peace; Will the Future Bring War?

The agreement would not come during the 1995 campaign and it wouldn't come during the 1996 regular season either. Randy Levine, the Player Relations Committee's (PRC) chief negotiator, and the Major League Baseball Players Association's Donald Fehr headed up the bargaining teams that accomplished little during 1995.

The seats at the negotiating tables were empty most of the time. There were many empty seats in the ballparks as well. Fans were slow to welcome the game back. By the end of May, 26 of the 30 clubs had reported having fewer people at the games than they had had during the same period the previous year. With 144 playing dates in 1995 compared to 162 in 1993, one would have expected lower total attendance figures for the post-strike season. However, the figures indicated an average of 82,643 fewer customers for each of the 144 playing dates—nearly 12 million for the season.

Early in the campaign two of the replacement players—pitcher Ron Rightnowar (Milwaukee) and Ron Mahay (Boston) were recalled and met with a mixed welcome from their teammates and an uncertain future with the Players Association.

The season also witnessed a series of postponements of the trial before the administrative law judge of the National Labor Relations Board (NLRB) on the unfair labor practices charges filed by the union against the clubs. The NLRB appeared willing to keep the issue out of court and was anxious for labor and management to settle their problems by signing a new collective bargaining agreement.

Discussions about baseball's antitrust exemption continued in the halls of Congress without any resultant ruling against the game. However, in August, the owners ruled against arbitrator George Nicholau, who was best known for the collusion hearings and his decisions against the clubs. They fired Nicolau and replaced him with Nicholas Zumas.

In September, a month after announcing a television deal, the United Baseball League (UBL) delayed the start of its first season from 1996 to 1997. That was to be the last major news about the potential threat to the two existing major leagues. The twentieth century would not witness another Federal League.

Before the end of the season, the owners agreed to put $49.1 million into the players' pension and benefit plan, but that was the only progress on the labor scene during the campaign.

On September 29, a three-judge panel of the United States Court of Appeals upheld Federal Judge Sonia Sotomayor's March 31 ruling, ending the appeal process for the owners.

The postseason was back in 1995. The Colorado Rockies and the New York Yankees were baseball's first wild-card teams. Neither made it beyond the first round and eventually the Atlanta Braves beat the Cleveland Indians, 4 games to 2, to capture the World Championship.

On November 15, the 277th day after the end of the strike, the two sides finally held their first formal post-strike bargaining session. The owners' new payroll luxury tax proposal offered a slightly different approach. It included an adjusting tax system which would provide some flexibility for future negotiations. A part of the plan called for a 2.5 percent tax on each player's salary, which the union had included in one of its earlier proposals.

The two sides did not make much progress during their sporadic meetings early in 1996. However, in January, the owners had looked ahead and approved interleague play for the 1997 season. Like all matters involving change, the union would have to give its approval before the new venture could become a reality.

On March 20, the owners voted to accept a revenue-sharing plan that included some modifications from the approach which had not worked out earlier. The earlier plan was tied to a salary cap; the new one would include a 2.5 percent tax on each player's salary the first year of the agreement and an increase to 3.5 percent for the second year.

The first serious movement toward an agreement came in August. The owners' labor policy committee authorized Levine to make a "last and final offer" to the union, and if, in his judgment, that did not show promise for breaking the deadlock, he was authorized to then proceed to the United States District Court in Manhattan to ask Sotomayor to lift the injunction, based on the position that the two sides were at a legal impasse.

Serious negotiations began and reports were soon coming out of the meetings that an agreement was near. But "near" in baseball bargaining had often proved to be a fair distance away, and that was the case once again. As a deal appeared imminent, the issue of crediting service time to the players for days lost during the strike became a new, complex, and divisive issue.

Jerry Reinsdorf, the owner of the Chicago White Sox, led the owners who were adamantly against awarding service time. Some who were more moderate on the issue were willing to allow the days of service to be counted for all players except those who would become free agents or eligible for salary arbitration as a result of the days logged during the strike.

The strike had wiped out 52 days in 1994 and 23 days at the start of the 1995 season. The regular season is 183 days in length but, for service accumulation, 172 days equals one year of service. The number of days the players were seeking credit for, based on the formula, was 41 in 1994 and 12 in 1995 (11 fewer than the number of days missed in each season).

If service time was awarded, 19 additional players would become eligible for free agency and a like number would become eligible for salary arbitration. In the long run, every player would benefit from having the additional days added to their service time.

Andy MacPhail, who was a member of the owners' labor committee, was an outspoken opponent of crediting the players with service time during the strike:

> It's difficult for me seeing any kind of agreement where we would agree to give any kind of service time. They didn't play, there was no revenue generated, the game suffered considerably because of the strike.... If we give them service time now, we will never have peace.[1]

The collective bargaining negotiations continued through the 1996 postseason and beyond. On November 6, the owners voted on the proposed agreement as it stood at the time—an agreement that Levine and Fehr had both approved. With a "yes" vote of at least three-fourths of the owners needed for passage, the 18–12 vote *against* fell far short.

Less than two weeks later, Reinsdorf signed Albert Belle to a whopping five-year, $55 million contract. On the one hand the owners were trying to negotiate an agreement that would control the spiraling increases in spending, and, on the other hand, one of their own gave out the largest salary in the history of major league baseball.

Some owners were angry about Reinsdorf's action, and, although it wasn't the only reason for the eventual change of heart on the part of many of them, it certainly was a factor. Bud Selig, who had been silent earlier, had strongly urged the approval of the collective bargaining package. On November 26, the owners voted overwhelmingly, 26–4, to ratify the new agreement. A week later, the players ratified it at a meeting in Puerto Rico.

Baseball's eighth Basic Agreement was a five-year deal, retroactive to the start of the 1996 season, with the players having an option to extend it after the 2000 season through 2001. The players made major strides as a result of the package. Their minimum salary was raised to $109,000 for 1996 with graduated increases to $200,000 by 2001. All players who were on the major league rosters at the time of the strike received credit for service time during the work stoppage. In a further step, the restriction against filing for free agency twice within a five-year period was lifted. Under the new agreement, a three-person panel would hear 50 percent of the arbitration cases in 1996, 75 percent in 1999, and all of the cases in 2000.

Revenue sharing would become part of baseball at the major league level for the first time. The thirteen clubs with the highest revenues would contribute to a pool that would be distributed among the 13 clubs with the lowest revenues. The two most recent expansion clubs, Colorado and Florida, would be exempt for the first two years.

The agreement included a payroll tax for players. Using money from licensing and other revenue, the players on the 25-man roster would pay a 2.5 percent tax in 1996 and 1997. Most of that money—estimated to be $40 million for the two years—would assist in funding the shortfall in revenue sharing.

A luxury tax would not be assessed in 1996, 2000, and 2001. During the three years the tax would be in effect, it would apply only to the clubs with the five highest payrolls. In 1997 those clubs would be taxed 35 percent on that portion of the payroll over $51 million. A year later, the percentage would remain the same, but the threshold would be increased to $55 million. In 1999 the threshold would become $58.9 million with a 34 percent tax on the portion of the payroll above that amount.

The Basic Agreement also provided for interleague play for the first time in 1997. Both sides would have to renegotiate a continuation of the games for future seasons.

Major League Baseball (MLB) had the assurance that there would be at least four championship seasons and perhaps five, if the Players Association decided not to reopen the agreement after the 2000 season. After that game would be ripe for a new round of negotiations and probably struggles.

Even during the off-season for collective bargaining, it was difficult to miss the ongoing language of potential discontent: revenue sharing; free agency; salary arbitration; payroll tax (or was that a disguise for salary cap?); television and Internet revenue; realignment; expansion (or contraction); and interleague play. Each area offered grounds for both discussion and discord.

On July 14, 2000, MLB's Independent Blue Ribbon Panel on Baseball Economics issued its 87-page report based on an 18-month study of baseball's financial situation. The members of the panel—Yale University President Richard Levin who chaired the committee, Pulitzer Prize–winning political commentator George Will, former U.S. Senator from Maine George Mitchell, and former Federal Reserve Chair Paul Volcker—studied the available financial material, met with 14 team owners, and held a *one-hour* interview with the MLBPA.

The panel urged MLB to impose a 50 percent luxury tax on payrolls above $84 million; to share 40 percent to 50 percent of local revenues after ballpark expenses; to split new national broadcasting, licensing, and Internet revenue unequally to assist low revenue clubs, provided that they meet a minimum payroll of $40 million; to include foreign born players in the annual draft; to institute an annual competitive balance draft; and, when necessary, relocate franchises to address the competitive issue of the game.

As expected, the report met with mixed reviews. Selig expressed cautious optimism; Fehr was taking a wait-and-see attitude.

Carl Pohlad, long-time owner of the small-market Minnesota Twins, called the report the "best thing that's happened to baseball in 50 years ... After this report, I feel more optimistic than in a while. I don't know what Yankee owner George Steinbrenner's reaction will be."[2]

On ESPN's *Outside the Lines*, Marvin Miller, the MLBPA's founder and former executive director, in a debate with Levin on July 17, said, "I've only skimmed the report. But I have to say I'm not impressed with the proposals. I had hoped that there might be some original ideas. And I had hoped that the report would be a lot more scholarly than it is."[3]

Four months later, Miller, speaking at a symposium entitled "Baseball's Future Competitive Balance and Labor Relations," which was held on November 17, 2000, at Smith College in Northampton, Massachusetts, questioned the "independent" nature of the Blue Ribbon Panel. In his remarks, he said:

They are all reputable people, but I wonder how this panel could be called independent. The four members of the panel were appointed by commissioner Selig, who is an employee of the owners. Each of the four has a long relationship with ownership and management. For example, George Will is a director of the Baltimore Orioles and the San Diego Padres. George Mitchell, who was one of the finalists for the job of commissioner when Selig was chosen, is a director of the Florida Marlins.

Throughout the study, all of the staff work was done by employees of the clubs and the commissioner's office.

To me, that doesn't sound independent.[4]

On August 28, the Players Association, as expected, exercised its option to extend the eighth Basic Agreement through October 31, 2001. The players had generally been happy with the package that had gone into effect in November 1996. Baseball would have at least five full seasons without canceled games during spring training or the regular season. That would be the longest stretch of uninterrupted seasons since the game had a six-season run from 1966 through 1971.

Stan Kasten, president of the Braves, saw the pact from the perspective of management and said:

> Certainly it's a wonderful deal for the players, and they would enjoy it continuing for many, many years…. If it's not good for the industry, it creates problems for everyone, and clearly, this deal creates problems for the industry.[5]

With a new economic report in hand and the guarantee of a complete 2000 season, the real world of financial reality was continuing to be stretched in all directions. The record for a major league payroll was broken in the Bronx. When the Yankees completed three trades that brought infielder Jose Vizcaino, outfielder David Justice and pitcher Denny Neagle to the club, their payroll rose to an all-time record $107.4 million—which was six times the payroll of the Twins.

At the Smith College Symposium in November, broadcaster Bob Costas and author of the current best-selling book, *Fair Ball: A Fan's Case for Baseball*, engaged Miller in a discussion about the financial disparity between the big-market and small-market clubs and what the future of the game might be if that disparity is allowed to continue unabated. Costas, focusing on the need for competitive balance in baseball, commented:

> I'm not saying that each major league franchise should be assured of winning the World Series once over the next 30 years.

My definition of competitive balance is that teams should have a chance to win, but there is a mountain of evidence today that baseball has a stacked deck favoring the wealthier franchises.

Baseball has two bottom lines—the competitive and the financial. The gaps between the have and have-not franchises were never as great as they are today.[6]

Miller countered Costas' position, saying:

It [competitive balance] is the new mantra.

People talk about the Yankees winning three World Series in a row, and four of the last five, but that's not new. They won four in a row in the '30s and five in a row in the '50s. The old Philadelphia A's dominated early in the 20th century, and the Oakland A's won three in a row in the '70s.

The lack of competitive balance has been part of baseball for its entire existence, and there is no reason for concern.

The Yankees now are the biggest draw in baseball on the road. The teams most likely to win draw best around the major leagues. This is nothing new.[7]

The 2000 free-agent crop, with the "fabulous four"—the New York Mets' left-hander Mike Hampton, the Baltimore Orioles' right-hander Mike Mussina, the Indians' outfielder Manny Ramirez, and the Seattle Mariners' shortstop Alex Rodriquez—heading up one of the best-ever groups of players available for the bidding, threatened to raise the salary ceiling even higher.

Many clubs had annually opened their checkbooks wide to sign the future saviors who had been taken in the annual amateur draft. The owners were usually not giving willingly; they were dealing from a one-down position. On May 15, 2000, Sandy Alderson, executive vice president of Major League Baseball Operations, invited the scouting directors of all 30 clubs to Atlanta for a meeting on negotiating salaries for the draft picks. The directors shared financial information about how much money they were planning to spend on the 2000 group of drafted players. The approach led to some success for the clubs as the agents and the draftees dug less gold out of their coffers that summer.

While the clubs were experiencing some measure of control in that area, agent Scott Boras had another youngster waiting to raise the bar on the amount of a signing contract. In 1996 Boras had been one of those who alerted some club executives that baseball rules required that a drafted high school or college player be offered a contract within 15 days or else he become a free agent. Boras had guided right-handed pitcher Matt

White, who had been picked number 7 by the San Francisco Giants and had not been offered a contract within 15 days, into the land of free agency where he obtained a long-term, big-money deal, signing for $10.2 million with the Tampa Bay Devil Rays. Three other amateurs were declared free agents that year because the drafting clubs did not follow the 15-day rule.

It had been Boras who had advised Georgia Tech catcher Jason Varitek, who had been a first-round draft pick of the Twins in 1993, to return to college for his senior year and wait for more money to flow his way in the next draft. Varitek was the Mariners' number 1 pick the following June, and he received a much larger contract from them than the Twins had offered a year earlier. From that and similar situations, some clubs learned that it was better to come up with a sizable bonus rather than lose a number 1 pick.

Boras was already set for the 2001 draft season. Landon Powell, a high school catcher from Apex, North Carolina, was projected as one of highest rated amateurs for the 2001 amateur draft. What Boras knew in 2000 and the major league general managers didn't was that Powell had passed a test for a general equivalency high school diploma. Powell was eligible for the 2000 draft—not needing another year of academic preparation. He went undrafted, and, besides his G.E.D., Powell received a ticket to free agency and offers from as many of the 30 clubs who want to send one his way!

During the off-season, the recurring issue of baseball's economics faced another round of scrutiny by the United States Senate. On November 21, the Senate Judiciary Committee's subcommittee on antitrust, business rights, and competition held its first day of hearings. Selig told the panel that it was time for sweeping changes in the game's economics, and he echoed one of Costas' themes, saying, "At the start of spring training, there no longer exists hope and faith for the fans or more than half our 30 clubs ... It is my job to restore hope and faith. I can assure you this system will be changed.[8]

The beat goes on. What will the ninth Basic Agreement bring? Only time will tell.

Notes

Chapter One

1. Albert Goodwill Spalding to O.P. Caylor of the *Cincinnati Enquirer*, January 1881, Paul Dickson, *Baseball's Greatest Quotations* (New York: Harper Perennial, 1992), 405.

2. Steve Mann, "The Business of Baseball," *Total Baseball*, Eds. John Thorn, et al. (New York: Warner Books, 1989), 629.

3. David Q. Voigt, "The History of Major League Baseball," *Total Baseball*, Eds. John Thorn, et al. (New York: Warner Books, 1989), 8.

4. *Ibid.*, 9.

5. *Ibid.*, 10.

6. *Ibid.*

7. *Ibid.*, 11.

8. *Ibid.*

9. Red Smith, "Tale of Yank Robinson's Dirty Pants," *New York Times*, 3 Apr. 1972, 51.

10. *Ibid.*

11. "The Brotherhood Meeting," *New York Times*, 7 Nov. 1889, 2.

12. "Ward's Test Case," *New York Times*, 17 Jan. 1890, 8.

13. *Ibid.*

14. Voigt, 14.

15. *Ibid.*

16. "Rusie Sues Freedman," *New York Times*, 13 Nov. 1896, 7.

17. Paul Dickson, *Baseball's Best Quotations* (New York: Harper Perennial, 1992), 24. [In 1900, quoted in *Baseball: An Informal History* by Douglas Wallop].

18. "New Baseball Agreement," *New York Times*, 6 Jan. 1901, 8.

19. "American League Organized," *New York Times*, 30 Jan. 1901, 7.

20. "Ball Players Gain a Point," *New York Times*, 27 Feb. 1901, 10.

21. *Ibid.*

22. "American League Baseball," *New York Times*, 25 Apr. 1901, 10.

23. Frederick Ivor-Campbell, "Team Histories," *Total Baseball*, Eds. John Thorn, et al. (New York: Warner Books, 1989), 57.

24. "Blow to American League," *New York Times*, 22 Apr. 1902, 6.

25. Gary D. Haley, "Baseball and the Law," *Total Baseball*, Eds. John Thorn, et al. (New York: Warner Books, 1989), 643.

26. "Blow to American League," 6.

27. "Baseball War at an End," *New York Times*, 12 Dec. 1902, 10.

28. Voigt, 15.

29. Bob Considine, "Mr. Mack," *The Fireside Book of Baseball,* Ed. Charles Einstein (New York: Simon & Schuster, 1956), 51.

Chapter Two

1. A. D. Suehsdorf, "Baseball Commissioners," *Total Baseball,* Eds. John Thorn, et al. (New York: Warner Books, 1989), 656.
2. *Ibid.,* 656–657.
3. Editorial, *New York Evening News,* 7 Oct. 1908.
4. "Baseball Players' Union," *New York Times,* 7 Aug. 1912, 7.
5. "What the Baseball Fraternity Really Is," *New York Times,* 8 Sept. 1912, Sec. 4, 2.
6. "Should Benefit Players," *New York Times,* 8 Sept. 1912, Sec. 4, 2.
7. "Cobb Whips Hilltop Fan for Insults," *New York Times,* 16 May 1912, 12.
8. "Johnson Answers and Fines Ty Cobb," *New York Times,* 26 May 1912, Sec. 2, 1.
9. Ty Cobb with Al Stump, *My Life in Baseball: The True Record* (New York: Doubleday & Company, Inc., 1961), 105.
10. *Ibid.,* 105.
11. "Congress Is Asked to Sift Baseball," *New York Times,* 23 Apr. 1913, 2.
12. *Ibid.,* 2.
13. "Cobb Must Settle His Own Case," *New York Times,* 23 Apr. 1913, 9.
14. "Ty Cobb Fined $50," *New York Times,* 15 May 1913, 9.
15. "Will Not Deal with Fultz," *New York Times,* 29 Oct. 1913, 9.
16. "To Restrict Players," *New York Times,* 30. Oct. 1913, 10.
17. "Commission to Get Busy," *New York Times,* 30 Dec. 1913, 10.
18. "Heydler on Tinker Deal," *New York Times,* 30 Dec. 1913, 10.
19. "Must Sign New Contracts," *New York Times,* 8 Jan. 1914, 12.
20. "Club Owners and Players," *New York Times,* 9 Jan. 1914, 12.
21. "Baseball Reserve Clause Is Invalid," *New York Times,* 11 Apr. 1914, 12.
22. *Ibid.,* 12.
23. "Major Leagues Hit in Chase Case," *New York Times,* 22 July 1914, 22.
24. Cobb with Stump, 108.
25. "Federals File Odd Petitions in Suit," *New York Times,* 16 Jan. 1915, 10.
26. "Deny Fed's Charge of Breaking Laws," *New York Times,* 17 Jan. 1915, Sec. 4, 1.
27. "Says Fed's Suit Is Serious," *New York Times,* 17 Jan. 1915, Sec. 4, 1.
28. "Johnson Scores Federals," *New York Times,* 25 July 1915, Sec. 3, 2.
29. "Long Baseball War Is Settled," *New York Times,* 23 Dec. 1915, 10.
30. John Eckler, Esq., "Baseball—Sport or Commerce?" *The Second Fireside Book of Baseball,* Ed. Charles Einstein (New York: Simon and Schuster, 1958), 108–109.
31. Gary D. Hailey, "Baseball and the Law," *Total Baseball,* Eds. John Thorn, et al. (New York: Warner Books, 1989), 644.

Chapter Three

1. "Landis Announces Code for Baseball Clubs in Dealing with Players," *New York Times,* 17 Jan. 1940, 26.
2. "Cardinals' Farms Rapped by Landis," *New York Times,* 24 Mar. 1938, 28.
3. John Kieran, "Letting Freedom Ring," *New York Times,* 16 Jan. 1940, 26.

4. "Landis Announces..." 26.

5. Joseph M. Sheehan, "Hearing on Yankees' Application to Restrain Pasquels Postponed," *New York Times*, 8 May 1946, 30.

6. "U.S. Ruling Restores Coast Veteran's Job," *New York Times*, 6 May 1946, 24.

7. Frederick Turner, *When the Boys Came Back* (New York: Henry Holt & Company, 1996), 136.

8. "Says Owen Is Not Wanted," *New York Times*, 3 Apr. 1946, 33.

9. "Majority Claimed on 6 Clubs by Guild," *New York Times*, 5 June 1946, 27.

10. "Chandler Sympathizes with Quest of Ball Players for Improved Lot," *New York Times*, 3 Aug. 1946, 9.

11. "Moguls, Players Agree on Reforms," *New York Times*, 6 Aug. 1946, 18.

12. Geoffrey C. Ward and Ken Burns, *Baseball: An Illustrated History* (New York: Alfred A. Knopf, 1994), 353.

13. *Ibid.*, 354.

14. "Baseball Exiles Oppose Gardella," *New York Times*, 11 Feb. 1949, 30.

15. "Congressman Fears Gardella's Action May Kill Baseball," *New York Times*, 11 Feb. 1949, 30

16. Arthur Daley, "From Abner Doubleday to Danny Gardella," *New York Times*, 11 Feb. 1949, 30.

17. "Ban on Major Leaguers Who Jumped to Mexico Lifted by Chandler," *New York Times*, 6 June 1949, 24.

18. *Ibid.*, 24.

19. "Baseball Inquiry Backed," *New York Times*, 19 July 1951, 18.

20. Luther A. Huston, "Baseball Players Are Not 'Peons,' Ty Cobb Tells Washington Hearing," *New York Times*, 31 July 1951, 1.

21. Gary D. Hailey, "Baseball and the Law," *Total Baseball*, Eds. John Thorn, et al. (New York: Warner Books, 1989), 645.

22. Luther A. Huston, "Baseball a Sport, and Not a Business, High Court Rules," *New York Times*, 10 Nov. 1953, 1.

23. "'We're Out of Fog,' Ford Frick Says," *New York Times*, 10 Nov. 1953, 40.

Chapter Four

1. John Drebinger, "Sales Increased on All Payments, *New York Times*, 2 Feb. 1957, 15.

2. Howard M. Tuckner, "Team Basis Cited in Sports Groups," *New York Times*, 26 Feb. 1957, 36.

3. "Frick Gets Invitation," *New York Times*, 20 Mar. 1957, 42.

4. Allen Drury, "Frick Sees Peril in Baseball Bill," *New York Times*, 20 June 1957, 1.

5. *Ibid.*, 1.

6. Ford C. Frick, *Games, Asterisks, and People* (New York: Crown Publishers, 1973), 188.

7. C. P. Trussell, "Feller Supports Some Baseball Trust Laws," *New York Times*, 26 June 1957, 17.

8. Arthur Daley, "The Rajah and the Draft," *New York Times*, 27 Aug. 1957, 38.

9. *Ibid.*, 38.

10. Paul Dickson, *Baseball's Greatest Quotations* (New York: Harper Perennial, 1992), 34.

11. John Drebinger, "Meetings at End, Disputes Remain," *New York Times*, 8 Oct. 1957, Sec. 5, 2.

12. Geoffrey C. Ward and Ken Burns, *Baseball: An Illustrated History* (New York: Alfred A. Knopf, 1994), 355.

13. *Ibid.*, 355.

14. *Ibid.*, 369.

15. "Rickey Sweeps Majors with Choice Metaphors," *New York Times*, 9 Dec. 1959, 62.

16. Marvin Miller, *A Whole Different Ball Game* (New York: Birch Lane Press, 1991), 6.

17. Dickson, 174

18. "Players Endorse Frick on TV Pact, *New York Times*, 6 Dec. 1959, Sec. 5, 4.

19. Bowie Kuhn, *Hardball: The Education of a Baseball Commissioner* (New York: Times Books, 1987), 21.

20. Lee MacPhail, *My Nine Innings* (Westport, CT: Meckler Books, 1989), 97.

21. "Wisconsin's Supreme Court Rules Braves Can Stay in Atlanta; Mets Win, 3–2," *New York Times*, 28 July 1966, 25.

22. Marvin Miller, Interview with author, July 1997.

23. MacPhail, 98.

24. Miller Interview, July 1997.

25. Ward and Burns, 388.

26. "Koufax and Drysdale Reject Dodgers' Offer of $210,000," *New York Times*, 30 Mar. 1966, 50.

27. Ward and Burns, 387–88.

28. Benjamin J. Rader, *Baseball: A History of America's Game* (Urbana and Chicago: University of Illinois Press, 1994), 188.

29. *Ibid.*, 189

30. Miller Interview, May 1997.

31. Miller, Telephone conversation, March 1998.

32. Miller, 47.

Chapter Five

1. Marvin Miller, *A Whole Different Ball Game* (New York: Birch Lane Press, 1991), 67, 68.

2. Marvin Miller, Interview with author, May 1997.

3. Bowie Kuhn, *Hardball: The Education of a Baseball Commissioner* (New York: Times Books, 1987), 34.

4. Miller, 95.

5. Joseph Durso, "Baseball Owners Deny They Are Using Delaying Tactics in Pension Talks," *New York Times*, 6 Dec. 1969, 63.

6. Kuhn, 40.

7. Miller, 105.

8. Miller Interview with author, June 1998.

9. Paul Dickson, *Baseball's Greatest Quotations* (New York: Harper Perennial, 1992), 324.

10. Dickson, 335.

11. Arthur Daley, "For Meritorious Service," *New York Times*, 28 Jan. 1973, Sec. 5, 2.

12. Curt Flood, "Why I Am Challenging Baseball," *The Armchair Book of Baseball*, Ed. John Thorn (New York: Collier Books, 1985), 130.

13. Flood, 125.

14. Miller, 40.

15. Miller, 191.

16. Leonard Koppett, "Baseball Is Sued Under Trust Law," *New York Times*, 16 Jan. 1970, 36.

17. Robert Lipsyte, "Expert Witness," *New York Times*, 11 June 1970, 59.

18. Thomas Rogers, "Flood Loses Suit to Bar Reserve Clause; Gentry of Mets Defeats Reds, 2–1," *New York Times*, 13 Aug. 1970, 39.

19. Leonard Koppett, "Baseball's Next Inning," *New York Times*, 20 Oct. 1971, 57.

20. Miller, 204.

21. Geoffrey C. Ward and Ken Burns, *Baseball: An Illustrated History* (New York: Alfred A. Knopf, 1994), 426.

22. Kuhn, 106.

23. Arthur Daley, "It Even Includes Maternity Benefits," *New York Times*, 30 Mar. 1972, 49.

24. Miller, 215.

25. Jerome Holtzman, "The Year of the Player Strike," *Official Baseball Guide for 1973* (St. Louis: The Sporting News, 1973), 271.

26. Holtzman, 271.

27. Miller, 215.

28. Holtzman, 274.

29. Miller, 220.

30. Irv Kupcinet in *Baseball Digest*, July 1972, *Baseball's Greatest Quotations* (New York: HarperCollins, 1991), 233.

31. Joseph Durso, "Game Wasn't Missed," *New York Times*, 16 Apr. 1972, Sec. 5, 3.

32. Miller, 194.

33. Dickson, 46.

34. Leonard Koppett, "Baseball's Exempt Status Upheld by Supreme Court," *New York Times*, 19 June 1972, 45.

35. Kuhn, 89.

36. Ford C. Frick, *Games, Asterisks, and People* (New York: Crown Publishers, 1973), 192.

Chapter Six

1. Joseph Durso, "Ruling Is Seen Raising Prospect of Baseball Strike Next Spring," *New York Times*, 20 June 1972, 45.

2. "Ruling Is Seen," 45.

3. Jerome Holtzman, "Review of 1973," *Official 1974 Baseball Guide* (St. Louis: The Sporting News, 1974), 260.

4. *Ibid.*, 261.

5. Basic Agreement, Article VI, Section F, Paragraph 12.

6. "Home Run in Baseball," *New York Times*, 28 Feb. 1973, 40.

7. Holtzman, 264,

8. Paul Dickson, *Baseball's Greatest Quotations* (New York: Harper Perennial, 1992), 388.

9. Marvin Miller, Interview with author, July 1997.

10. Miller Interview, July 1997.

11. Marvin Miller, *A Whole Different Ball Game* (New York: Birch Lane Press, 1991), 235.

12. Leonard Koppett, "A's Hunter Ruled Free Agent," *New York Times*, 16 Dec. 1974, 51.

13. Lee MacPhail, *My Nine Innings* (Westport, CT: Meckler Books, 1989), 134.

14. Bowie Kuhn, *Hardball: The Education of a Baseball Commissioner* (New York: Times Books, 1987), 140.

15. Miller Interview, July 1997.

16. Kuhn, 142.

17. Dickson, 134.

18. "A's Fingers Wins Raise in Arbitration," *New York Times*, 16 Feb. 1975, Sec. 5, 5.

19. Dickson, 79.

20. Rich Marazzi, "Dave McNally Had an Impact on Baseball On and Off the Field," *Sports Collectors Digest*, 20 June, 1997, 111.

21. MacPhail, 161.

22. "Baseball to Appeal Free-Agent Ruling," *New York Times*, 11 Feb. 1976, 66.

23. Kuhn, 108.

24. "Baseball to Appeal," *New York Times*, 11 Feb. 1976, 66.

25. John Helyar, *Lords of the Realm* (New York: Ballantine Publishing Group, 1995), 164.

26. *Ibid.*, 165, 166.

27. *Ibid.*, 166.

28. Edmund Fitzgerald, Letter from Fitzgerald to author, October 1997.

29. Dickson, 453

30. Murray Chass, "Baseball Owners Delay Spring Training Start," *New York Times*, 24 Feb. 1976, 43.

31. "Miller: Kuhn to Rescue?" *New York Times*, 7 Mar. 1976, 3.

32. Murray Chass, "Baseball Is Divided on Early Settlement," *New York Times*, 11 Mar. 1976, 50.

33. Miller, 266.

34. Kuhn, 175, 176.

35. *Ibid.*, 176.

36. *Ibid.*, 177.

37. Joseph Durso, "Finley Defends Sales in Hearing by Kuhn," *New York Times*, 18 June, 1976, 17.

38. From a copy of Commissioner Bowie Kuhn's June 18, 1976, statement.

39. Joseph Durso, "Baseball Takes Head Counts, Then Sets Sights Ahead," *New York Times*, 7 Nov. 1976, Sec. 5, 5.

Chapter Seven

1. Bowie Kuhn, *Hardball: The Education of a Baseball Commissioner* (New York: Times Books, 1987), 331.

2. Paul Dickson, *Baseball's Greatest Quotations* (New York: Harper Perennial, 1992), 404.

3. *Ibid.*, 12.

4. *Ibid.*, 232.

5. "They Said It," *Sports Illustrated*, 18 Dec. 1978, 12.

6. Marvin Miller, Interview with author, July 1997.

7. Miller Interview, July 1997.

8. Murray Chass, "Miller Advises Owners to Negotiate in Earnest," *New York Times*, 15 Jan. 1980, Sec. 3, 12.

9. Miller Interview, July 1997.

10. *Ibid.*, July 1997.

11. Red Smith, "The Strike Some Owners Want," *New York Times*, 22 May 1980, Sec. 2, 19.

12. "The Strike Some Owners Want," Sec. 2, 19.

13. "Baseball's Little Miracle," *New York Times*, 24 May 1980, 18.

14. Murray Chass, "Accord Averts Baseball Strike; Free Agent Issue to Be Studied," *New York Times*, 24 May 1980, 18.

15. Joseph Durso, "Mets Skeptical Over Settlement; Beat Braves, 2–1," *New York Times*, 24 May 1980, 17.

16. "Accord Averts Baseball Strike; Free Agent Issue to Be Studied," 18.

17. Lee MacPhail, Interview with author, June 1997.

18. Edmund Fitzgerald, Telephone conversation, October 1997.

19. Kuhn, 169.

20. Steinbrenner: Strike Threat Unifies Owners," *New York Times*, 19 Feb. 1981, Sec. 2, 14.

21. Joseph Durso, "Carpenter's Motive: Prod Other Owners," *New York Times*, 8 Mar. 1981, Sec. 5, 4.

22. George Vecsey, "In Sports, Money Is the Main Issue," *New York Times*, 16 Mar. 1981, Sec. 3, 1, 2.

23. Jim Kaplan, "No Games Today," *Sports Illustrated*, 22 June 1981, 20, 21.

24. Marvin Miller, *A Whole Different Ball Game* (New York: Birch Lane Press, 1991), 288.

25. Kuhn, 343.

26. Miller, 289, 290.

27. Miller Interview, July 1997.

28. Kuhn, 348.

29. Miller Interview, July 1997.

30. Jerry Kirshenbaum, "Scorecard," *Sports Illustrated*, 6 July 1981, 8.

31. Miller Interview with author, May 1997.

32. Lee MacPhail, *My Nine Innings* (Westport, CT: Meckler Books, 1989), 177.

33. MacPhail, 177.

34. *Sports Illustrated*, 10 August 1981, front cover.

Chapter Eight

1. "Text of Kuhn Statement," *New York Times*, 4 Aug. 1983, Sec. 2, 14.

2. Peter O'Malley, Letter from Peter O'Malley to author, November 6, 1997.

3. David Q. Voigt, "The History of Major League Baseball," *Total Baseball* (New York: Warner Books, 1989), 47.

4. Murray Chass, "Yankee Appeal on Belcher Is Denied," *New York Times*, 16 Feb. 1984, Sec. 2, 19.

5. Marvin Miller, Interview with author, July 1997.

6. Murray Chass, "Baseball Owners Ask Players' Help," *New York Times*, 28 Feb. 1985, Sec. 2, 9.

7. Lee MacPhail, *My Nine Innings* (Westport, CT: Meckler Books, 1989), 199.

8. "Baseball Owners Divided," *New York Times*, 8 Mar. 1985, 28.

9. "Money Talks," *New York Times*, 30 May 1985, Sec. 2, 14.

10. MacPhail, 202.

11. Murray Chass, "Owners Ask Curb on Free Agency," *New York Times*, 21 May 1985, Sec. 2, 7.

12. "A Look Inside Baseball's Contract Negotiations," *New York Times*, 23 June 1985, Sec. 5, 2.

13. Robert McG. Thomas, Jr., "Ueberroth Orders Wider Tests for Drug Use in Pro Baseball," *New York Times*, 8 May 1985, 12.

14. Michael Goodwin, "Meeting on Drugs Spurned by Players," *New York Times*, 17 May 1985, 22.

15. "One Small Step in Baseball Talks," *New York Times*, 12 July 1985, 18.

16. Murray Chass, "Baseball Players Set Aug. 6 as Date for Strike," *New York Times*, 16 July 1985, 17.

17. Murray Chass, "Action by Ueberroth Opposed," *New York Times*, 29 July 1985, Sec. 3, 21.

18. Dave Anderson, "Commissioner on the Spot," *New York Times*, 30 July 1985, Sec. 2, 7.

19. Lee MacPhail, "Memorandum to All Chief Executives—Major League Clubs," 29 July 1985, 1.

20. *Ibid.*, 1, 2.

21. Murray Chass, "Behind the New Baseball Pact, Compromises," *New York Times*, 9 Aug. 1985, 18.

22. George Vecsey, "The Best of Times," *New York Times*, 9 Aug. 1985, 19.

23. *Ibid.*, 204.

24. Marvin Miller, *A Whole Different Ball Game* (New York: Birch Lane Press, 1991), 338, 339.

Chapter Nine

1. Taken from the PRC Presentation at the General Managers' Meeting, Scottsdale, Arizona, November 5, 1985, Sec. 1.

2. Bud Selig, Interview with author, August 1997.

3. Lee MacPhail, Interview with author, June 1997.

4. Marvin Miller, Interview with author, May 1997.

5. "The Matters Put at Issue by Grievance No. 86-2," Ruling by Thomas T. Roberts, 21 Sept. 1987, 1.

6. *Ibid.*, 2.

7. *Ibid.*, 12.

8. "Post-Hearing Brief Submitted on Behalf of the 26 Major League Clubs," 4, 5.

9. *Ibid.*, 5, 6.

10. "The Matters Put at Issue," 14.

11. Murray Chass, "Baseball Owners Lose Arbitration on Free Agents; Football Players' Union Strikes on a Parallel Issue," *New York Times*, 22 Sept. 1987, 32.

12. "Brief for Major League Baseball Players Association, Vol. II: Brief on the Merits," 46.

13. Murray Chass, "Baseball Ruling Favors Free-Agent Players," *New York Times*, 10 Feb. 1987, Sec. 4, 31.

14. "In the Matter of Arbitration Between Major League Baseball Players Association and the 26 Major League Clubs, Grievance 87-3, Panel Decision No. 79," 31 Aug. 1988, 74, 79.

15. "Brief for Major League Baseball Players Association...," 33.

16. In the Matter of the Arbitration Between Major League Baseball Players Association and the 26 Major League Clubs, Grievance No. 87-3, Panel Decision No. 79, 51.

17. *Ibid.*, 52.

18. *Ibid.*, 53.

19. "Brief for Major League Baseball Players Association...," 34.

20. Before the Major League Baseball Arbitration Panel..., 54.

21. *Ibid.*, 54, 55.
22. Murray Chass, "Once Again, Labor Problems Threaten to Overshadow Game," *New York Times*, 18 Dec. 1988, Sec. 8, 3.
23. Murray Chass, "Lockout's On, but Vincent Has Suggestions," *New York Times*, 14 Feb. 1990, Sec. 2, 9.
24. Joseph Durso, "Back to Work with Mixed Views," *New York Times*, 20 Mar. 1990, Sec. 2, 15.
25. Durso, "Back to Work...," Sec. 2, 15.
26. Murray Chass, "Players Can Share Information Bank's 'Assets,'" *New York Times*, 13 Nov. 1988, Sec. 8, 2.
27. Chass, "Players Can Share Information...," Sec. 8, 2.
28. Claire Smith, "Arbitrator Finds 3d Case of Baseball Collusion," *New York Times*, 19 July 1990, Sec. 2, 9.
29. Murray Chass, "Players Get $102.5 Million in Collusion Case," *New York Times*, 18 Sept. 1990, Sec. 4, 25.
30. Claire Smith, "Major Leagues Enlist Outside Advice," *New York Times*, 18 Dec. 1990, Sec. 4, 25.
31. Smith, "Major Leagues Enlist...," Sec. 4, 25.

Chapter Ten

1. Murray Chass, "Owners' Labor Agent Doesn't Favor Lockout," *New York Times*, 14 Jan. 1993, Sec. 2, 13.
2. Murray Chass, "Owners Link Salaries to Revenue Sharing," *New York Times*, 18 Feb. 1993, Sec. 2, 17.
3. *Ibid.*, Sec. 2, 17.
4. "Resignation Cites 'Best Interests,'" *The Boston Globe*, 8 Sept. 1992, 30.
5. "Bunning Issues a 'Bribe Alert,'" *New York Times*, 12 June 1993, 28.
6. Claire Smith, "Players Must Wait for Owners to Settle Their Differences," *New York Times*, 12 July 1993, Sec. 3, 4.
7. Murray Chass, "Fehr Raises Possibility of Late Work Stoppage," *New York Times*, 24 July 1993, 31.
8. Claire Smith, "TV Contract Spurs Soul-Searching," *New York Times*, 3 June 1993, Sec. 2, 15.
9. "Owners Promise No Lockout," *The Boston Globe*, 13 Aug. 1993, 29.
10. Larry Whiteside, "This Restructuring Is Restrictive," *The Boston Globe*, 12 Feb. 1994, 31.
11. "Antitrust Hearings to Begin Again," *New York Times*, 25 Feb. 1994, Sec. 2, 12.
12. Tom Verducci, "In the Strike Zone," *Sports Illustrated*, 1 Aug. 1994, 28.
13. Murray Chass, "Officials Decide to Discuss Fights," *New York Times*, 6 May 1994, Sec. 2, 10.
14. "What's in the Cap?," *New York Times*, 15 June 1994, Sec. 2, 13.
15. Murray Chass, "Players Union Delays Strike Vote," *New York Times*, 17 June 1994, Sec. 2, 11.
16. Murray Chass, "Owners and Players Stand Still; Clock Runs," *New York Times*, 19 July 1994, Sec. 2, 9.
17. Murray Chass, "Labor Secretary's Plea Is Hardly a Solution," *New York Times*, 9 Aug. 1994, Sec. 2, 15.
18. George Vecsey, "The Owners Are Trashing Themselves," *New York Times*, 12 Aug. 1994, Sec. 2, 7.
19. George Vecsey, "Baseball Is Dead Issue; Get a life," *New York Times*, 14 Aug. 1994, Sec. 8, 1.

Chapter Eleven

1. Murray Chass, "Economist Hired by Union Disputes Owners' Loss Claims," *New York Times*, 25 Aug. 1994, Sec. 2, 9.
2. Claire Smith, "Take 700 Players and 28 Owners and It Winds Up to 0 Solution," *New York Times*, 15 Sept. 1994, Sec. 2, 13.
3. Jim Bunning, "Repeal That Antitrust Exemption," *New York Times*, 3 Oct. 1994, 15.
4. Lee MacPhail, "Keep That Antitrust Exemption," *New York Times*, 3 Oct. 1994, 15.
5. Murray Chass, "A Hint of Hope by Baseball Owners," *New York Times*, 20 Oct. 1994, Sec. 2, 17.
6. Larry Whiteside, "United They Don't Stand—Just Yet," *The Boston Globe*, 2 Nov. 1994, 66.
7. Murray Chass, "Replacement Players May Play Ball Next Year," *New York Times*, 30 Nov. 1994, Sec. 2, 15.
8. Murray Chass, "Players Try to Block Foreign Fill-ins," *New York Times*, 2 Dec. 1994, Sec. 2, 9.
9. Murray Chass, "Clubs Say Offer Is New, But Players Say It Isn't," *New York Times*, 12 Dec. 1994, Sec. 3, 3.
10. Larry Whiteside, "Salary Cap in Place," *The Boston Globe*, 23 Dec. 1994, 73.
11. Keith Bradsher, "Congressmen Pledge to Revoke Baseball's Antitrust Exemption," *New York Times*, 24 Dec. 1994, 1.
12. Murray Chass, "Players Get Anti-Union Letter from the Owners," *New York Times*, 8 Jan. 1995, Sec. 8, 10.
13. Murray Chass, "Selig, Fehr Take Part in Civilized Exchange," *New York Times*, 23 Feb. 1995, Sec. 2, 16.
14. Murray Chass, "Negotiating Teams Move to Night Round of Talks," *New York Times*, 2 Mar. 1995, Sec. 2, 14.
15. Larry Whiteside, "Talks and Clock Keep Running," *The Boston Globe*, 2 Mar. 1995, 54.

Chapter Twelve

1. Hal Bodley, "Cubs' MacPhail Speaks Too Soon," *USA Today*, 26 Mar. 1996, Sec. 3, 3.
2. Carl Pohlad, "MLB's Blue Ribbon Report: Sides Take Time to Digest Findings," *Minneapolis Star Tribune*, 16 July 2000.
3. Marvin Miller, *Outside the Lines*, ESPN, 17 July 2000.
4. Marvin Miller, Symposium entitled "Baseball's Future Competitive Balance and Labor Relations," Smith College, Northampton, Massachusetts, November 17, 2000.
5. "Union Extends Deal with Owners Through 2001," *The Philadelphia Inquirer*, 29 Aug. 2000, Sec. 6, 4.
6. Bob Costas, Symposium entitled "Baseball's Future Competitive Balance and Labor Relations, Smith College, Northampton, Massachusetts, November 17, 2000.
7. Miller, Symposium entitled "Baseball's Future..."
8. "Selig Sounds Call for Change," *Springfield [MA] Union-News*, 22 Nov. 2000, Sec. 4, 7.

Index

213